EVANGEL

Redemption in Christ

EVANGEL
Redemption in Christ

BOOK ONE

Apostle Curtis L Schulze

A Pauline Revelation
info@pathfinderfellowship.org
PO Box 3352
Stafford VA 22555

ReadersMagnet, LLC

Book I - EVANGEL: Redemption in Christ.
Copyright © 2023 by Apostle Curtis L Schulze

Published in the United States of America
ISBN   Paperback: 979-8-89091-419-4
ISBN   eBook: 979-8-89091-420-0

All rights reserved. No part of this publication may be reproduced, stored in a retrieval system or transmitted in any way by any means, electronic, mechanical, photocopy, recording or otherwise without the prior permission of the author except as provided by USA copyright law.

The opinions expressed by the author are not necessarily those of ReadersMagnet, LLC.

ReadersMagnet, LLC
10620 Treena Street, Suite 230 | San Diego, California, 92131 USA
1.619. 354. 2643 | www.readersmagnet.com

Book design copyright © 2023 by ReadersMagnet, LLC. All rights reserved.

Cover design by Brittney Phillips
Interior design by Daniel Lopez

TABLE OF CONTENTS

Dedication vii
Introduction ix

1   Another Gospel? 1

    The Deeds of the Law 11
    Grace of Christ 25
    The other side of Grace no one told you about 29
    Grace or Mercy 36
    My Gospel 44
    St. Augustine on Grace 54
    Original sin, human Depravity, and free Will 61
    Why Do Men deny the Existence of God? 69
    Revelation of the Mystery 78

2   Redemption in Christ 90

    What the Gospel has accomplished [the finished work] ... 92
    Redemptive Terms 102
    Divine Exchange 113
    The Cross of Christ 145
    The Mercy Seat 170
    How much more shall the blood of Christ 184
    Believing and Prevailing Prayer 198

3   In Summary 205

    Part One 211
    Part Two 233
    Imputed or infused? 258
    Part Three 265
    The Resurrection 268

    Final Thoughts 286
    Additional Materials 290
    About the Author 291

DEDICATION

I would be remiss if I did not dedicate this book to the Grace of our Lord and Savior Jesus Christ. The Grace of God has taught me to flee all ungodliness and the wickedness [enticements: worldly lusts] that is so prevalent throughout our world (Tit. 2:11-12). "God's marvelous **grace has manifested in person**, bringing salvation for everyone. This **same grace teaches us how to live each day** as we turn our backs on ungodliness and indulgent sinful lifestyles; and, it [grace] equips us to live self-controlled, upright, godly lives in this present age" (Tit. 2:11-12 TPT). Paul said, "I am crucified to the world [by the Cross], and the world is crucified to me [by that same Cross] (I am dead to the world; and, the world is dead to me) (Gal. 6:14). Only by the abundant [His abounding] <u>grace</u> [the redemptive work of His Cross] and, the free gift of his righteousness [now only made possible by the resurrection that imparts new life] do any of us stand here free and justified before God our maker [delivered, healed, and made whole] (Rom. 1:16; 5:15-17). All of this is (only) made possible **by** and **through** Jesus Christ and Him crucified!!!

I am so grateful for the gospel of our Lord and Savior JC for it is the power of God unto salvation to all who will *simply* believe and obey. His Redemptive Work on the Cross-is the ground [from which] [that God used] to give us his precious Holy Spirit. Now the Holy Spirit, who is the "Spirit of Christ" [within us], has become to us both the ***Sanctifier*** and the ***Perfecter*** of our faith. He is the POWER of God within. May God Be Praised Forever MORE!!!

By the **Grace** of Christ [by the power of His Cross] and, with the help of his precious Holy Spirit, God has made me to be more than a conqueror through him who loved us and died for us on the Cross (Rom. 8:31-39). Now [in Christ] and, with Him [Christ and him crucified], God has now freely given us/me all things that pertain to **life** and **godliness** (2 Pet. 1:1-4). For God has made Him who knew no sin to be made sin for us, that we might be made the righteousness of God in him (2 Cor. 5:21). For God has made him [Christ] to be for us wisdom, righteousness, sanctification, and redemption (1 Cor. 1:30). I dedicate the writing of this book to my Lord, and His wonderful, awesome, and matchless GRACE!!! I praise you Lord Jesus.

From the start; I want to cast down the idea we can have the grace of God but at the same time reject His Lordship [the lordship of JC]. Listen carefully to the text written by Paul that puts the **grace** of God and the Lordship of JC together as ONE, "from whence also we **look for the Savior, the Lord Jesus Christ**" (Phil. 3:20 KJ). Our Savior is not Jesus Christ, but: **the Lord** Jesus Christ. In order to have the **grace** of God we must call Jesus Lord. To claim JC as Savior but not Lord is a false gospel!!! May God help us all too truly see this and come into agreement with God, or, you will not be saved!!! The Grace of God and the gospel of our Lord and Savior JC are identical concepts. You cannot have the Grace of God *apart* from the gospel of our Lord JC; and, the *gospel* of our Lord JC is the vehicle through which God manifests and bestows His grace [to all who believe on the Lord JC, which are those who called upon Him as LORD to be saved] (Rom. 10:9, 13). God help us all to see this!! We are to look upon the Lord JC who is the Savior!!! We are saved when we look to him to save; and, we bow our knee to him as Lord.

INTRODUCTION

Truth worth fighting for, "the gospel of our salvation." Before the close of Martin Luther's ministry near the end of his life, he, this great reformer of the 16th century, came to realize the need to forewarn the next generation of believers for/of its responsibility to safeguard (protect) the true gospel message. Luther recognized (realized) that this newly rediscovered and recovered **Evangel** [the gospel] was in danger of reverting [back] to apostasy (error). **Apostasy** *means* departure from the truth [this is the abandonment of a right and proper understanding and right application of the gospel message]. It is at this point that Luther realized each generation of the church would have to contend [struggle] for "the faith," if the true gospel message was to survive. We find in Jude 3, "Beloved, when I gave all diligence to write unto you of the *common salvation*...that you should *earnestly* contend for **the faith** which was once delivered unto the saints." The Passion Translation [TPT] says it this way, *"Dearly loved friend, I was fully intending to write to you about our amazing salvation we all participate in, but felt the need instead to challenge you to vigorously **defend** and **contend for** the beliefs that we cherish. For God, through the apostles, has once for all entrusted these truths (the gospel) to his holy believers."* Here, **"the faith"** *means*, on behalf of "The faith" and, encompasses the entirety of the body of truth we received from the inspired Word of God [TPT]. You will notice from the text, that, Jude is speaking specifically about our *common* salvation. The word common here in the GK *means*, "That which is *shared* by all." No doubt, what is written here in the text concerns the **defense** of the True Gospel Message, "For there are certain men crept in unawares...ungodly [corrupt] men, ***turning*** [perverting; changing] the **grace** [gospel] of our God [of our Lord JC] into <u>lasciviousness</u> (into the participation of evil desire and evil practices)..." (Jude 4). *"There have been some who have sneaked in among you unnoticed. They are depraved people whose judgment was prophesied in Scripture a long time ago. They have* **perverted the message of God's grace [the gospel]** *into a license to commit immorality and* **turn against our only absolute Master,** *our Lord Jesus Christ"* [Jude 4 TPT]. Here, in Jude 3-4, refers to the fact that the Saints must defend the Doctrines of Christianity with intense effort. Here, in Jude 3-4, refers to the fact that no other Faith will be given; the idea is that <u>God gave the Christian Doctrines to the Saints as a deposit of Truth to be guarded</u>. False teachers had crept into the Church. They came in by stealth and dishonesty, and refers to the fact that "Grace" [the gospel] had been turned to <u>license</u> [permission to sin; excess liberty, "freedom abused"]. If we deny the CROSS, which puts an end to sin and to the sinful lifestyle, which is God's plan for eternal Redemption, we are at the same time denying *both* the Father and the Son [Page 999, The Expositor's New Testament (TENT) Jimmy Swaggart Counselor's edition copyright 2008 www.jsm.org]. In Galatians 1:6, Paul, calls this spiritual counterfeit as, "**...unto *another* gospel**" which in the GK is translated as an *altered* [different] gospel, making it **different** [altered] from the one he preached. Here, Paul called *both* the **gospel** and the **grace** of Christ one and the same. Notice Jude said, that, these truths [of the gospel message] was given through the apostles but <u>entrusted</u> to all the saints [all believers]. The responsibility to safeguard the faith [the true gospel message] was [is] placed upon all Christians regardless of station, calling, gifting, anointing, or office [position or status]. God help us all!!! It is clear from Paul's writings that there was more than one gospel being preached in his day; so, it is not strange that we find many today preaching an incomplete and even counterfeit gospel. A gospel that may present some of its facts as true, and yet, rejecting all that the gospel entails. The preaching of a gospel of forgiveness, however, a gospel that neglects and/or rejects repentance as necessary and required for true biblical Christian salvation. Paul taught that, there was only one true Christian gospel!!!

Every other *gospel* **was a false presentation of the Christian faith** and, a **false representation** of the true biblical Christian gospel of our Lord and Savior JC. God help.

*"But felt the need instead to challenge you to vigorously **defend** and **contend for** the beliefs that we cherish"* (Jude 3 TPT). I especially like the way this translation has identified the dual application [implication] of the faith [the logical relation between two propositions that hold both the *first* and *second* to be true]. We both **defend** the *gospel* and as well **press** into the *gospel*. The word contend here in Jude means to struggle for [it]; it comes from another GK word that means to *compete for* a prize, and as well, to *contend with* an enemy (#75 NT Strong's Concordance). In 1 Timothy 6:12, we find the same GK word translated as **[Fight] the good fight of faith**, lay hold on [to apprehend] eternal life. "Strive to enter in at the strait gate: for many, I say unto you, will seek to enter in, **and shall not be able**" (Lk. 13:24). Here, this same GK word [for fight] is translated, "to strive." The Christian is called of God to *both* give a **defense** for the gospel, as well to **contend** for [it] [or, to press into it] the true faith that he/she might bring forth the fruits of righteousness [the fruits of their spiritual transformation]. The Christian must continue to STAND [defend the faith] all the while [at the same time] PRESSING into the deeper **gospel** truths in order to harvest its promised provision. Today, many in the church have fallen away from [abandoned] the true gospel message. She no longer defends it nor, seeks to press into it!!

It is to this admonition [admonishing of history: the warning given to us by the early Protestant Reformers] where this book concerns [points]. Paul's [Apostolic] warning [2 Thess. 2:3-17; 2 Tim. 3:1-17] of a Church in crisis [great apostasy] just prior to Christ's return [Second Coming] is most evidently seen today in the Church's misunderstanding and misapplication of the gospel. Most Christian's teeter-totter **between legalistic and lawless living [its tendencies]**. **Legalism** places primary emphasis on legal principles [do's and don'ts] or, on a formal structure **[the traditions of men]**; while **Lawlessness** *means* unruly or not restrained. A **Legalist** is one who strictly adheres to law or letter, rather than the Spirit. In Christian Theology, it is the act of putting the Law of Moses above the Gospel by establishing requirements for salvation beyond simple obedience, repentance, and faith in Christ and the message of the Cross. **Lawlessness** in Christian Theology is, paying no attention to the biblical standard for Moral living. It is asserting that the Law of God has no place or demand any longer on the life of the Christian. It asserts that the Christian is no longer under or obligated to the biblical standards for biblical morality. Most *err* in their understanding of the **right** [and proper] relationship between **Law** and **Grace**. Many are living by and relying upon a false religious system of faith and practice [a form of godliness], without having an ongoing personal experience with the promised *power* of the gospel. Others, who call themselves Christian [believers], **are living very disorderly** and **dysfunctional lives**, who as well are rejecting the same promised *power* of the gospel designed **to reorder their lives** in keeping with the scriptures. Many have lost the *power* inherent within the **gospel** message that sets them [the believer] apart from the world, and, that sets one right before God: a righteousness that demonstrates [proves] itself [its presence] through holy [separate] and fruitful [right and proper] living. Many are abandoning the holy scriptures [are rejecting the bible as divinely inspired] [as God's standard for Christian living][as the standard for biblical morality] [this is lawlessness]; while others [the legalist] **who hold** to the scriptures are abandoning **the place** the *gospel* must hold [the part it must play] in the sanctification of the believer (that part the **power** of the *gospel* must hold in our spiritual growth, development, and the spiritual transformation of the believer, *"But grow **in grace** [the gospel] and in **the knowledge** of our Lord and Savior Jesus Christ"* [the knowledge of the Cross] (2 Pet. 3:18). This word "knowledge" here refers not only to who Jesus Christ is [the Lord of Glory], but as well, to what He did, in order that we might be Redeemed from sin, which points to the Cross [Page 977, The Expositor's New Testament]. Remember, the gospel is the death, burial, and resurrection of our Lord and Savior Jesus Christ. *"But continue to grow and increase in God's grace and intimacy with our Lord and Savior, Jesus Christ"* [2 Pet. 3:18 TPT]). We continue to be nourished in grace [in the gospel] and in the intimate **knowledge** of our Lord and Savior, Jesus Christ, and of God the Father. Spiritual growth is, you and I yielding to the **grace** of God [you and I yielding to the *gospel* of JC in his death, burial, and resurrection] and, having a passion [having a strong desire] to know Jesus Christ our Lord intimately [in *both* his presence, and, in his redemption] (TPT Pg. 696). "But grow in [the] **grace** (of our Lord and Savior JC) [grow in the gospel: underserved favor and, spiritual strength] and in the recognition and knowledge and understanding of our Lord and Savior Jesus Christ [the Messiah] (you and I growing in our understanding of him and his redemptive works)." (AMP).

How should we understand this relationship between law and grace?? The **Law** of Moses best understands the Old Testament; and, the **Life** of Christ best understands the New Covenant [The best way to understand the two Covenants is by defining them as **Law** and **Life**. In this way, the NT Doctrine of Grace would not be misunderstood and misapplied. Grace must be understood as having two distinct and separate sides: *both* belonging to the same one truth. Like a coin, having two distinct and different sides but *both* belonging to the same one coin. Grace will both, extend *mercy* to the sinner for justification, as well extend power to the saints for their sanctification. To fail to see and to hold onto *both* sides of this truth will end up *perverting* the gospel, the grace of Christ]. The Christian does not live by the **Law** but, by the **Life** of Christ. It is not Grace [mercy] contrasting [or opposing the] Law; but, it is how the Law corresponds [relates] to [His] Life. The Law of God reveals *both* His Divine Character and His Moral Will [His, God's holy (righteous) standard]. The word correspond *means*, to be **in conformity to**, to be **in agreement with** [to compare closely: to be equivalent or, parallel: to be in a perfect match]. Law and Grace are not adversarial [nor designed to be opposites]; the **Life** [of Christ] is the fulfilment of the

Law [of Moses]. The **Grace** [of Christ] corresponds [relates] to the **Life** [of Christ]. Grace is not the *covering over* of a sinful life, but the *empowerment* of the new life!! The **gospel** of Jesus Christ [the **grace** of God] is the **power** of God unto **salvation** to all who believe [deliverance, healing, and wholeness] (Rom. 1:16). The Life of Christ, under the Law of Moses, finished [perfected] forever its righteous demands!!!!! Grace [**the Cross**: his **death**, **burial**, and **resurrection**] [is the putting to death of the old life, and] is the impartation of this New Life in Christ [to and *within* the believer] (Rom. 6:3-15). It is through the New Life [given to us] that the *righteousness* of the law might be finished [accomplished] in us, when we walk after the Spirit [and live in agreement with this new life (within)] (Rom. 8:1-17). Paul said, "I am *crucified* [on the cross] with Christ: nevertheless I live; yet not I [I died], but Christ *lives in me:* and the life which I now live in the flesh [in this mortal human body] I live by the faith of the Son of God, who loved me, and gave himself for me" (Gal. 2:20). *"My old identity [old self] has been co-crucified with Messiah and no longer lives; for the nails of his cross crucified me, with him. And now the essence **of this new life is no longer mine**, for the Anointed One **lives his life through me. We live in union as one!!** My new life is empowered by the faith of the Son of God who loves (us) me so much that he gave himself for me, **and dispenses his life into mine**"* (Gal. 2:20/Jn. 15:1-27 TPT *"I am the sprouting **Vine** and you're my **branches**"*). Grace [the gospel of our Salvation] points to what he did for us to both *forgive* [our sins] and to *change* our lives [walk] [our lifestyles]. To reject sanctification [the demand put on a changed life] is to reject [deny] justification [the forgiveness of sins].

Paul goes on to say, "I do not *frustrate* the grace of God: for if righteousness comes by the law, then Christ is dead in vain" (Gal. 2:21). Where Paul called the Legalistic *"frustrating the grace of God,"* [or, frustrating the gospel]; Jude called the Lawless, *"turning [changing] the grace of God [the gospel] into a license to sin."* The New Covenant is not Grace contrasting [opposing] Law, but it is Law corresponding [relating] to Life!! Grace points to the New Life [perfected by Christ under the Law] that we all have received in Christ Jesus. This [treasure] New Life in us [not me] will accomplish the righteous standard of the Law [when we walk in the Spirit (or, live in agreement with the new life); because, it is His life living *in* and *through* us, not me, or mine]. This is how Law corresponds [relates] to Life. Not my life, but Christ [His Life] within me the *hope* of glory [expectation for change]. The Law corresponds [relates] to His Life. To <u>correspond</u> means as well, to harmonize, to <u>cohere</u> **[to hold together firmly as parts of the same whole]**. This perfectly matches the testimony of the scriptures *"...and the Word [the Law of God] was made flesh [was made a Man] and dwelt among us"* (Jn. 1:14). His *life* in me [as a treasure *within* the earthen vessel] would **never violate the Law of God**!!! How could it??? The Law of God is not opposed to the **purposes** of God. Again, Not I, but JC who lives his **life** *in* and *through* me this is the hope [of glory] for all [every] change [regeneration and **transformation**]. The *law* corresponds [relates] to His Life [which corresponds to His Grace] [His <u>earned</u> FAVOR (deserved blessings): His perfect obedience to the Law]; and this Grace expresses His Life [that was under the Law of Moses] that which has *fulfilled* the Law of God [every *jot* and *tittle*]. The *unmerited* and *undeserved* **grace** that we all received from God was earned by JC through his *sinless* life, and, *sin-bearing* death. These are the redemptive **works** of Christ [His earned favor and blessings] all done on our behalf. <u>Grace</u> must never be seen as **opposed** to [as an enemy of] the <u>Law</u> of God [or, even as it's opposite]. Law and Grace are fighting for the same team. **Grace is opposed to <u>legalism</u> [the wrong use of the law] but, it is not opposed to the Law of God.**

The New Covenant is not about Law, but Life!! *"Is the **Law** [of God] then against [contrary and opposed to] the promises of God?? God forbid [of course not]...wherefore the Law [of God] was our schoolmaster [teacher; guide] to bring us [to lead us] to Christ [His Life]"* (Gal. 3:21, 24 KJ/AMP). Here, Paul is not saying, "The Law was given to <u>confer</u> **[to bestow, or, to impart]** spiritual life, but rather, to *point* to [Christ] the **Life** that was to come, *"Since that's true, should we consider the <u>written</u>*

*law to be contrary to the promise of new life: How absurd! Truly, if there was a law [of Moses] that we could keep which would give us new life, then our salvation [our justification] would have come by law keeping. But the Scriptures make it clear that since **we were all under the power of sin**, we needed Jesus [His life]! And he is the <u>Savior</u> [the message of the Cross] who [that] brings the promise [of new life] to those who believe…**The law becomes a gateway [a guide] to lead us to the Messiah [his life] so that we would be saved by faith [in his crucified and resurrected life]**. But when faith comes the law [of Moses] is no longer in force [in charge over us], since we have already **entered into [new] life [found only in Christ and, in him crucified and, resurrected and ascended]**"* (Gal. 3:21-22, 24-25 TPT). The **new life** we have received [in Christ Jesus] would never **violate** [transgress] the Law of God, ever (1 Jn. 3:9). Law and Grace are not opposed to each other; nor, are they standing on opposite sides of the fence. It is the law pointing to the need for grace, and, it is grace [his life] that finishes and completes law.

    The Grace of God is all about the Life of Christ (and his **passion**: his death, burial, and resurrection), *"For sin shall not have **dominion** [rule] over you: for you are…**under grace**"* (Rom. 6:14). Under Grace *means*, under the BLOOD and now a partaker of his death, burial, and resurrection unto new life. The Law Points to [His] Life, and Grace becomes the very expression of that Life. This is Why Paul called the Law [of God], holy, and just, and good, and ordained [appointed] to life (Rom. 7:10, 12), *"I once lived without a clear understanding of the law, but when I heard God's commandments, sin sprang to life and brought with it a death sentence. The **commandment that was intended to bring life** brought me death instead. Sin, by means of the commandment, built a base of operation within me, to overpower me [to deceive me and lead me astray] and put me to death. So then, we have to conclude that **the problem is not with the law itself, for the law is holy and its commandments are correct and for our good**"* (Rom. 7:9-12 TPT). This is the right and proper way GRACE is understood in the New Covenant. Yes, the Law [of Moses] gives the believer knowledge of sin, but this same Law [of God] gives us the knowledge of His Life. The Law cannot possibly be the opposite of Grace!! The Law of God points to the Life of Christ, and the **Life of Christ becomes the very Grace** of God received within and, is expressed through the believer whose whole self-life now yielded over to the Holy Spirit [the Spirit of Christ within them]. If the Law of God is holy, and just, and good, and ordained [appointed] to life, then what does that make Grace if it is the opposite of the Law. This is why it is impossible to believe, or, even to make the NT set Grace against Law [to set into opposition or to turn into a rivalry]. The Law of God is not against the promises of God; this would make Grace and Law actually working together. If the bible calls Grace "the **promise**" [promises], and the Law not against those promises, wouldn't that put them both on the same team (Gal. 3:17-29)? Even though the Law [of God] *reveals* His Life, we do not look to the Law; we look away from it [the *law*] to the New Life [in Christ] that comes to all who through faith of Jesus Christ receives this Eternal Life [this ZOE: the God quality/kind of life]. God Be Praised!!!

Today, the church still lacks a *clear* and *precise* understanding of the [right and proper] relationship between **Grace** and **Truth** [Law and Gospel]. In these series of books, I am going to attempt to bridge the gap between Law and Gospel in order to bring a clear and precise message on the Grace of Christ. My prayer is, that, the Spirit of Christ will rest upon me to help me to rightly-divide the Word of truth: to clear up the confusion many believers have between Law and Grace. In this trilogy, I will explain Biblical Redemption [Salvation] and the Sanctification of all believers. I will *contrast* the **gift** with the **fruit**, and show how the **fruit** verifies the **gift**. No fruit, no gift!! The *fruit* is the proof of the gift; the *gift* is what brings forth the fruit. God help us!! May His Grace [favor, and mercy] be with me in this endeavor. In these series of books, I will work to clear up any misconceptions about the Pauline Gospel. If you ever truly wanted to know what the Apostle Paul had in mind when he wrote *his* gospel this book is for you. Paul was the Apostle of grace; however, Paul in his writings never once gave us permission to participate in vice. Paul, never taught a grace that would ever willingly and blatantly violate the law of God [His holy and righteous standard for moral conduct and Christian living]. Paul's gospel, and his teaching on the grace of Christ was a **perfect balance of the power** of God and, **the wisdom of the Cross**. The gospel <u>supersedes</u> the law; however, this same gospel upholds the righteous standard of that law. Its takes the power of the Holy Spirit to make *real* and *alive* the gospel's promised result [the gospel's purchased provision: its redemptive supply]. The law of God is the command to obey; the gospel is the power and redemptive supply that makes obedience to God, possible. The law is the command to obey; the gospel is the power to perform it!! The law of God communicates the holy standard; the gospel and the grace of JC makes holy living possible and acceptable to God. The word <u>supersede</u> means, **to cause to be set aside**; to force out of use as inferior. It means to **take the place or position of the former: to displace** in favor of another. The NT Covenant of Grace [the NT gospel of JC] has *displaced* and *replaced* the dispensation of the giving of the law [of Moses] and, the Old Covenant faith. Despite this; the law is not set aside as invalid, nor, is it to be looked upon as no longer useful as if it has lost its eternal value [we are speaking in respect to the law of God, which is universal and eternal, that which reflects HIS MORAL CODE. The Law is eternal; however, the gospel of JC has forever fulfilled [finished] its righteous demands. The law of God is no longer the divine standard; the gospel of JC that has fulfilled [finished] the law of God is now His divine eternal standard. The gospel alone upholds *both* His divine mercy and His divine justice!! The Law could only define and demand divine justice; the gospel can and will and has *both* satisfied divine justice and provided divine mercy. The gospel is God's new holy standard for moral conduct and Christian living. The gospel is *both* a provision for reconciliation between God and men [the forgiveness of sins]; and, the power of God to enter into holy and sanctified [set apart] living [the **new power** and **provision** for moral conduct, and for true Christian living: not by the letter of the law, but, by the power of His indwelling Spirit]. In this book we are going to highlight and expound upon **what Paul called the wisdom**

of the Cross. Paul taught that the <u>wisdom</u> of the Cross is the <u>power</u> of God toward us who believe!! Only the gospel [alone] can provide for *both* the redemption of man and, power for holy living!!! This is why the gospel of JC by necessity must be understood and applied as *both* Christian justification, and, as well, Christian sanctification: as *both* <u>forgiveness</u> and <u>power</u> for new living.

I am well aware that the introduction to this book is quite weighty; please do not be discouraged if this was difficult to fully comprehend. Please be [very] patient with the material in this book. It is not that it is going to get any easier but, it is necessary for a true and complete understanding of the Gospel. We are **saved** [born again] by the *simplicity* that is in Christ Jesus; but, just because **faith** in the *gospel* of His **grace** is <u>simple</u>, this does not mean it is not as well complicated. Because so many have under estimated the Grace of Christ, and the Gospel of His Grace, this is why so many false gospels were *formed* and **promoted** over the many centuries of the Church. Do you understand?? In our **ignorance**, we have **over simplified** the gospel!! This is why Peter said of Paul, "...**even our beloved brother Paul** also according to the *wisdom* given unto him hath written unto you; as also in all his epistles, speaking in them of these things; **in which are some things hard to be understood**, which they that are *unlearned* and *unstable* <u>wrest</u>, as they do also the other scriptures, unto their own destruction" (2 Pet. 3:15-16). The word *wrest* here means to twist and to pervert the scriptures [the gospel of His grace]. Peter said this was being done by the <u>unlearned</u>, and as well by the <u>unstable</u>. The **unlearned** *refer* to those who are **untaught**, or **improperly** taught the gospel of His Grace. The **unstable** *means* those who are **uncommitted** to the *holiness* of God, these are <u>vacillating</u> between the *world* and Christ. Today, we are seeing much of the very same things happening in the Church: **leaders** and believers alike **not fully informed** of the Gospel of His Grace *promoting* an <u>incomplete</u> and <u>distorted</u> gospel; as well the lack of true biblical <u>consecration</u> to JC for true sanctification [true holy living]. We are clearly living in the closing moments of the last days of this age of Grace, just before the return of the Bridegroom for His bride. The misunderstanding of, and, as well, the misapplication of the true biblical gospel is the long awaited prophesied falling away [apostasy] of the Church. God help us all!!! My prayer is, that, you and I will not be found wanting on that day of His Return, "...when the Son of man comes, shall he find **faith** [GK-the faith] on the earth" (Lk. 18:8).

ANOTHER GOSPEL?

"... So your minds should be <u>corrupted</u> [seduced; distorted] from the <u>simplicity</u> [singleness and pure devotion] that is in Christ. For if he who comes preaching *another* [a different] <u>Jesus</u>, whom we have not preached, or if you receive *another* [a strange] <u>spirit</u> which you have not received, or *another* [an altered] **gospel**, which you have not accepted..." (2 Cor. 11:3-4).

Surprisingly, the gospel today has become, to today's church, a lost truth!!! Few truly understand the biblical gospel. Many, who claim to be Christian, only understand parts of it (the gospel), and those parts they do understand are watered down, or, entirely misapplied. It is possible to have only parts of the truth, and then to take those parts [truths] and make them the whole. This would <u>pervert</u> *entirely* those parts of the gospel, because of all those missing pieces! The integrity (or balance) of the gospel would be found in all those missing pieces. What we do not know or, what we fail to understand about the gospel, could cause us to interpret, or attempt to apply the gospel in ways God had never intended. To <u>pervert</u> in the Old English [OE] means to turn from the truth; to twist or distort from its true use: to misinterpret and to misapply. The problem is never found in the things we know but, in those things we do not know [as of yet]. We often see the part as a whole; instead of understanding the whole through its many parts. The part maybe true, however, it is fully understood and properly balanced and made complete by the whole, with all of its many parts. Many are now falling away because they have taken a part of the gospel and have made it the whole. Repentance, faith, grace, forgiveness, redemption, reconciliation, and new life, sanctification, transformation, and so much more are the so many different parts of this ONE GOSPEL WHOLE. God help us to desire and receive the full gospel.

Paul, in his epistle to the Galatians warned the believers of a counterfeit gospel. "I marvel that ye are so soon removed from him that called you into the **grace** of Christ unto *another* gospel..." (Gal. 1:6). Here, Paul is speaking of a *different* gospel, one **altered** from its original form. This word *another* in the GK means, different, *altered*, or strange [the word *strange* in the OE means foreign; or, not belonging to the other]. Paul, when speaking of the believing Jews [the Christian Jew] revealed a **bent** *toward* legalism [the word Christian in the GK simply means a *follower* of Christ]. The word counterfeit *means* **to forge, fabricate,** or **imitate** with the view to deceive or defraud, by passing a false copy for the genuine article or for the original. *"I am shocked over how quickly you have strayed away from the One who called you **in the grace of Christ**. I'm frankly astounded that you now embrace **a distorted gospel!!** That is a "fake gospel" that, is simply not true. There is only one gospel, the gospel of the Messiah! Yet you have allowed those **who mingle law with grace to confuse you** with lies. Anyone who comes to you with **a different message than the grace [gospel] that you have received** will have the curse of God come upon them!"* (Gal. 1:6-8 TPT). This speaks of those [persons] who put *law* above *grace*, who place their primary emphasis on legal principles [do's and don'ts], or, on a **formal structure [the traditions of men]**. A **Legalist** is one who strictly adheres to law or letter, rather than the Spirit. In Christian Theology, it is the act of putting the *law* [or, some set of rules, or any other religious system for that matter] above the Gospel by **establishing requirements for salvation** over and beyond simple obedience, repentance, and faith in Christ and the message of the Cross. Today, this is just as prevalent in the church as it was in Paul's day. In the *four* Gospels, it is called the **traditions** of men [of the Elders] (Matt. 15:2-9). In these scriptures, Jesus called these *traditions* the doctrines and commandments of men [the *teachings* and *rules* of men]. "Not giving heed to **Jewish** fables [myths], and

commandments of men, that turn from the truth" (Tit. 1:14). In the Amplified Bible, it is stated this way, "...or to **rules** [laid down] by [mere] men who reject and turn their backs on the truth [of the gospel]." [This presents the fact that anything that turns men from the Truth **of the Cross** must be rejected out of hand (TENT Page 879)].

Legalism is the opposite *heresy* of Antinomianism. Antinomianism rejects all moral standards including biblical morality; while Legalism, either exalts Law above Grace, or, rather, adds to grace some set of rules or ritual discipline necessary for salvation [justification]. The problem with Legalism [the problem with this error] [which is the fundamental distortion of Legalism] that makes it a *false gospel* is its belief that one must earn acceptance with God. This is outright denial [rejection] of the gospel. These hold to **the letter** *apart* from **the Spirit**!! Here, you will find men adding to the Law of God. Just as the Pharisee's of old, these add to the word of God their own distinctive traditions. Here, **traditions** would be understood as **any additional thing** *added* to the gospel message for our *justification*, and, even for our *sanctification*. Faith in the gospel *alone* **is the power** of God unto salvation [the gospel alone is the power of God to enter into our justification and sanctification]. Nothing else is required, or necessary!! To **add to the gospel**, or [to even] **subtract** from it we would run the risk of distorting the gospel. These who deal in the commandments [systems] of men raise their traditions to a status equal to the word of God. These *traditions* [systems] of men rob the people of God of their **blood bought freedoms** [their God given rights]. These put chains on people where God has left them free. Legalism [the commandments of men] have plagued the Church in every generation. Legalism often occurs as an overreaction against the sins [false doctrines/teachings] of the Antinomian heresy. Legalism then is the church [the believer] [without being fully aware of what he/she is doing] overreaching to make sure no one is allowed to slip into moral laxity [by putting the people under some set of rules or, some discipline] [a particular discipline or some practice that distracts from the gospel] [some specific religious restraint]. This creates a dictatorship [a lordship] *within* the local church [a separation between leadership and laity], and, will become very oppressive. It is **legalism** that is always *adding* something to the gospel; **antinomianism** is always subtracting. There are many different *forms* [expressions] of the antinomian heresy [lawlessness]. Often, these many different forms of lawlessness arise as an overreaction to legalism. Christians who are guarding against legalism have to be careful not to slip into the many different forms of **libertinism**. This is the *heresy* of self-indulgence [excessive freedoms]. These teach that to be under grace *means* to have a license to sin [one devoid of moral principles, and, are given over to experiencing the senses]. **Its cry for freedom against all oppression is a cry for moral liberty [freedom to sin].** These teach that the **remission** of sins [forgiveness] *means* to cover sins [and not the removal of sin] (Rom. 6:14-16). The only solution or correction necessary for either heresy is a clear and precise understanding of the gospel as *the power* [ability] of God that makes one righteous, and brings men *into* salvation [that which *empowers* men for sanctification and transformation] (RSB Page 1713). God, help us to break free from these very deceptive and destructive heresies!!

Paul's entire Epistle to the Galatians was dedicated to combating Legalism. The Judaizers in the scriptures were [Jewish followers of Christ] religionists [legalists] who adhered to a strict observance of the Law [the letter]. These would often put [promote] the **law** above **grace**, or mingle *law* with gospel [adding something to the gospel]. "Beware [take heed] lest any *spoil* [deceive] you through philosophy [through some wisdom] and vain deceit [through some empty pride], after the *traditions* of men, after the rudiments of the world [through some human logic], and not after Christ," [here this speaks of any **rule** or *doctrine* that pulls the believer away from the *message* of the Cross] (Col. 2:8). Here, **spoil** means to *distract* or intimidate ["strip you naked" or "take you captive"] (TPT Page 558 *f*). All of these things are intended to distract from the message of the Cross!!! Which the Bible calls "...the *simplicity* [the singleness] that is in Christ."

We find further in Colossians 2:18-23, Paul addressing the "Stoics" and other Greek disciplines. A *Stoic* or Stoicism in Paul's day was a system of logic promoting personal ethics. This philosophy at times would apply extreme discipline, what the bible calls "will worship *and* humility, and neglecting of the body; not in any honor [respect] to the satisfying of the flesh." [Stoicism is a passive determinism of emotional indifference that elevates the virtues of self-control. By mastering human passions and emotions one could realize peace within himself. The Greek Stoics believed that humans can only reach their full potential when they live by sheer reason and the divine principle, or the spark of divinity, which they called logos (TPT Page 359 *g*). This philosophy was the basis for many Gnostic Cults. The so-called Christian Gnostics rejected the Wisdom and Power of the Cross. Gnosticism comes from a GK word "gnosis" which *means* having knowledge. Many of these early so-called Christian and Jewish Sects emphasized personal spiritual knowledge and personal discipline over the orthodox teaching of the Church that included the Preaching of the Cross. The early church of the first three centuries encountered many false **gospels** [the so-called Christian Gnostic Cults]. These [persons] would often mix the gospel message with other religious disciplines [with other schools of thought].

Paul goes on to say, "Wherefore if ye be **dead** with Christ [on the Cross] from the rudiments [elements] of the world, why, as though living in the world, are ye subject to ordinances [rules], after the **commandments** and **doctrines** of men? (Touch not; taste not; handle not; which all are to perish with the using) [Which things indeed have a show of wisdom]. The Amplified Bible says it this way, "If then you have **died** with Christ [on the Cross] **to material ways of looking at things** and have escaped from the world's crude and elemental notions and teachings of externalism, why do you live as if you still belong to the world? [Why do you submit to **rules** and regulations? Such as] Do not handle [this], Do not taste [that], Do not even touch [them], referring to things all of which perish with being used. To do this is to follow *human percepts* and doctrines. Such [practices] have indeed the outward appearance [that popularly] passes for wisdom, in promoting [putting forth a] **self-imposed** rigor of devotion and delight in self-humiliation and **severity of discipline of the body**, <u>but they are of no value in checking the indulgence of the flesh</u> (the ***lower*** nature)." Only the CROSS-and the Divine Exchange [the atonement] can deal with the LOWER NATURE [the fallen human condition]. Listen to the way The Passion Translation states it, *"For you were included in the death of Christ and have **died with him to the religious system** and powers of this world. Don't retreat back to being **bullied by the standards and opinions of religion**-for example, <u>their strict requirements</u>, "You can't associate with that person!" or, "Don't eat that!" or, You can't touch that!' These **are the doctrines of men and corrupt customs that are worthless to help you spiritually**. For though they may appear to possess the promise of wisdom in their submission to God through the deprivation of their physical bodies, <u>it is actually nothing more than empty rules rooted in religious rituals</u>."* These are all those things we add to the ***gospel*** of His Grace [the preaching of the Cross]. This clearly corrects the so called Christian Ascetic's of the last 2000 years. Ascetic *means*, practicing strict self-denial as a measure of personal and especially spiritual discipline.

Jude in his epistle verse four [Jude 4] warned of false teachers who preach a *gospel* that turns the **grace** of God into a license to sin. In both cases, Paul and Jude warned the churches of the many different gospels altered in some way. Jude, when speaking of the believing Gentile spoke of a **bent** toward <u>lawlessness</u>, or lasciviousness (wantonness OE, negligence of restraint, or indulging freedom to excess). **Lawlessness** *means* unruly or not restrained. **Lawlessness** in Christian Theology is paying no attention to the biblical standard for Moral living. It is asserting that the Law of God has no place or demand any longer on the life of a Christian. It asserts that the Christian is no longer under or obligated to the biblical standards for biblical morality. Jude said, "For certain men have crept in stealthily [gaining entrance secretly by a side door]...persons who *pervert* [corrupt] the **grace** (the spiritual blessings and favor) of our God into <u>lawlessness</u> and wantonness and immorality, and disown and deny our sole <u>Master</u> and Lord, Jesus Christ" (Jude 4 Amp). From this, we can see that Lawlessness is tied [connected] to those who *deny* and *reject* His Lordship. The words Master and Lord here *implies* Slavery [servitude]. The believer is **bought** [was purchased] with a precious *price* that being the shed blood of Christ on the Cross!! Paul taught, that, all true believers have lost their **right** to themselves!! The true Christian has no *right* to deny [to turn a blind eye to] his Lordship, *thus* **has no right to live lawlessly [without restraint]** (1 Cor. 6:19-20). "For the love of God <u>constrains</u> us [fuels our passion and motivates us to obey God, TPT]...that they which *live* [have received a new life] should not henceforth live unto themselves, but unto him which died for them, and rose again" (2 Cor. 5:14-15). The word *constrain* here means to seize, compel, urge, and to control, to lay hold of, overwhelm, and completely dominate. Paul is stating that, the motivating passion of his life is Christ's love filling his heart, leaving him no choice but to surrender everything to God (TPT Page 493). Today, many in the church [who have laid claim to the Christian faith] have embraced a *false* **gospel** [a corrupted and distorted **grace**] that denies the Lordship of JC, and that welcomes a life <u>without restraint</u> or *self-control*, and now living a life in agreement with the moral standards and worldly values of this present evil age. Both Second Peter Chapter 2, and Jude, warn against preaching a **gospel** that *promotes* [allows for] loose **morals!!** "Then certain *philosophers* of the <u>Epicureans</u>, and of the <u>Stoics</u>, encountered him..." (Acts 17:18). These *persons* called the **Epicureans** were a branch of Greek philosophy that promoted self-indulgence, the gratification of the **appetites**, and material pursuits [not much different with many today **who preach a prosperity gospel**]. This *philosophy* denied the after-life, and was a type of humanism. This *branch* of Greek philosophy crept into the Church *turning* the **gospel** of His Grace into a license to sin [a permission and the promotion of vice]. Only the CROSS-and the Divine Exchange [the atonement] can deal with the LOWER NATURE [the fallen human condition]. While the gospel is not against the material realm [the body], at the same time, it is not the preaching and promotion of material things.

Peter, in his second epistle chapter two warned of false teachers who turned from the truth, from the true knowledge (gospel) of our Lord and Savior Jesus Christ, who subtly (slowly) brought in (introduced) destructive heresies, even denying the Lord who bought them (by his own precious blood), <u>bringing the way of truth into disrepute</u> (dishonor or discredit). These *false* gospels misrepresent the way of salvation, causing many to fall away from the truth about Jesus Christ and, the CROSS. Notice, the teachings of these teachers slowly moved away from the truth about the gospel, as they began **to alter** in some way the truth about the way of salvation. These *false* gospels have a tendency to either <u>center</u> [revolve around] the **law** [the letter] [rules], or give too much attention to **[externals/** outward things] appearances/observances [the traditions of men]; or, they will move in the opposite direction and take Christian liberty (freedoms) to an extreme [and indulge in loose morals]. *"Many will follow immoral lifestyles. Because of these false teachers, the way of truth will be slandered...Consumed with the lusts of the flesh,* **they lure back into sin those who recently escaped from their error.** *They promise others freedom, yet they themselves are slaves to corruption, for people are slaves to whatever overcomes them"* (2 Pet. 2:2, 18-19 TPT). This is an apostolic warning concerning false gospels.

Today, religious **traditions** *mixed* in with the **gospel** in so many churches have hidden its true meaning causing many to lose it [the gospel] altogether. Others, in their attempt to be relevant (germane) have introduced false freedoms into the church, which have caused many to allow the world and its ways, thinking, values, and <u>secularism</u> to crept in and corrupt its true message. S*ecularism* [nonreligious] (temporal) *means* indifference toward sacred things. These churches show no respect for the things of the past [having no interest and showing contempt for all *traditions* whether good or bad], and treating with contempt [all] anything that has the appearance of being old, as irrelevant. These *forge* new ideas [traditions] often based on worldly principles, and based [steeped in] modern values. Modernism is the tendency in theology to accommodate traditional religious [thinking] teaching to contemporary thought, which devalues [and reduces] the supernatural, and/or they devalue biblical moral standards. Both the *rejection* of the **supernatural** and the lowering of biblical standards of morality are in vogue for many contemporary churches. These popular or seeker friendly churches who lower biblical standards, and who deemphasize the Authority of Scripture are distorting (altering) the true gospel. They are watering down the message of the gospel [the message of the Cross], in order to appeal to (to attract, to lure) the world around them. They use secular methods of evangelism to attract the sinner (unbeliever) to Christ. Paul called this the preaching of *another* [a different] Jesus, the receiving of *another* [a strange] spirit, and believing on *another* [an altered] gospel (2 Cor. 11:3-4). God help us all!!! Today, there are more *tares* than **true wheat** in our churches!!!

The true gospel will *both* embrace the supernatural, and as well uphold biblical standards for morality. For the **grace** (gospel) of God that brings *salvation* hath appeared to all men, teaching us that, **denying ungodliness** and **worldly lusts,** we should live soberly, righteously, and **godly** in this present world (Tit. 2:11-12). The *preaching* of the true gospel of Jesus Christ will always uphold, in its entirety, the biblical standards for godliness (holiness) without compromise. Never once should grace (the gospel) be seen, or understood as a license to sin, or as a covering for a sinful lifestyle. Paul said, "Who gave himself for our sins, that he might ***deliver*** us [set us free] from this present evil world" (Gal. 1:4). *"He has taken us out of this evil world system and set us free through our salvation"* (Gal. 1:4b TPT). This "evil world system" would include not only the *irreligious* or the lawless, but as well, would include the **religious systems of men** based on some performance [duty] to some set of rules or religious traditions of men instead of the gospel of His grace [the power and wisdom of the Cross] (Pg. 514 TPT). For example, we find just prior to the Protestant Reformation of the 16th century many penitential religious works practiced by so called Christian monks all throughout Europe. Fastings, and prayers, self-flagellation, etc. all these things were *invented* and ordered by the [traditions] and commandments of men. Martin Luther called these doctrines [and religious practices] self-chosen works!! It is not that prayer, fasting, and the like, are wrong in and of themselves; but when applied, and understood as a *means* for justification [acceptance] with God, it is error [it is a false gospel].

In 2 Peter 1:4; 2:20, the apostle calls the believer, now a partaker of His divine nature, one who has escaped the corruption (the pollutions) that is in the world through lust, through the knowledge (of the gospel) of our Lord and Savior Jesus Christ. The warning that Peter gives in the text makes it clear that there is no wiggle room for compromise or distortion, "(If) they are **again** *entangled* therein (in the world), and **overcome** (to turn back to the old habits of sin), the latter end is worse with them [the believer] than the beginning." Many today are preaching an ***altered*** gospel that allows for modern ways, ideas, and values that has worked incessantly within our modern day culture to redefine and to change standards of morality. Paul warned the church that in these last and evil days there would be a great falling away from biblical standards, while maintaining a form of *godliness* (a form of the gospel) [but an altered gospel]. Paul spoke of these [persons] as those who would turn away their ears from the truth, drawing to themselves ***teachers*** who do the same (2 Tim. 3:5, 4:2-4). *"For the time is coming when they will no longer listen and respond to the healing words of the truth because they will become selfish and proud. They will **seek out teachers with soothing words that line up with their desires**, saying just what they want to hear. **They will close their ears to the truth**..."* (2 Tim. 4:3-4 TPT). Today, I have found many so called bishops, prophets, pastors, and leaders in Christendom all in agreement with the prevailing moral worldly trends of our modern present evil age. God help us all!!!

THE DEEDS OF THE LAW

"Knowing that a man is not justified [accepted] **by the works** of the law, but by faith of Jesus Christ...for by the *works* [deeds] of the law shall no flesh [man] be justified in the sight of God" (Gal. 2:16; Rom. 3:20). Just recently, I took out some time to watch on cable TV a program that highlighted the *histories* of both the Chinese and Japanese cultures. In this program, I [saw, and] came across **Confucius** a Chinese philosopher and politician. He was a Chinese sage; and, would later be recognized as a major religious figure within *both* the Chinese and Japanese cultures. He was an early Chinese ethical teacher promoting **a moral** and **social code of conduct** that worked to reform man **from the outside, in**. He was a man [a person] that practiced **an outward** *form* of **ritual discipline** designed to change the **outward habits** of the body, and **inward attitude** of the mind. Through constant **effort** and **practice** [ritual discipline], [constant repetition] a man would *transform* from what he was to the very thing he practiced. This is exactly what the Apostle Paul *meant* by the **deeds** of the Law. This is exactly what Paul had in mind when he said, by the deeds [works] of the law shall no man be *justified* in the sight of God. No moral code, ethical teaching, set of rules, religious system or, traditions [practices] of men can **convert the soul** [no works of self-discipline in and by themselves can **convert the heart**] and change the fallen inward nature and character of man in order to bring him/her into new life. Man is spiritually dead because of trespasses and sins [and separated from the life of God] (Eph. 2:1-9). No outward work, system, code of conduct, and/or religious practice can convert him, whether Greek, Roman, Chinese, nor Jewish, or any other source or type of ritual discipline, set of rules, or moral principles can justify man before God [these things cannot convert the heart nor change his inward nature]. Yes, it can **reform** [change] the *habits* of men from the outside, but it cannot change who he really is on the inside: it cannot change his fallen nature [fallen human condition on the inside]. No matter what we do or, no matter how hard we try, the outside cannot change the inside; only the gospel of His Grace **[the message of the Cross]** can forgive sins and covert the heart, **and bring men** into new life, which is found only in the **Person** and **work of** JC through faith in the gospel [through faith in that Cross: His divine-human redemptive works that makes this great exchange, possible].

This is exactly what Paul was getting at in Romans and Galatians; only the gospel can covert the heart [soul] of a sinner and bring about a spiritual rebirth. The gospel is all about a spiritual regeneration!!!!!! Man is *totally* depraved, which *means* he is affected [infected] by sin in all the different parts of his being: his spirit, soul, heart, mind, will, emotions, and body. This is why, no matter how much or how well he **obeys** a set of rules, a moral code, ritual discipline, or religious system it still will not and cannot cancel nor alter the old fallen human adamic nature within [that fallen human condition]. Man still is who he is by that inward nature; no matter how outwardly obedient [disciplined] he might be in his outward conduct. God looks not to [at] the *outward* appearance of man's endeavors [efforts], **but to the inward man of the heart**. The outward disciplines of man's efforts cannot and will never change his inward nature: **no matter how successful or effective he might be in the discipline of his mind and body**. The outward application of man's efforts cannot convert the heart and change who he is by nature [that fallen human condition within]. The fallen *spirit* of man must **be reborn**, and, must under-go a spiritual regeneration [must be made alive, and brought into new life], which only the gospel of His Grace can achieve [the message of the Cross]. The Jews under the Old Covenant did not understand this; today, most of the Church has forgotten this fact of man's entire moral depravity. Today, the *likes* of those who put their *trust* in the disciplines of the Buddha; and, the moral and social teachings of Confucius and, the many different Greek philosophies and disciplines that have influenced the moral and ethical principles of America and our western culture, is exactly what the bible *means* by the **deeds** of the law shall no flesh be justified in His sight [accepted with God]. It is not by a man's outward performance, duty, or moral obligation [even to the scriptures themselves] that changes a man and makes him/her right with God, **but only in the gospel of His grace**, and through faith in His blood that has made atonement for man's sins and rebellion before God can we be accepted. Not faith and *works* [Grace mingled with Law], but by faith **alone** in the gospel alone [His redemptive works on the Cross] can a man be justified [accepted before God]. This is why men must *first* come to understand his **true sinful condition**, before the *gospel* will make any real sense to his **mind** and understanding. This is exactly why Christ was sent: to *seek* and **to save** that which was lost [lost and fallen away through man's sin and sinful condition]. If man had the *power* in and of himself to keep a set of rules, moral principles, ritual discipline, and/or religious system [in order to change the fallen human condition within] and to earn his/her acceptance with God then **righteousness** [new life] would have come by the keeping of the Law [by man's outward performance of his body and his mind] (Gal. 3:21).

This is exactly what Paul was *addressing* in the church, in his letter to Colosse. For the first three centuries of the church Gnosticism was a major problem [opponent] of the gospel. This was for the most part a **moral** code and *religious* system [in many cases a ritual discipline] rivaling true Christianity; other aspects of Gnosticism moved into debauchery and threw out all moral restraints [this is what Jude was addressing in his epistle]. Here, I am specifically dealing with that form of [false] gospel that applied a **false humility** and **will worship** [that which exalted and promoted the religion of the *power* of the human will] based on the basic elementary principles of the world's moral and ethical beliefs [that rejected the bible's testimony of man's total moral depravity]. It in-stills a works-merit basis of acceptance with God in opposition to a faith-grace basis founded on the all-sufficiency of Christ's Person and work [on the Cross]. The tendency [of these people] is for these elementary principles **to produce a legalistic asceticism** [which relies **on the power of the human will to perform**], in contrast to faith alone in JC and our union with him through the spiritual **circumcision of the heart**. This new position for men [the believer] is the true authentic spiritual circumcision, i.e. the putting off of the body the <u>sinful nature</u>. The true Christian is now able to live a life of victory over sin and sinning because he has been made alive by the resurrection life Christ has *imparted* to him/her through faith in the gospel. The remedy to false religion **[the spiritual counterfeit]** and to any and every other false system of belief and practice centers on JC and what he did on the Cross to redeem men [The New Unger's Bible Handbook, by Moody Press]. In Paul's day, the two *groups* he was confronted by the most [outside of the Jews] were the Epicureans, and the Stoics. The <u>Epicureans</u> were given over to the present pleasures, and would line up with Jude's rebuke in his epistle to those who changed the grace of God into a license to sin; but the **Stoics** *embraced* a philosophy **of stern self-repression** based on human self-sufficiency [the power of the human will **and the belief in man's innate human goodness**]. These held to the high moral principles **of a life of self-denial** [King James Bible commentary, Thomas Nelson Publishers, Page 1370]. The belief in the **moral freedom** of the **human will** and the **innate goodness of man** has *infiltrated* the church and, the gospel message. Today, the church no longer believes in the total depravity of the human **person**. This is why today the *gospel* message is weaken, and, **no longer preached in its entirety**. Many no longer believe in the necessity of the Cross!! Many have turned the New Testament into a **moral guide**, and into just some *principles* to follow to win acceptance with God. Many today *preach* a Cross-less Christ!!! Many today preach a *gospel* without the need for the Cross!!! Many today preach a bloodless Gospel!!!!!!!!!!!! Many today preach a gospel of good works, **seeing no need for the atonement**. This can be traced back to those who began to reject the bible's testimony of man's total moral depravity, and then began

to preach the [false] *gospel* of man's innate [inherent] goodness. In Romans chapters 1-3, Paul started out by building the case against man's total inability to seek out and to serve God. Then Paul's remedy for man's total inability to obey God is found in Chapters 3-8. The gospel of His Grace is the message of the Cross that is necessitated because of man's inability to morally choose [through his own volition] to obey and to serve God. Paul said, "...there is *none* righteous, no, not one: there is *none* that understands, there is *none* that seeks after God. They are all gone out of the way, they are together become unprofitable; there is *none* that does good, no, not one... there is no fear of God before their eyes [all are guilty before God]" (Rom. 3:10-19). Here, in the first three chapters of Romans Paul was addressing men from all occupations. He first addressed the **pagan man** in Romans 1. Second, Paul addressed *both* **the moralist** [the moral man] [this is the *Gentile* living by some moral code in pursuit of virtue], and the *Jew* [the **religionist**] in Romans chapters 2 and 3. These [all] three groups Paul is addressing here becomes the audience of Romans 6 and 7. Knowing this will help us to understand Paul's mindset [and his meaning] in these chapters [in Romans six and seven] applied to our Christian sanctification. The *gospel* is the **power** of God to enter into salvation!!

Secular Humanism believes man is inherently good; this way of thinking has crept into the church and the gospel message. Today, many so called Christians have lost the true and genuine testimony of the Scriptures concerning man's true condition before God. Man is a fallen creature, a creature that must be born again!!! The bible says, all men are spiritually **dead** to the true God through their many trespasses and sins. All these trespasses and sins against the Law of God, is found as to its true source **in the fallen sinful nature** [the fallen human condition passed down from the first man, Adam] (Eph. 2:1-5; Rom. 5:12-21). Man is not inherently good, but is clearly inherently evil [corrupt to his core] and in rebellion against God his maker [creator]. Man is dead morally and spiritually and **unable to use [exercise] his human free will** to choose that which is good. Even

his good works [his good deeds] [apart from God] **are evil** [corrupted and tainted by the presence of sin and the sinful condition]. Because of the fallen human condition within, all of humanity, **his human free will is as well fallen [and corrupted]**. It is not that man is not free to choose, **just not free to choose the good** [the perfect Will of God in obedience from the heart]. Man is only **free to choose in accordance with his fallen nature.** Man has no ability in and of himself to choose God apart from the grace of God; this is the testimony of the Apostle Paul in Romans chapters 1-8. Man in his pride and fallen human condition will attempt to earn [work] for his acceptance with God. A justification or acceptance with God through an outward code of conduct [set of rules] and religious system [ritual discipline] that cannot change him [that fallen human condition and the corrupted human will (heart)]. No matter how good or altruistic he may appear to be to others, the *motives* of the **heart** cannot escape the *corruptions* of the fallen sinful nature within [fallen human condition]. This is why Jesus said, "...neither can a corrupt tree bring forth good fruit" (Matt. 7:17-20). Jesus said, "Either **make the tree good, and his fruit good**; or else make the tree corrupt, and his fruit corrupt: for a tree is known by its fruit" (Matt. 12:33). JC said, "...neither **can a corrupt tree bring forth good** fruit" (Matt. 7:18). No matter how hard a man attempts to change himself on the outside, who is born into an inward sinful nature, this will never take, and this can never overturn that sinful inward condition. If the tree is corrupt *within* it can only produce evil works [bear corrupt fruit] no matter how true and genuine [and good] these works may appear to be on the outside [for all to see]. All their good works and deeds are corrupt and tainted by the stain and influence of sin [that fallen human adamic condition (root-nature)].

The human will is in bondage to sin and the sinful condition within, and cannot properly respond to God and His Will apart from the **power** provided by the *gospel* of His Grace [that divine exchange- the message of the Cross]. The fallen human will is free to choose, just not free to choose God [the good] apart from the intervention of

His Divine Grace. This is why the *gospel* of His Grace is like no other religion, philosophy of men, or moral code of conduct: for with men [by the human will of man] salvation is impossible, but with God **[by his grace, alone]** salvation is made possible, *"So then it is not of him that wills, nor of him that runs, but of God that shows mercy"* (Rom. 9:16). All these things are made possible by the help and strength of His divine Grace [this is the helplessness of man in his sin, and the sovereignty of God in His Grace]. This is the sinner's [man's] moral inability to obey God apart from His Divine Grace. This is why the bible says, man has to be spiritually *quickened* and make alive with Christ; because man himself apart from His [God's] divine Grace [in and of himself alone, and his own dead religious works] is helpless and unable to respond to God without GRACE [Eph. 2:1-10]. The Gospel that men preach today is seriously lacking the power of God to transform the sinner. It is more of a works based [oriented] gospel based on the innate [inherent] goodness of man; and/or it is a gospel that **rejects the basic biblical standard for morality** [a license to live contrary to the Law of God]. Self-effort and self-reliance *plagues* the church and hinders the **power** inherent within the gospel message alone. The power of God will not *work* apart from our **total abandonment** to the grace of God. Grace will not fully work unless one understands their total inability to help themselves! It will take God to open our eyes to see this is so, *both* scripturally and experientially. God, help us to abandon ourselves and our understanding of things, and our labor, over to the grace of God.

Some have taught that the **two trees** in the garden in Genesis 2 represent both law and gospel. Ever since the fall of Adam, men would rather **live by the law** rather than simply receive God's grace through faith in the blood of His Cross. Men today would rather **live by some set of rules** [by some religious system] then simply receive the gospel. Men would rather rely upon their own human efforts and strength then simply, trust God. The reason for this is that men believe in their **own innate** [inherent] **goodness** within them. Men reject the testimony of the scriptures where it concerns his total moral depravity [his fallen sinful human condition within]. Men strive by an outward effort to prove themselves good, and worthy of divine acceptance. Because of this, man would rather live by his own principles, and by his own ideas of a higher moral good. It is this knowledge of the good that men strive to prove their inherent goodness. Today, men see no need for a gospel; men believe in their own innate goodness and, through his own moral efforts he will earn God's approval. Men would rather devise their own schemes [methods] and, would rather create their own devices, then put their trust in God, and surrender their will to Him. Men would rather invent a way to God, then simply receive God's way!! Men seek to **improve** themselves in order to **prove** themselves to God, and to men. Today, many men who call themselves Christian, who put their trust in some outward [external] restraint have simply **reduced the gospel** to some outward religious work, or some moral code, or a set of rules to follow applied to outward works.

In Genesis, God created in 6 days all we see today in our material world. After each day of creation, God said, "it is good." On the 6th day when God created man, He said, it was very good. The knowledge of the good is tied into *both* the **created order of things** and, **man's conscience**. The conscience within communicates **what is right** from what **is wrong**; because of this built in knowledge of the good, many men strive to live by a higher moral standard [principle of truth]. It is in the garden where man was first introduced to the tree of the knowledge of good and evil. It is not just the knowledge of the evil, but as well, it is the knowledge of the good. All would agree today, that to live a life of vice, or, to pursue a life of pleasure and self-seeking, is the knowledge of the evil. Very few today see a life that is lived by the high ideals of man's moral and religious standards, as nothing more than just eating from the same corrupted tree. Many men throughout the history of the world have sought after the highest good, to live by principles of truth based upon the **elementary principles** of the world **[the created order of things]**. These who have sought after truths and principles to live by, based on the knowledge of the truth [based upon the knowledge of the good] found both **in nature**, and **conscience**, have rejected the **person of truth** and the **author of life [the One, (the only one) who made all these things possible]**. These have attempted to live by the **principles** of truth, but have rejected the **<u>Person</u>** of truth [Jesus Christ]. Man can reach their highest good, in keeping with some set of rules, some moral principles, in a code of conduct, and in the adherence to some school of thought: both a religious and philosophical system, and keep it perfectly, and yet, he is lost, spiritually dead in trespasses and sins. Man cannot save himself!! Man cannot and will never reach the highest good and attain to the highest truth without first putting their trust in the Person of Truth [the Good Shepherd].

"For I am not ashamed of the *gospel* of Jesus Christ: for it is the **power** of God unto <u>salvation</u> to everyone that believes; to the Jew first, and also to the Greek" (Rom. 1:16). Here, Paul is calling the **gospel** of Jesus Christ a POWER. This word <u>power</u> is the GK word *dunamis* where we get our English word dynamite. This speaks of explosive power. The true gospel is explosive power!!! This ***power*** is the mighty sanctifying and perfecting work of the Holy Spirit in the life of the believer (Acts 1:8). This **power** will *both* work the works of God (operate the *gifts* of the Spirit) and bring forth the *fruit* of the Spirit (reproduce the character of Christ in the life of the Christian). All of this is contingent upon a right understanding and right application of the gospel of Jesus Christ. The Holy Spirit will not recognize nor work through a spiritual counterfeit. This is why so many are ***weak*** in spiritual things, and susceptible (in bondage) to carnal vices (things of the flesh). No power!!!!!!!!! The power (of the Holy Spirit) will work, but it will only work in conjunction with the preaching of the true gospel "For the preaching of the *Cross*...unto us which are **saved** it is the ***power*** of God" (1 Cor. 1:18). Notice, for the saved person, the Christian, the preaching of the Cross continues to be the POWER of God. This <u>salvation</u> where of Paul speaks, means *deliverance* (rescue) from sin, *healing* from bodily sicknesses and diseases, *soundness* or wholeness a complete **redemption** that will affect (impact) not only the spirit's <u>regeneration</u>, but the soul's <u>transformation</u>, and the body's <u>subjugation</u>, and future <u>resurrection</u> (1 Thess. 5:23). This salvation or *gospel* where of Paul speaks must include both <u>Justification</u> and <u>Sanctification</u>. This true gospel *promises* both the **power** of God to save us, then through that same *power* to continue to keep us through sanctification and honor unto God. **The grace (gospel) of Jesus Christ is a ruling power!!** Keep in mind; a **bent** toward either <u>legalism</u> or <u>lawless</u> tendencies could disqualify you from accessing both this justifying and sanctifying [perfecting] **grace** in your own personal life and spiritual growth, creating a <u>form of godliness</u> [a counterfeit gospel]. Notice, this gospel is for both the <u>Jew</u> and the <u>Greek</u> [the Gentile]. This is not only the answer to Moses, and the law of God [Judaism: Jewish law keeping and Jewish customs]; but as well is the answer to every Gentile **philosophy, morality**, ethics, religions, **rituals**, symbols, **practices**, and any other **discipline** and **belief** in the pursuit of the higher good [in the pursuit of virtue]. <u>Greek</u> here refers to the **sophisticated** Gentile, the one in pursuit of virtue and self-improvement. Paul speaks of the Jew [the religionist], as well the Greek, and the <u>barbarian</u>. Here, **<u>Barbarian</u>** would reflect every other Gentile [every other people group] in the pagan world who are taken up by pagan ideas and pagan customs and, practices based upon superstitions and any other elementary elements of the natural material world of animate and inanimate objects [natural things]. A crude living; and, a belief system based on the lower animal nature of man's fallen human condition; these see themselves as no different, as animals. They live as one with nature; as those who are only a part of the natural order of things; and not as a higher order of being that was **made in the image** and *likeness* of God: having a **human spirit higher and unlike any of the other** living creatures (Gen. 1:20-28; 2:7-9; Zech. 12:1; Rom. 1:13-17). We find in Ecclesiastes 3:18-22, how man in his fallen human state fairs no better than the beasts of the field. As one dies, so dies the other!! They *both* **share in the same one breath** [require the same physical air to live]; so man in his fallen state is seen and look upon as no different: as one having no preeminence above a beast: for all is vanity [all is empty] [all is futility] in man's fallen human state. This is the pagan ideal and the pagan experience in this life of fallen creation. All, go unto the same one place; all are of the dust and, all turn to dust, again. This is the reality of the pagan world and the pagan man of the 5 physical senses: **the sense ruled man!!** To them the supernatural is the various superstitions of the various workings of all the elements of those things both animate and inanimate [the forces of nature and the natural forces of this life] interacting within all things that were and are created upon planet earth. This **is a nature worship and a natural religion, and a practice** that draws its power and strength from that fallen human state within [the fallen adamic spirit and root-nature]. You will notice, despite the negative and fallen condition of man in the text, when a man dies his spirit goes upward and returns to God, and the beast of the earth: their spirit goes downward and will return to the earth from which it came: proving man to be the higher order of being despite his fall from grace [despite his fall from his privileged position]. This is the difference between the Greek and the Barbarian, one is in the pursuit **of the highest good**, while the other is content to live in agreement with the lower nature; and yet, both, are in that same fallen human condition!! The word <u>sophisticated</u> *means* highly developed, refined in knowledge, and finely [tuned] experienced and made aware of the good [the evolution of man]. <u>Barbarian</u> means one who is inferior; one who is lacking refinement, learning, knowledge, sophistication, and culture. This gospel of JC is not only for the unrefined, and unlearned, and those who are hopelessly lost; but, as well for all those who are educated, learned, refined, successful, cultured, sophisticated, and experienced in this present world; who do not know they are just **as helpless** and **hopelessly lost** as all others (how all these things cannot and will not save themselves). God help us to see the gospel of JC as the only hope and help for man!!!! All men are in the same condition and status in this life where it concerns eternity. This gospel is for the Jew *first*; then it is for the *Greek*: all those who through the pursuit of the highest good whose goal of self-improvement [personal achievement] have attempted to earn them favor with God [or, to earn the right, and, a place in the afterlife]. Last but not least; the majority of this world live under a very low moral standard of living. Most would be considered pagan, heathen, and inferior by all standards of moral men. This world is completely fallen with no innate or inherent goodness to found in any, whether Jew, Greek, or Barbarian. The Christian is called a NEW CREATION!!! The highest good and the highest truth is found only in Christ and him crucified.

What, I have attempted to do in these books is, to bring back to the preaching of the gospel that balance of power, which still heals the sick, cleanses the leper, raises the dead, and casts (drives) out devils (Matt. 10:1-8); but as well, causing all men who believe in Christ and him crucified to become partakers (full participates) in the divine nature, being fully conformed to in character to the image of the Son, unto the measure of the stature of the fullness of Jesus Christ, which Paul called the **perfect** man (the maturing of sons: 2 Pet. 1:3; Rom. 8:29; Eph. 4:13). The true UBER man [superman] is the BORN AGAIN believer who is now in Christ Jesus. The one who is **now growing** and **increasing** in the knowledge of God, and **in the full stature of** Jesus Christ (Rom. 8:29-30). We see today, in the world, the **new age movement**, the **free masons**, and the many other different **eastern** and **western** schools of thought; the many **meditative practices of the east**, and the many other philosophical schools of thought coming from the west that influences our western culture today, all perishing with the using!!! The power to change; and, the power to overcome these fallen forces of darkness, and fallen beggarly elements of this fallen evil world is found in our simple **baptism** *into* Jesus Christ: we put into his death, burial, and resurrection. The power of God is found in Jesus Christ and him crucified, alone!!! God help us all to see and believe!! It is in our simple baptism by Spirit into his death and resurrection that has turned the ordinary man into an Uber-Man: all because of our new union with him, Christ.

God has put it in the *gospel* this inherent ability (capacity) to forgive sins, empower service, and transform character, which the bible reveals will be the hallmark or distinctive characteristics of the BRIDE **who will make herself ready** for the return of the bridegroom. The *gospel* and the **preaching of the Cross will have its final act played out in the last scene on the world stage** before Christ returns to the earth. This will be a gospel of power that will demonstrate both what is of him, and who truly belongs to him. This will take place during a time when many will fall away from the faith [the true gospel of our salvation], some rejecting its power (miracles), others, denying its godly character, while still, even others **will demonstrate a willful rejection** of both. In these three series of books called EVANGEL [the GOSPEL], I will attempt to paint a full picture of redemption, though not exhaustively, but completely, in order to *equip* and *prepare* the saints to shine forth as the sun in the preaching and demonstration of the kingdom of God "and this *gospel* of the **kingdom** shall be preached in all the world **for a witness unto all** nations; and then shall the end come (Matt. 13:34; 24:14) [the end will not come until the bride has prepared herself in all her glory and splendor (both the *gifts* and *fruits* of the HS) as one belonging to the GOD-Man Jesus Christ]. The Spirit, has given us all these giftings and callings of God in order that the true Church of the Lord Jesus Christ might grow up in him [Jesus Christ] in all things for the edification and increase [and transformation] of his bride.

My prayer for these books, "That the God of our Lord Jesus Christ, the Father of glory, may give unto you the spirit of wisdom and revelation in the knowledge of Him: the eyes of your understanding being enlightened; that ye may know what is the hope of his calling, and what the **riches of the glory of his inheritance in the saints**, and what is the exceeding greatness of his power to us-ward who believe, according to the working of his mighty power, which he wrought in Christ, when he raised him from the dead, and set him at his own right hand in the heavenly places," **be with you all** (Eph. 1:17-20). Paul here is speaking of the *knowledge* of Jesus Christ [the knowledge of His Grace], which we receive through the knowledge of his **word** that enables the Holy Spirit to increase our "Wisdom and Revelation," the eyes of our heart being enlightened [illuminated; to receive light]. This illumination is the power to live a holy life; a power given to all those who believe on the Lord Jesus Christ and what He has done at the Cross. This spiritual wisdom and knowledge from God works in the believer's life according to the power of His/the indwelling presence of the HS, and works for us [on our behalf] according to the precision of our faith in that Finished Redemptive Work of Christ: in his death, burial, and resurrection, and in our knowledge of it and, in our trust in it [TENT Page 784]. God help us to see these things!!!

GRACE OF CHRIST

"To the praise of the *glory* of his **grace**, wherein he hath made us acceptable in the beloved. In whom we have redemption through his blood, the forgiveness of sins, **according to the** *riches* **of his grace**" (Eph. 1:6-7). God Be Praised For His/this wonderful and matchless Grace!!!

"Through **Him** also we have [our] *access* (entrance, introduction) by faith into this **grace** (state of God's favor) in which we [firmly and safely] stand" (Rom. 5:2 Amp). Grace is a **position** [*place* of favor; provision] we stand in before God. "Who, when he came, **and had seen the grace of God**, was glad, and exhorted them all, that with purpose of heart they would cleave unto the Lord" (Acts 11:23). What Barnabas saw was the visible tangible **power** and *moving* of God's Spirit among them, and He called it the Grace of God. The *testimony* of the Scriptures make it clear, that, the Grace of God is a POWER that converts and transforms. We find in Hebrews 4:16, that, grace is given **to help [to aid] us** in our time of need. It is not a covering [or exemption] given to us for **failure**; but, a *power* to help aid us in our time of temptation that we might overcome. It is a provision [supply] given that *enables* the believer toward victory!! The grace of God is not a covering for failure but a promise and power [provision] for victory [a power and provision for our success]. I'm not saying that Christians cannot fail, but, grace is given to help us to overcome failure and defeat, not to succumb to it. In Hebrews 12:14-17, we find the writer warning Christians not to FAIL the Grace of God. We are called **to holiness**, and must look diligently to the Grace of God lest we fail the grace of God, and thereby be identified with the **fornicator**, or any <u>profane</u> person [worldly, sensual, and compromised person], that, when he/she would have inherited the blessing, he or she, was rejected. "Wherefore we receiving a kingdom which cannot be moved, **let us have grace**, whereby we may serve God **acceptably with reverence and godly fear**" (Heb. 12:28). Did you see that? The Grace of God *enables* us to serve Him in an acceptable manner through godly lives that expresses godly fear. The bible tells us that, by **the fear** of the Lord men depart *from* evil (Prov. 16:6). It is clear from the scriptures that **grace** and sin [wickedness] do not mix!! Being under Grace and living in sin should not have a part in the same sentence, "But the Lord is faithful, who shall establish you [in the faith; in holiness] and keep you from evil" (2 Thess. 3:3). In John 17:15, Jesus prayed to the heavenly Father [for those who belonged him] to keep them from the evils of sin and the evils of this world. All of this is made possible by the *infused* grace of God [and the sanctifying work of the HS] within the life of the true born again spirit filled believer, "For it is a good thing that the **heart** [of the believer] be established [strengthened for his journey] with **grace**" (Heb. 13:9). Luke wrote in Acts 20:32, "...and to the word [message] of his grace, which is able to build you up [grow you up in the things of God], and to give you an inheritance among all them <u>which are sanctified</u>." Notice in the text, grace, is working on your/our behalf in order to bring you/us into sanctification. This inheritance whereof Paul speaks is only realized [by the believer] through his/her sanctification; and that, **this grace** is working diligently to do [accomplish] in your life: to build you up and to bring you into your spiritual inheritance in JC. Grace is not passively waiting around until you sin in order to cover up [or clean up] your sinful mess; Grace is always **active** and moving [working] **to empower**, enable, and transform all who are willing to receive its work [its part] in the sanctification process. The sanctification process involves the **active grace**, the work of the HS, and the cooperation [yielded life] of the believer. This is why Paul and Barnabas encouraged the believers **to continue** <u>in the Grace</u> of

God (Acts 13:43). Why would they counsel believers to continue in something [passive] that could not help or change them? There is no doubt; grace is a power and provision made available to us in our union with Christ. **Sin should not reign** [or rule over us] in our mortal body, that we should obey it [sin] in the lusts thereof (Rom. 6:12). Why, because we are dead to sin, and now living under the Grace of God, and walking according to the Spirit's empowerment (Rom. 6:2, 14-15; 8:13).

*"God's marvelous **grace** has manifested **in person**, bringing salvation for everyone. This same **grace teaches us** how to live each day as we turn our backs on <u>ungodliness</u> and <u>indulgent lifestyles,</u> and it equips us **to live self-controlled, upright,** and **godly lives** in this present [evil] age"*(Tit. 2:11-12 TPT). The GK word for "ungodliness" is singular, while the word for "indulgent lifestyles" is plural. This has led some scholars to believe that we are to turn our backs on both the ***root principle*** for ungodliness [which would be the sinful nature] and the ***specific acts*** that result from ungodliness [the body of sin]. These three specific adjectives "self-controlled," "upright," and "godly" refer to our behavior [conduct] toward God and toward others. In verse 13 and 14, Paul says, *"For we continue to look forward to the joyful fulfillment of our hope in the drawing splendor [appearing] of the glory of our great **God** and **Savior**, Jesus Christ…[who] sacrificed himself for us that he might <u>purchase our freedom from every lawless deed</u> and to purify for himself a people who are his very own, passionate to do what is beautiful in his eyes"* [TPT]. Notice in the text the four great truths of Grace: <u>Grace</u> is a person; <u>Grace</u> brings salvation; <u>Grace</u> educates us on how to live pure lives; <u>Grace</u> brings an [End-time] hope of the manifestation [appearing] of Jesus Christ [We are a people encircled by God himself. The compound Greek word *periousios* is translated from "around," as a circle, and the verb "to be." It can mean something surrounded by something else. It can be charted by a dot within a circle. As the circle surrounds the dot, so God is around each one of his saints. The circle has the dot all to itself. Therefore, God has his very own all to himself.

We are unique in that we belong only to him. Uniquely his, we are monopolized by God, ***taken into himself by grace*** through faith and surrounded by his love]. [TPT Page 613-614; **footnotes** h,i,j,k,m,n]. The bible says, "...your life is hid with Christ in God (Col. 3:3). God surrounds us as we are in union with Him [Christ].

THE OTHER SIDE OF GRACE NO ONE TOLD YOU ABOUT

"I marvel that ye are so soon removed from him that called you into the **grace** of Christ unto another **gospel**" (Gal. 1:6). You will notice in this text, both, the *grace* of Christ and the *gospel* are used as interchangeable terms **"...into the grace of Christ *unto* another gospel?** When we speak of the grace of God, we are speaking of the gospel of Jesus Christ. All that the *gospel* means, and all that the *gospel* provides for the believer comes by the **grace** of God. It is through the preaching of the true gospel [the message of the Cross] that the *grace* of Christ is available to all who believe. Remember, the *gospel* of Christ is the power of God unto salvation to everyone who believes (Rom. 1:16). The *gospel* is the means by which the Holy Spirit will move [act] and work through in power to perform and provide the believer with all that is necessary for salvation and sanctification [for victory over sin, the world, and the devil] which, is a work of His grace [is performed by His Grace]. May God be praised and honored forevermore because of His Grace!!

To alter the gospel in any way is to exchange it for another!! Jude said, "...**turning** the *grace* of our God into carnal vice or into a license to sin, and denying the only Lord God, and our Lord Jesus Christ" (Jude 4). To alter the gospel in any way is to deny, refuse, and reject his lordship over one's life. The word *turning* in the GK, means, to, **change** the gospel in any way, is, to, **exchange** that same gospel for a different one. Of course, Paul stated in Galatians 1:6-9, that, there is no other gospel available or acceptable. The grace of Christ and the preaching of the true gospel are inseparable!!!!!! You cannot have the one without the other!!! You cannot claim to be under the grace of God, if, you are putting your trust and hope in a different gospel [or, you are putting your trust and hope in a spiritual counterfeit]. The grace of Christ is only available to those who place their trust in, only, the true biblical Evangel (the gospel). This is why Paul said, "That if thou shalt confess with thy mouth **the <u>Lord</u> Jesus,** and shalt believe <u>in</u> thine <u>heart</u>...thou shalt be saved" (Rom. 10:8-10). Notice, we *confess* Jesus as **Lord** in order to be saved. Anyone who **alters** the gospel, or, receives an **altered** gospel, will end up denying **his Lordship** through rejecting the one and only **true gospel**. Confess with your mouth the **Lord Jesus**, and then you will be saved. This confession of his lordship in the life of the believer is, **the right** [authority] [legal ground] the *grace* of Christ has **to save** [justification] and **to rule** [sanctification] through righteousness by JC our Lord (Rom. 5:21). Grace, is God's ruler, it is not, your/our slave!!

"Moreover, brethren, I declare unto you the **gospel** which I preached unto you, which also ye have received, and wherein ye stand; by which also ye are saved, if ye keep in memory what I preached unto you, **unless ye have believed in vain**. For I delivered unto you first of all that which I also received, how that Christ **died for our sins** according to the scriptures; and that he **was buried,** and that he <u>rose again</u> the third day according to the scriptures" (1 Cor. 15:1-4). Paul defined the **gospel** as the DEATH, BURIAL, and RESURRECTION of our Lord Jesus Christ. Notice, Paul, is warning in the text, *"By which also ye are saved, if ye <u>keep</u> in memory what I preached unto you,* **unless ye have believed in vain.**" To **keep** the *gospel* means to hold to it and to continue therein. The warning the scriptures give is, that, many who believe at first, will not continue to hold to the truth of the gospel; but they will rather, **begin to drift away** toward some spiritual counterfeit, or, just walk away altogether. Too many separate the *grace* of God from the *gospel* of Christ, as if, they, can continue in the **grace** of God even though they moved away from the **gospel** of Jesus Christ. In Romans 1:16, Paul calls it the GOSPEL of Christ; in Galatians 1:6, he calls it the GRACE of Christ. Both the *gospel* and the *grace* of God are found in the same one person and redemptive work of our Lord and Savior Jesus Christ on the Cross. To *deny* the **one** (the gospel of Christ) is to *reject* the **other** (the grace of Christ). No wonder Paul said, "But we preach Christ [the person of His Grace] crucified" (1 Cor. 1:23). You cannot separate the ***grace*** of God from the ***gospel*** of Christ!!! The **ONE** [the grace of God] depends totally and entirely on the **OTHER** [the gospel of Christ]. God, help us all to see this!!!!!!!

Many lay claim to the *forgiveness* of God, but separate that forgiveness from the Lordship of Jesus Christ "And **that repentance** and the *remission* of sins should be preached **in his name** [the Lord Jesus Christ] among all nations, beginning at Jerusalem" (Lk. 24:46-47). The word *remission* in the GK means forgiveness, not just **pardon** for sin, but as well **deliverance** from sin [remember, *mercy* is God not doing something or, not giving you what you deserve; but *grace* is God doing something or, giving you what is undeserved]. The grace of God is not a covering for a sinful lifestyle but an empowerment of a new life of righteousness by One Jesus Christ, "...much more they which receive abundance of *grace* [favor] and of the **gift** of righteousness shall reign [rule] in life by one, the Lord Jesus Christ...that as **sin** hath reigned [ruled] unto death, **even so might grace reign** [rule] [now] through righteousness unto eternal life by Jesus Christ our Lord" (Rom. 5:17, 21). You will notice, it is by Jesus Christ who is our Lord, that, God is now doing something. You will notice they preached **repentance** for the forgiveness of sins!!!! Repentance comes before forgiveness. To *repent* means to think differently about yourself and your sins, and to change your mind, and reverse your decision and the course of your life (the direction you are moving in). Both the true gospel and the grace of Christ will always honor and uphold the Lordship of Jesus Christ over the life and choices of those who believe. "That the *name* of our <u>Lord</u> Jesus Christ may be ***glorified*** in you, and ye in him, according **to the grace** of our God and the <u>Lord</u> Jesus Christ" (2 Thess. 1:12). "Wherefore we receiving a kingdom which cannot be moved, **let us have grace,** whereby we may serve God acceptably with reverence and godly fear: for our God/Christ is a consuming fire" (Heb. 12:28-29). There is no doubt; grace has imparted something brand new to us that, has **changed absolutely everything** in our life. This is why Paul, **called us a new creature/a new creation!!** In the GK this *means* a "**new thing**, and is as well, a new spiritual genesis/a new spiritual (re)generation] (2 Cor. 5:17). Thanks be to God!!

Peter said, "For if after they have escaped the pollutions of the world *through the knowledge of the Lord and Savior Jesus Christ,* (if) they are again entangled therein, and overcome, the latter end is worse with them than the beginning" (2 Pet. 2:20). Notice, it was through **the knowledge** of this *gospel* of JC as *both* Savior and Lord that they were saved. They escaped the corruption of this world [and Satan], and came into true salvation that will always bear the fruits of sanctification (a life victorious over sin, the world, and the devil), and they were enabled to do this through the power and performance of the Holy Spirit in their lives, working through the knowledge (of the gospel) of Christ as *both* Savior and Lord. Just as you cannot separate the grace of God from the gospel of Christ, you also cannot and must not separate his Savior-ship from His Lordship. "[For it is He] who *delivered* and **saved us** and called us with a calling in itself holy and leading to holiness [to a life of consecration, a vocation of holiness]; [He did it] not because of anything of merit that we have done, but, because of, and, to further His own **purpose** [His Will] and *grace* (unmerited favor) which was given us in Christ Jesus...[It is that purpose and grace] which He now has made known and has fully disclosed and made real [to us] through the appearing of our **Savior** Christ Jesus, **who annulled death** and made it of no effect and brought [new] *life* and immortality (immunity from eternal death) to light through the **gospel** [of Christ]" (2 Tim. 1:9-10 Amp). It is clear; the reason for the bestowing of His Grace [Divine Favor] on the life of the believer is for His Divine Eternal Purposes (for his good pleasure, not ours). Grace is extended for His own purposes and not for our personal pleasure. He saves us not for us, but for Himself!! We are saved according to his own purpose and grace!!! Not just grace, but, as well, his, own, divine, eternal purposes are we saved!! We are saved by grace, through faith, for his own divine eternal purpose and glory [we are saved for his good pleasure]. Help!!

The grace of God is not a covering for a sinful lifestyle but an empowerment of a new life of righteousness by one Jesus Christ "...much more they which receive abundance of **grace** and of the *gift* of righteousness shall reign [rule] in life by one, Jesus Christ...that as sin hath reigned [ruled] unto death, even so might *grace* reign [rule] through righteousness unto eternal life by Jesus Christ our Lord" (Rom. 5:17, 21). It is clear from this text, that, most believers (Christians) have completely misunderstood the very purpose for His Divine Grace. His Grace is given [to hold] divine authority for one purpose alone to **govern** and to **guide** the entire sanctification process. This is why the Holy Spirit is called the Spirit of Grace; just as He is called the Spirit of Truth (Heb. 10:29; Jn. 16:13). Did you know the Bible also calls Him the "Spirit of Holiness?? "And declared to be the Son of God *with power*, according to the **spirit of holiness**, by the <u>resurrection</u> from the dead" (Rom. 1:4). What does **"with power"** mean?? The GK word here is *dunamis* "But ye shall receive **power** [dunamis] after that the Holy Ghost is come upon you" (Acts 1:8). This scripture in Romans 1:4 is referring to the Holy Spirit when he [the Holy Spirit] raised Jesus Christ from the dead, "But if the **Spirit** of him [God] that *raised* up Jesus from the dead" (Rom. 8:11). Of course, this text in Romans 1:4 is declaring Jesus Christ as Eternally Holy!! The Holy Spirit or the Spirit of Holiness is sent into the earth to declare it, "But when the **Comforter** is come, whom I [Jesus] will send unto you from the Father, even the Spirit of Truth, which proceeds from the Father, **he shall testify of me**...He shall **glorify me**; for he shall receive of mine, and shall show it unto you

(Jn. 15:26, 16:14). Just as Jesus is the Christ, the Holy Spirit is the Spirit of Christ. Just as Christ is the personification of His [God's] Grace, the Holy Spirit is the Spirit of Grace. Just as Jesus the Christ is the Person of the Holiness of God, the Holy Spirit is the Spirit of Holiness. This is why the Holy Spirit will wait, and will only work in and through the ***mediumship*** of the Gospel [Grace of Christ] [the Cross] of Jesus Christ. The Holy Spirit has come to take that which belongs to Him, the Lord Jesus Christ [what is his], and to declare it/him [and to show it] unto you. The **power** of this *gospel* is experienced in/by the Spirit and the Cross.

You will notice in the two scriptures of Romans 5:17 and 21, the **believer** [who received the abundance of *grace* and of the *gift* of righteousness] shall rule [reign] in life [in this life] by this one Jesus Christ; and **grace** [through that same given righteousness by the power of the Holy Spirit] shall rule [empower; guide; govern] the believer through this righteousness [a given righteousness] to spiritual victory by that same one Jesus Christ our Lord. Grace [both] comes from the Lord, and is the Lord. Grace is *both* **a principle** [a supply], and **a person**!! It speaks to both who he is, and what he does. Notice that *both* **grace** and the **believer** shall *rule* together in this life by that same one Jesus Christ our Lord. Both **grace** and the **believer** *cooperate* [work together] in bringing forth a spiritual harvest [a spiritual result]. "Whereunto I also labor, striving (struggling; laboring; fighting) according to his working (the operation of his grace), which works in me mightily" (Col. 1:29). *"But God's amazing **grace** has made me who I am! And his **grace** to me was not fruitless. In fact, I worked harder than all the rest, yet not [I] in my own strength but [in] God's, for his **empowering grace** is poured out upon me [the grace of God which was with me]"* (1 Cor. 15:10 TPT/KJ). Grace **rules** and **leads**, and the believer **submits** and **follows**!!!!!! Grace rules, and grace rules through righteousness by the indwelling presence and internal working of the Spirit of Christ from within [by the ***person*** of the Spirit of Grace who is the ***person*** of the Spirit of Holiness] [the HS], bringing men *into* eternal life and bringing forth eternal life *from* within men [as fruit brought forth from *within* the believer] (Jn. 4:10, 14; 7:38). Who is the Spirit of Christ, but, the person of the *indwelling* presence of the Holy Spirit [it is He who works within men]. The Spirit of Holiness is the One within who **sanctifies** and **prefects** all.

GRACE OR MERCY

Many confuse the different role of His Mercy, with His Grace. Mercy is you and me not receiving what we deserve; while Grace is you and me receiving what is undeserved; there is a vast difference!! Even you and me receiving **mercy** from God, is God, [Grace] extending what is underserved. God by His Grace will extend His mercy to the sinner; but then, God will go to work by that same Grace to lift the sinner, now saint, out of sin [and darkness] placing him/her into Christ Jesus. Grace will send **mercy** into that place of darkness and sin in order to rescue and deliver the sinner from the captivity of sin and, out from under the power of darkness. Grace operates as a **ruler** appropriating and directing *mercy* as a **servant** to minister to the needs of the sinner, as well, to use this same mercy to accomplish the work of his divine grace. Grace will use mercy, but **mercy** will not and cannot violate the operating principles of His divine [sovereign] grace. Grace will not personally nor directly get involved with sin, but will indirectly come to the rescue through the *means* of using [his] divine mercy, "who is holy, harmless, undefiled, separate from sinners, and made higher than the heavens" (Heb. 7:26). This is quite different!! Grace will never get its/his hands dirty; grace will never focus on the defeat [of sin] in a Christian; but God [his grace] has extended his mercy to minister to the Christian in times of defeat or sin. Grace is a power that will directly focus upon and draw attention to the Christian's victory in Christ Jesus. Remember, Grace is you and me **receiving** what we do not deserve [what is undeserved]. Vine's Expository Dictionary calls <u>grace</u>, being, that which **bestows** or, **favor bestowed**; to *endue* with grace [favor]. To <u>endue</u> *means* **to furnish; to supply with**; to endow; to enrich. I do understand, that, this is simply a play on words, but a necessary play on words, in order to make it very clear that the bible makes a deliberate distinction between God extending his **mercy** by grace, and his **grace empowering the new life** *through* righteousness in [by] Christ Jesus. Many confuse these two, and as a result, **wrongly apply it to the way of salvation** [Justification and Sanctification]. Grace extends mercy to *justify* the sinner [in order to provide forgiveness for sins], and then [He] Grace will *empower* the believer for sanctification [transformation]. [He] Grace imparts a divine supply for spiritual transformation. Grace *both* saves [forgives] [through the mercy of God] and sanctifies [empowers] [by the **power** and **work of the HS** made possible *through* **the provision** and **supply** of His grace]. The reason why I am saying it in this way is, because of the way many have taught Grace and, have turned the message of the Cross, the gospel, the grace of God, into a license to sin [into permission to commit vice]. Many treat the grace of God as a lowly servant in subjugation to the sinner. When in fact, Christ, who is the **personification** of the grace of God is, a **ruler**, a **sovereign**, a victor, a champion, **a conquering** king. Paul, in his letter to the Church at Rome taught, when speaking of the grace of God, it, the grace of God, **will abound** *unto* many, it **will abound** *within* many and, it will rule and reign *in* and *through* the life of the Christian by [in agreement with] [according to] the righteousness of Jesus Christ *unto* [eternal] life. Again, this is speaking of the grace of God as the **abounding life** of Jesus Christ *within* all those who believe!!

Grace, must be understood as having two distinct and separate sides all belonging to the same one truth. Like a coin, having two distinct and different sides but both belonging to the same one coin. Grace will both extend *mercy* to the sinner for their justification [to clear them of all guilt, providing for the forgiveness of sins], and as well, extend *power* [empowerment] to the saints for their spiritual sanctification [spiritual growth and transformation]. To fail to hold to *both* sides of this same one truth will end up *perverting* the gospel, or the grace of Christ. Grace [the gospel of our Salvation] points to what he did for us to both *forgive* [our sins] and to *change* our lives [our lifestyle]. To reject sanctification [the changed life] is to reject justification [the forgiveness of sins]. Remember, to alter the gospel in any way is to exchange it for another!! Grace will point to *both* his **sin-bearing death**, and as well, his **resurrected** [new] **life**. Grace must be understood in terms of *both* **his actual death on the Cross** and, his resurrection life [New Life]. Grace must be understood in *both* terms that not only **extend mercy to the repentant** sinner but as well, **power** [empowerment] [divine ability, given] to the believing saints!!! Grace has provided for both our justification and our sanctification. Grace is power!!! Grace is an empowerment: a supply we are endued with [are given] that will enable us to live this overcoming Christian life in our Christian sanctification. Remember, mercy, is you and I not receiving **what we deserve**; Grace, is you and me **receiving what is underserved**. Through faith in the gospel of JC, we have received a Grace from God that is undeserved, which, **is a divine supply that will empower** and **enable us** to live out this new life experience through a victorious Christian faith. Through the gospel of his grace, we have been made more than **conquerors** *through* the One who loved us and died for us. Help!!

The Grace of God is all about the Life of Christ [and His great **passion:** his death, burial, and resurrection]. For sin shall not have **dominion** [shall not rule] over you: for you are, under grace (Rom. 6:14). Under Grace means, under the BLOOD and now a partaker of his death, burial, and resurrection *unto* **new life!!** This salvation or *gospel* where of Paul speaks must include *both* our Justification and Sanctification. This true gospel of God *promises* both the **power** of God to save us, then, through that same power, it promises to continue to keep us through sanctification and honor unto God. The **grace** [the gospel] of Jesus Christ is a ruling power!! Keep in mind; a bent toward *either* legalism [trusting in one's own self-effort] or, lawless tendencies [to accept loose morals as common place and acceptable to God] could disqualify you and others from accessing His [this] sanctifying [and perfecting] **grace** in your personal life and spiritual growth, creating a **form of godliness** [an appearance of the gospel]; however, it denies the power. God has put it in the *gospel* this inherent/innate ability (capacity) to forgive sins, **empower service**, and transform character, which the bible reveals will be the **hallmark** or **distinctive characteristic** of the Bride who will **make herself ready** for the return of the Bridegroom [the maturing of sons]. This is the Pauline revelation of JC: his Pauline gospel. A grace that *both* forgives sins, and empowers holy living!!! You cannot have the *first* without the *second*!!! You cannot lay claim to the *former*, and at the same time outright right the *latter*. You cannot call JC Savior, and, at the same time, refuse to bow your knee to Him as Lord. Grace, will *both* extend **mercy**, and, impart **power**!!! There is absolutely no room for the Antinomian heresy. There is absolutely **no tolerance** for a <u>doctrine</u> in the Church [for a religious tradition] that *teaches* the **grace** of God as a license to sin. God, help!

Many treat **grace** as their own personal <u>slave</u> [indentured servant] sent to obey them, and, to follow behind to clean up any sinful mess [situation] the Christian may fall back into; no, that is not the job of grace, that is the job of mercy, which grace will extend, if, the reason behind that extension and the <u>motive</u> *within* the Christian is repentance. The word *indentured* means to bind one party into the service of another. Grace is a Ruler, not some yielding lowly slave doing the bidding of an unrepentant sinner, Christian or otherwise: Grace is a LORD!! Grace is no other than the person of the Lord Jesus Christ himself, the very personification [embodiment] of God's very own Grace. This is why **grace** must not be taken lightly or handled [treated] with disrespect, "For if we **sin willfully** *after* that we have received the knowledge of the truth, there remains no more sacrifice for sins...of how much sorer punishment, suppose ye, shall he be thought worthy, **who hath trodden underfoot the Son of God, and hath counted *the blood* of the covenant**, wherewith *he was sanctified*, an **unholy thing**, and hath done **despite** *unto* the Spirit of Grace" (Heb. 10:26, 29). Notice, to trodden underfoot the Son of God, and to show disrespect toward the Spirit of Grace are synonymous terms, or rather, are used and applied interchangeably. The word *despite* in the GK means, to **insult**. You do not *insult* a thing, but a person. The Spirit of Grace is the sanctifying and perfecting *work* of the Holy Spirit in the life of the believer: to *frustrate* the grace of God as **ruler** [over the entire sanctification process] or, to *receive* this grace of God **in vain** [without any tangible visible or identifiable results] is the same as to trodden underfoot the Son of God (Gal. 2:21; 2 Cor. 6:1). This is exactly what it means to *insult* the Holy Spirit or the Spirit of Grace. To receive or believe on the **blood** of the covenant [grace of God] wherewith we are [set apart] sanctified [made holy and consecrated for sacred service]: to violate its principles of godliness and holiness is to **insult** the Person and Work of His Grace. The bible is quite clear; the Grace of God is a **power unto salvation** for all *those* who believe. God expects to get results [receive fruit] "And this I pray, that your love may abound yet more and more in knowledge [of this gospel] and in all judgement (understanding); that ye may approve things that are excellent; that ye may be sincere and without *offence* till the day of Christ; **being** *filled* with the **fruits** of righteousness, which are by [come by] Jesus Christ" (Phil. 1:9-11; Matt. 21:33-44). To reject His Holiness, is, to reject His Grace, because, it is the same **one person** and **work** of God. You can't have his **grace** without having his **holiness** as well. For these, *both* His Grace, and His Holiness, come, from the same One Source, which is Jesus Christ, our LORD. God, help us to see this!!!

Grace will use mercy, but mercy will not and cannot violate the operating principles of His divine grace. Many apply *mercy* to the violation of his divine grace. Many preach a *forgiveness* without deliverance; and, preach a *mercy* without repentance "...but whosoever *confesses* and **forsakes** them [his sins] shall have mercy" (Prov. 28:13). The word *forsake* in the OE means to abandon in full; to renounce; to reject; to quit; to leave entirely. The bible commands all persons everywhere to [repent] ***depart*** from sin, and ***believe*** the gospel [depend on the **grace** of Christ] [to depend on his death, burial, and resurrection: his sin-bearing death and, on the bringing forth of new resurrected life]. Unless we *believe* the gospel and, have **faith** [confidence] in his death, burial, and resurrection, and, is followed by a departure from sin, we will not be forgiven. Many have separated his Lordship from his Saviorship. This just will not work!! Many want to accept him as **Savior** but reject him as **Lord** this is a spiritual counterfeit. "To open their eyes, and *to turn them from* darkness to light, *and from* the power of Satan unto God, ***that they may receive forgiveness of sins,*** and inheritance among them which are **sanctified**..." (Acts 26:18). In order to receive the forgiveness of sins you have to turn from darkness to light, from the power of Satan to God; and notice, those who are forgiven are also the sanctified. I am not trying to make this too difficult; but the bible places an emphasis on the Work of the Spirit: how can the practice of sin and the work of the Spirit co-exist? They cannot!! The One [the believer] must give way to the Other [the sanctifying and perfecting Work of the Spirit]. The bible says, **you know a tree by its fruit.** "Whosoever *abides* [continues] in Him [Christ] does **not sin** [does not practice sin]; whosoever continues in sin *hath* not seen him [has not the gospel of Christ]...He [the person] that *commits* sin [the person that practices sinning] is of the devil; for the devil [Satan] sins from the beginning... whosoever is born of God does not commit [does not practice] sin; for his **seed** [the **new life in righteousness**] remains [abides] [continues] in him: and he cannot sin, because he is born of God [because he is reborn from above]...whosoever does not [practice] righteousness is not of God" (1 Jn. 3:5-10). The Bible teaches that, the believer will have spiritual battles, so it is not impossible for a Christian to sin, but, notwithstanding, it is impossible [not possible] for true born again believers [true Christians] **to continually** give themselves **over to the practice of sin** [to give themselves over to an immoral lifestyle]; the Holy Spirit *within* them would never allow this to happen, or, to continue to happen on a consistent basis (James 4:4-10). God, help us all!!!

I do not want to diminish that side of Grace that will extend mercy to the sinner in need of forgiveness; nor do I want to diminish or even ignore that side of Grace that will extend God's mercy to the believer on a continual basis throughout the entire sanctification process until they grow in grace and knowledge. I just want too especially draw attention to the empowerment that grace [the gospel] provides the believer for spiritual growth and transformation that must not be ignored or denied!! When I look at the many different ways grace is defined and applied in the Old [Webster's] English Dictionary of 1828 [OE], it is clear; Grace is so much more than just God's mercy being extended to the sinner for the forgiveness of sin. Grace in the OE means, goodwill, free unmerited love and favor of God. [Grace] the **spring** and **source** of all the benefits men receive from God. [Grace] favorable influence of God: Divine influence or the influence of the Spirit, in renewing the heart and restraining from sin. [Grace] the application of Christ righteousness to the sinner. [Grace] a state of reconciliation to God. [Grace] favor, mercy, and pardon conferred (extended and invested within). [Grace] virtues, faith, religious affections, liberal disposition, meekness, humility, patience, all proceeding from Divine influence [are all coming from His Grace]. There is no doubt; Grace [his divine favor] is so much more than just God extending his mercy to forgive the sinner; or, mercy being extended to cleanse the Saint. Grace is a power [a force] and empowerment that will equip and enable the believer to receive more of God, and, grow in that grace [divine favor] received and bear its fruit [to bring forth a harvest in/of righteousness]. *"Yes, God is more than ready to overwhelm you with every **form of grace** [able to **make all grace abound** toward you], so that you will have more than enough of everything every moment and in every way [that ye always having all sufficiency in all things, may abound to every good work]"* (2 Cor. 9:8 TPT/KJ). This is why Paul called Grace *both* a "gift," and "abundance." It is a <u>principle</u> and a <u>person</u>, and a <u>**supply**</u> [a supernatural provision].

God, is a good God!!!! He is a generous God. God is merciful, and gracious. However, we are the saved of God, and called according to His divine purpose and grace (2 Tim. 1:9). Not just His grace, but His purpose!!! We cannot and must not separate His Grace from His divine purposes. **His divine eternal purpose in Christ was established from the foundation of the world.** It is wrong; and, impossible, to interpret and apply His divine grace outside of this eternal purpose in JC. It is important we do not underestimate and misunderstand the purpose for His divine Grace: toward the <u>sinner</u> and the <u>saint</u> alike. So many have misunderstood and misapplied the principles of His divine grace, to their own destruction!!!! Grace will extend mercy and, empower all who believe!!!! The *love* and *mercy* of God is found [and seen] in the redemptive works of the Cross. God's love and the Cross are inseparable (Jn. 3:16; 1 Jn. 4:10; Rev. 1:5). To attempt to win favor with God, or, to try to earn his love through any other way or means will end in failure and eternal death. The blood of His Cross is the only way to [reach] the love and heart of God!! Furthermore, the justice of God is only realized and actualized at the place of the Cross [the Atonement]. It is at the Cross where God can be [and remain both] the JUST [maintain His justice] and the JUSTIFIER [extend His mercy toward the sinner]. It is at the Cross [the grace of God] that both the *sinner* and His *mercy,* meet. And, it is at that same Cross [the grace of God] the saints are empowered by the gospel to live holy lives [and bear its fruit]. God help us all!!!

MY GOSPEL

"Now to him that is *of power* to stablish you according to **my gospel,** and the preaching of Jesus Christ..." (Rom. 16:25). What does the apostle Paul mean by "my gospel? Paul said, "How that by **revelation** he made known unto me the *mystery*... whereby, when you read, you may understand **my knowledge** in the mystery of Christ" (Eph. 3:3-4). Paul here is emphasizing those aspects of the *gospel* of Christ [the **grace** of God] revealed unto him. Therefore, what does Paul mean when he says "my gospel?? Paul, made a point of preaching the **Cross**-as both the **wisdom** and **power** of God. His death on the Cross [the gospel] contains [holds] a *wisdom* from God, and a **power** through which all who believe could enter into a **victory,** and an **authority** that will give them the right to rule [over] in every circumstance and in all situations. This is why Paul said, "For I determine not to know anything among you, except Jesus Christ, and him crucified" (1 Cor. 2:2; 1:18, 23-24). "For if by one man's offence death reigned [ruled] by one; much more they which receive abundance of **grace** and of the **gift** of righteousness shall reign [rule] in life by one, Jesus Christ...that as sin *hath* (past tense) reigned [ruled] unto death, even so *might* (present tense) grace reign [rule] through righteousness unto eternal life by Jesus Christ our Lord" (Rom. 5:17, 21). Paul spoke of the **gospel** as containing [hidden] within, the *mystery* of Jesus Christ. This speaks of the **grace** of Christ as a ***ruler*** made possible through the **gospel** of Christ. Grace is the empowerment of a new life of righteousness that exercises [takes] authority over every circumstance through the power and wisdom of the CROSS!! The preaching of the Cross is foolishness to them who perish; and to them that believe not [who do not understand the true gospel], see the grace of God as just an exemption or immunity from prosecution [a get out of jail free card; a covering for a life still subject to and under the powers of sin and the fallen human condition]. Paul, revealed in his epistle [letter] to the Corinthians [to those who struggled under the pressures and temptations of sin, the world, and the devil] the secret to true Christian emancipation: **the power and wisdom of the Cross.** To those who really [truly] know him; who came into a true and genuine saving faith and knowledge of the gospel of Jesus Christ as both Savior and Lord: **to them the preaching of the Cross is the very *wisdom* and *power* of God.** Paul said, "But we preach Christ **crucified**...Christ the power of God, and the wisdom of God" (1 Cor. 1:18, 23-24). Paul is saying, Christ **crucified** is *both* the **power** and the **wisdom** of God!!!!

"The Grace of our Lord Jesus Christ be with you all. Amen" (Rom. 16:20, 24). In Paul's epistle to the Romans, he repeated this statement twice. Why, because it was presented by Paul to the Christians in Romans as a simple prayer. Paul is simply presenting the church at Rome with a simple prayer. "(May) the grace of our Lord Jesus Christ be with you all." Wow, what a simple, powerful prayer!! Paul is saying, "(May) the **grace of Christ** be with you (always)." Paul is saying, May, the **grace** that belongs to Christ be with you all, always! Did you catch that? Paul prayed that the believers at Rome would have with them at all times the **grace** of Christ resting upon them, and ruling, and providing for their lives. Not a grace that is separated: taken from his grace, and given to me but, receiving the GRACE [favor] without distinction that belongs only to him (Christ alone). Paul is praying that, we would receive what is his, and through that grace: we [me] might freely receive all things. "He that spared not his own Son, but delivered him up for us all, *how shall he not with him also freely give us* all things? (Rom. 8:32). With Him: He, freely gives us all things!! With Christ, God, freely gives us all things that pertains to HIM. Paul is not asking God that we might receive something from Christ, but that we might receive Him and all that is His!!! What a great prayer, and, what endless possibilities to behold!!!! God, help us all to see this grace as HIM [received, from God]. God, multiply your grace [HIM] unto me!!!

The word <u>grace</u> is the GK word *Charis,* which means favor, gift, joy, liberality, benefit, pleasure, and so much more. Grace especially means ***divine influence upon the heart, and its reflection in the life.*** When Paul said, "The *grace* of our Lord Jesus Christ be with you all" he is saying, May His favor, gifting, generosity, joy, benefits, pleasure, etc. be with you all (always). May His **favor**, that which belongs only to Him, that which He [worked for] **earned** through a perfect sinless life of obedient to God under the law, now made possible [now made available to us all] through his sacrificial death, burial, and resurrection be with you, and rest upon you. A *life* of perfect obedience to God, which earned him the ***right*** to every spiritual blessing promised to those obedient to God under the Law as found in Deuteronomy chapter 28. The ***right*** to every spiritual blessing, benefit, promise, joy, gifting, pleasure, generosity, etc., now belongs to you, through the knowledge of him (his gospel), who has made you meet (who has qualified us) to be partakers of the inheritance of the saints in light (Col. 1:12). To be a *partaker* of the **grace** of our <u>Lord</u> and <u>Savior</u> Jesus Christ means **to share in** what he has earned [won] by the conquest of the Cross. This inheritance we all share in, as the saints in light, is the very same **plunder** and *spoils* of war [of conquest] accomplished by our Lord and Savior Jesus Christ through his death, burial, and resurrection. "For we are *made* partakers of [Him] Christ [Crucified]..." (Heb. 3:14). "For as by one man's sin/disobedience many were made sinners, so (as) by the obedience of one (Jesus Christ) shall many be made <u>righteous</u> [reconciliation: to be restored to divine favor] (Rom. 5:11, 19). We are reconciled to God, and restored to divine favor through his obedience, not by the *deeds* of the flesh, or by the *works* of the Law [of Moses]. This obedience: speaks *both* to his obedient *life* under the Law, and, to his obedience in *death* on the Cross (Phil. 2:8); As a result, we are made through [faith in] the **gospel** [grace] of Christ, heirs of God, and joint-heirs with Jesus Christ: heirs of God because we are joined to the Heir

(Rom. 8:17). May God be praised through JC our Lord!! This is "My Gospel," being, my confidence in the Cross of Jesus Christ.

Paul said, "But by the *grace* of God I am what I am: and his *grace* which was bestowed upon me [given to me] was not in vain; but I labored more abundantly than they all: yet not I, but the *grace* of God which was with [in] me" (1 Cor. 15:10). But I labored? Yet not I, but the **grace** of God which was with me, what does this mean? "Whereunto I also labor, striving according **to his working**, which works in me mightily" (Col. 1:29), what is this working? When Paul said, "Which **works in me** mightily," in the GK it means, God who is *active* within him: He works mightily, "For it is God which works in you (active within) both to **will** and to **do** of his good pleasure" (Phil. 2:13). What is his working? And, what does this mean, "Works in me mightily? All of this speaks to the *activity* of His **grace** bestowed upon us: active *within* all who believe on JC and he crucified; and, it is through the knowledge of this *gospel* of his **grace**: the Holy Spirit works to bring into full fruition [manifestation] in the life of the believer every benefit, blessing, promise, joy, pleasure, generosity, gifting, etc., that belongs to Jesus Christ. Grace means ***divine influence upon the heart, and its reflection in the life.*** What is working on the inside of us will show up on the outside: it does not cover sin, but takes it away: it does not cover all our character flaws, it removes them; it does not charge [command] us to change, it provides the **power** and *ability* to change, "(For) I am crucified with Christ: nevertheless, I live; yet not I [I died], but Christ [His Grace] lives [is alive; active] in [within] me" (Gal. 2:20). What shows up, or, fails to show up on the outside becomes the evidence that grace is at work within or, is received in vain, "(For) I do not frustrate the grace of God" (Gal. 2:20; 2 Cor. 6:1). "(We) beseech you also that you receive not the grace of God in vain." Either, we choose to cooperate [agree] with the grace of Christ, the way God intended, or, we could end up *altering* the **gospel** and *frustrate* the **grace** of God. God forbid: that we should frustrate the grace of God!!! God forbid, that, we should receive this Grace of/from Christ in vain to no profit [that which brings no change]. God help!!

No wonder the New Covenant has such a high expectation for godliness [holiness], because it is not the strength and ability (effort) of the Christian himself [alone] that is expected, but [the grace of] Christ within: the hope of glory (Col. 1:27). You will notice, that, Paul, worked in conjunction with [in cooperation with] the **grace** of Christ that was *active* within, "Whereunto I also labor, striving according **to his working**." Paul goes on to state that this *grace* of Christ was mightily at work [active] within him. The GK word for "mightily" is *dunamis* and points to the **sanctifying** and **perfecting** work of the Holy Spirit [Spirit of Christ] within the life and conduct [the fruit and works] of the believer [Eph. 2:8-10]. The *activity* of his Grace at work within is a dynamo acting [operating] for our good. It is *both* the privileges [benefits] of His **grace** and its power that makes Holiness possible. There is no doubt; the *grace* of GOD is an active power [and, a force active] within. In 2 Corinthians 12:9-10, Paul ties "His Grace" to "His Strength," God said, "My Grace is sufficient for you: for My Strength is made perfect in [your] weakness." Paul goes on to say, "...that the ***Power*** of Christ may rest upon me," clearly; based upon the context of this statement, Paul is connecting the Grace of God to the Power of Christ [the *inner* activity (and operation) of the HS, the "Spirit of Christ" from within]. God clearly corresponds [equates] His Grace with His Power. God's *power* comes to us through the gospel of His Grace by the Divine Working of the Holy Spirit. The Holy Spirit [the Spirit of Christ] is the one who applies the ***benefits*** of His Grace to us and within us. In 2 Timothy 2:1, Paul, exhorts his spiritual son Timothy to be, "...Strong in the **Grace** that is *in* Christ Jesus." Paul is telling Timothy, that, the *source* of your strength [vigor; power] to live this Christian life and, to live the overcoming Christian life, on an on-going basis, is this Grace of Christ that ***strengthens*** you from within. It is by this Gospel of his unmerited Grace that **we are enabled to live** and to walk-out this victorious Christian living [this power to save/transform]. Praise God for his glorious and unmerited Grace.

The *gospel* is not applied to the outward conduct. The gospel is applied to the **heart**; and, from a ***converted*** heart, man's outward ***conduct*** is changed. The law or the letter is applied to the outward conduct [the external]. Many apply the gospel today to the outward conduct. Many treat the ***gospel*** as if they would **handle** [were handling] **the law**. This is why there is so much error or misunderstanding in doctrine, today. One's attitude toward the gospel is the key!!! If we look at the gospel [of His Grace] as an outward application this creates a legalistic approach to the faith. If we understood the **gospel** as an application to ***convert*** the heart, this would draw men to trust and rely upon the Spirit [His promises]. This would rightly be called the New Birth and spiritual growth, which is both our **justification** and our **sanctification**. Thanks Be to God!!!

"Being born again...by the **word** [seed] of God, which lives, and continues, and abides forever" (1 Pet. 1:23). This is an inward conversion!! This is the inward application of the gospel by the Spirit to the regeneration of the inward man, the hidden man of the heart (1 Pet. 3:4). What has begun *in* the Spirit, as well, must be allowed to continue and finish *with* and *by* the Spirit (Gal. 3:3). God is both the Arthur and Finisher of our faith. What He [God] has begun through Christ in us, he will perform and complete it [finish it] by His Holy Spirit (Heb. 12:2; Phil. 1:6; Col. 1:22; 1 Thess. 5:23). It is not by the works of the Law [it is not by one's own religious efforts] that a man is justified before God: but by the hearing of faith. The hearing of *faith* points to a life *lived* by the Spirit of God (Gal. 3:1-5). This life of walking in the Spirit by faith must be applied to *both* our justification and our sanctification. Hallelujah!!! What has *first* begun in the gospel, must finish with the gospel!!! To add anything to the gospel [message] as necessary for our salvation, as well, to add anything to the gospel [message] [of the power of his death, burial, and resurrection] as applied to our Christian sanctification is to frustrate the grace of God. To add anything to the gospel is to turn outward, and attempt to apply the gospel as an outward work applied to our Christian sanctification in some outward form, such as you and I keeping some code of conduct, the outward application of some ritual discipline or Christian practice as a part of our Christian sanctification. Many have created various religious systems to assist men in their obedience to God, which only works to distract men from the true power inherent in the gospel, alone. God ministers to His people, by His Holy Spirit, and works His miracles in us and among us, how?? These things come to us, and are worked within and among us by simply hearing and believing the gospel!!! It is by the Spirit *through* the simple hearing of faith, through the gospel, that the power is manifested and the spiritual provision obtained!!! It all begins and ends and, it is all performed simply by believing on the gospel. Thank God!!

In the parables of the kingdom, Christ revealed the **operation** of the Spirit. The sower went out to *sow*, seed. These **seeds** fell upon four different types of soil. The soil *typifies* the human heart and the **seed** the word of God. "For the earth brings forth fruit of herself; first the blade, then the ear, after that the full corn in the ear" (Mk. 4:26-29). We find this Parable of the Sower in Matthew 13; Mark 4; and Luke 8. If the seed is put into the ground; or rather, if the **word of God is simply planted into the human *heart* it will produce fruit**, or, it will bring forth change. The power is found in the potency [and force] of the seed. It is this divine *power* that is inherent in the **gospel** and, when believed, that transforms all outward conduct: not by some religious creed, or by some religious tradition, nor religious practices [not by the wisdom of men; and, not by their vain philosophies, even if they are basing it on the word of God, which becomes nothing more than just a private interpretation]. It is not the religious systems of men. **It is the power of the gospel of JC alone that changes the outward conduct of men by the full conversion of the human heart.** If the seed of God's word is planted into the human heart through the *hearing* of faith, it will produce the promised spiritual result. For

God's word cannot and will not return to Him, void. This is why the walk of the Spirit and the hearing of faith are inseparable!!!! It is by the word of God [the gospel] [alone], and, it is by the Spirit of God working in the human heart, and now, through a converted heart that all of the outward conduct of men is completely transformed [now converted and changed, by the gospel, alone]. God help us all to see this!!

"We were reconciled to God by the death of his Son, much more, being reconciled, we shall be saved by his life...by whom we have now received the atonement" (Rom. 5:10-11). The word *reconcile* in the GK means to change. The word *atonement* in the GK is the same word that is translated elsewhere in the NT as reconciliation, and means *exchange*. Paul is saying, "We are changed by his death on the Cross, and we are changed by his resurrected life: by whom or by Him (Christ) we have all now received this Divine Exchange. Paul is making it quite clear; the ***gospel*** is a DIVINE EXCHANGE. We are not trying to change; we simply yield to the exchange. This is the method, operation, and power performed, which is inherent within the gospel. Faith in the gospel, is the inherent power within [this gospel] to experience this [its] divine exchange!!!

The **gospel** is not just a call, from God, for men to change; but rather, a provision made in JC for this divine exchange [to take place between God and the sinner]. Do you see it?? We do not work toward a **change**: we do not work for a change; we *yield* to **a divine exchange** [that takes place between <u>Christ</u> and <u>us</u>]. We do not labor, we yield!! It is not by our **might** (our own human effort and strength); and, it is not by our own **power** [by our own human ability and ingenuity], but by my Spirit (Him alone) says the Lord. The gospel is not an outward application toward [to] the outward conduct of men. The gospel is the application of the provision of Christ's death on the Cross, and His subsequent resurrection to the inward life and to the inward man; and then, it will find its expression in the outward life of those who place their confidence in this gospel for Christian sanctification. The gospel is the provision that God has made in Jesus Christ: **has made for the human heart for its full and final conversion.** This is why Paul said, with boldness and with the utmost confidence, "I am not ashamed of the *gospel* of Jesus Christ, for it is the **power** of God to enter into salvation for all who will just believe" (Rom. 1:16). This GOSPEL is the power of God that works within to transform!!! This power is designed by God to *convert* the hearts of the ungodly [sinners]. The gospel goes after the *inward,* not the *outward.* If the gospel has *reached* and *converted* the **inward**, then the **outward** [it] will change. Thanks be to God!!!

It is not what I do; it is what he has already done. This **divine exchange** is only possible by faith; and, it continues through a life and walk by the Spirit. A life, focused on the letter [or, on some outward restraint; some outward standard, or religious system of some so called Christian practice] removes one from this present reality of a DIVINE EXCHANGE. People struggle with change!!! Every day we struggle with change. People apply the gospel to their outward lives and to their outward conduct with little to no success. They struggle with the flesh, the world, and the devil having little to no power to resist. Why?? Because **the letter** puts *pressure* on change, but provides no power to effect that change, which, you and I, in and of ourselves, have no power to make that change. This must be understood as the application of some outward conduct, system, standard, practice, ritual discipline, and the like, which depends entirely upon the performance of the man [the believer] [and not upon that divine power inherent in the gospel, to save, to sanctify, transform, and to perfect the one who believes]. While the gospel has already made provision for this divine exchange, **we do not labor, we YEILD**, and receive by faith. We have failed to enter into this **kingdom reality** that has been *purchased* for us, by His own blood. "He that spared not his own Son, but delivered him up for us all, how shall He not, with him, **also freely give us all things**" (Rom. 8:32). "Now, we have received, not the spirit of the world, but the spirit which is of God; that we might know the things that are freely given to us of God" (1 Cor. 2:12). Praise Be to the LORD!!!!!!!! If we could only see that the gospel alone is the only standard, method, operation, and power provided by the LORD for this overcoming life. Thank You Jesus!!!

ST. AUGUSTINE ON GRACE

I would like to say a little bit about some of the comments [writings] of St. Augustine of Hippo, about GRACE, about 1600 years ago. He called the believer sons and daughters by the GRACE of adoption, not by nature, though we are given His *imparted nature* at the New Birth, and through this **imparted nature**, we all become *partakers* of [participates in] His Divine Nature. This *gift* of His Grace has *changed* our nature and has given us eternal life. So, this would make the gift of His Grace given to all of us who believe as well, the Gift of His own life. Keep in mind, I am *paraphrasing* [putting into my own words] much of what he said. To become a partaker means, to participate in, or to share in His divine nature through union with Christ. We are **united** with Jesus Christ [joined to Him] and we **share in** what He is, through our "spiritual adoption," this is why the bible calls us **"heirs of God,"** and **"joint-heirs of JC."** This *means* it is through faith in JC and him crucified we have now received New life, and this New life is now accomplished through a spiritual adoption, and within this spiritual adoption we are joined to the heir [Christ] and now become partakers of His divine nature [his Holy Character]. This does not mean we become divine, but rather, joined to Him who is Divine. Through faith in Christ, we are united [joined] to Him and **now share in who He is** [and all that He has], as the Person of God's Grace, and through Him [His Grace] we partake of eternal life. This eternal life is in Him!! This *understanding* of God and His Grace is nothing new to the Church. This concept of God and His Grace is wide spread throughout the writings and teachings contained within the Historic records of the Christian Church. Therefore, if this is somewhat strange to you, you are in the minority. In these books, when exhorting on the Grace of God, I am coming from 2000 years of *rich* Church history on the subject. Only in today's church, because of the departure from the faith [the truth] these things have been lost by most who are a part of this contemporary scene [modern church].

St. Augustine taught, Grace makes an inner-change within **the heart** that works to overcome sin. This is God by His Grace [Christ] overcoming the sin within us. Again, these are the rich ***traditions*** of the Church throughout its history, reflecting its Apostolic Teaching. In this sense, here, **tradition is seen as positive**. These **traditions** here speak of all the *beliefs* and *practices* about holiness passed down to us dating back to the early Apostles. Grace is not just a ***gift*** bestowed upon the believer, but as well, becomes an **inner-force** of righteousness that *bears* its fruit. This happens [takes place] when one yields their life [over] to the work of the Spirit of Grace [Christ] within. St. Augustine said, **"This inner-gift of Grace transforms us inwardly."** This is called an **assisting** [and **abounding**] **Grace** that helps us. This Grace of God strengthens us from within *enabling* us to bear its fruit!!! He said, "Grace helps to strengthen our will, to choose God's Will." In Philippians 2:13, Paul said, "For it is God which **works** *in* you both **to will** and **to do** of his good pleasure." God works **on our will**, and, **in our will**, even without our will!!! God works in our will, and will work with our will; He will work with us, and even within us, even without us [or, he will work outside of *both* human cooperation and participation], and this is His Grace. This must be understood in its balance. God works in cooperation with the human will, and at other times, **He works apart from the human will** [without violating its volition]. God works **with our** will, and **in our** will!!! God [His Grace] has come into our lives [hearts] turning it in a certain direction [by its divine influence] through the *sanctifying* and *perfecting* work of the inner presence of the Spirit of Grace [Christ within] [the Holy Spirit who now resides-dwells *within* the believer's own reborn human spirit]. One of the word meanings for grace, which is the GK word *charis* is, the divine influence upon the human heart and its reflection found at work in the outward life of those who believe. Paul said, "For it is a good thing that [for] the heart [to] be [set in, and] established with grace..." (Heb. 13:9). Grace is a power from God for change!! Grace becomes a power from God at work within for change!!!

Again, the inner presence of the Holy Spirit is the presence of Christ within. Inner Grace speaks to both His person within and as well the inner presence of His very own life. Romans 6:14 tells us, that, this **new life** we all have and hold is no longer under sin [under the law] but is now under Grace [in Christ]. This is why sin cannot dominate it, and this is why sin does not have to dominate us ***"For sin shall not have dominion over you...for you are under Grace."*** We are no longer under the Law [under sin] [in the Old Adam] we are now under Grace [in Christ]. St Augustine said, "Grace turns our will through an active delight [an active delighting in God] without violating the will [not through any form of coercion or by force]. St Augustine believed that **Grace** and **Free will** are compatible. How much of God's direct action [divine intervention] upon the soul [the will] and man's response to it [our cooperation with His Grace] is, still a very deep mystery few can agree upon. **How free, is Free Will??** How does the Grace of God **rule** [guide, and govern] in the life of the believer without violated man's Free Will?? St Augustine said, "The righteousness of God *infused* [imparted] within is the active Grace of faith, hope, and charity bearing its fruit *within* and **through** the believer." However, he taught **the necessity for the active cooperation** of our will, which God *enables* [our will] by His grace *within* the heart [human volition]. So, which is it, Grace first, or, human free will??? The bible is quite clear; we all were spiritually dead in trespass and sins, **and if dead** [which *means* to be entirely spiritually inactive], we are unable to respond to the call of God to believe and obey. Therefore, Grace must come first before our will can ever be free to choose and respond to God. Grace is what enables us to respond to God, and without this Grace, a response from man to believe and obey would be an absolute impossibility [man is *both* spiritually and morally dead in his sins unable to respond].

Grace is clearly not some weak and beggarly slave subject to the whims of an unconverted unregenerate sinner [or, backslidden Christian]; Grace is a sovereign and **ruler** *empowering* the new life for righteousness, and as well taking full responsibility for the overall process for our sanctification and transformation at work in the life of all true believers. To reject the *sanctifying* Grace that bears its fruits of **holy** and **set apart** living is to forfeit the *justifying* Grace for the saving of the soul. God help us all!!! [The Great Courses, the History of Christian Theology, by Phillip Cary "The Doctrine of Grace" Lecture 12]. It is clear; **human will is, free to choose**, but has lost all moral strength to choose God. Any choice man makes toward God without the help [aid] of His divine grace is corrupted and tainted by sin and the sinful condition. The bondage of the human will to the fallen adamic nature is the true testimony of the scriptures. Today, the error of those who violate the operating principles of His divine grace, are reaching an all-time high!! Those who err to the left of center are those who treat His divine grace as permission to continue to live in that fallen state, bearing fruits unto death; those who err to the right of center are those who do not accept [believe] the witness of the scriptures concerning the true condition of fallen men before a Holy God. The bible describes the fallen human condition **as a spiritual death**, the inability [impotence] of man in his unregenerate state to respond to the holiness of God. Any attempt by man to obey or adhere to moral principles apart from His divine grace are at best simply pomp and circumstance. **Man is incapable of true moral and spiritual fruit produced apart from** the power of the Cross. Any moral action, obedience, discipline, ethical stance, **and virtue is impossible without contamination** by the sinful nature. This is why men judge by the outward appearance [by the outward performance]; but **God looks into the heart** [looks into his **true inner condition and state of being**]. We, are either fallen, or redeemed men. We are both spiritually and *morally* dead in all our trespass and sins, or we are <u>forgiven</u> men [cleansed of all unrighteousness], quickened, **and made alive [to serve and obey God]** by His divine grace. All the goodness of men apart from His divine grace is filthy rags!! Every ritual discipline, religious systems of men, set of rules, moral principles, code of conduct, and the many secular and carnal religious traditions of men that enforce various rules and laws for religious order and discipline is nothing more than a cloak [fig leaves] and a covering for the fallen human condition within.

Man in his human pride will never admit of his own volition that he is totally depraved having no redeemable qualities within or without. Man is fallen through and through, every part of his total being is affected and infected with sin: in his spirit, soul, mind, heart, will, and body. While it is true, man is not as bad as he could be, but this is as well an act of His divine grace upon the world and the society of men. If God were to lift his general overall grace, upon this world and all humanity, it would plunge the world into utter chaos, and darkness would fill the earth. His Divine Grace is the restraining force upon the earth, and the Spirit of Grace [the Holy Spirit] is the restrainer. The great tribulation that is prophesied to come upon this world at the closing of this age is a world without this residing grace. The church in this world is supposed to be the **standard** that God raises up to resist [stand against] the tide [onslaught] of evil [and evil forces] in this world. It is *in* and *through* the <u>manifestation</u> of His divine grace *in* and *through* the lives of true believers, who **bearing [bringing forth] [harvesting] the fruits of righteousness** as a demonstration of His glory and virtue. The fact that many who claim to be Christian but still live unchanged lives is the proof that they are not under Grace. To be under Grace, means, to be under His divine influence: we could not do anything other than change!! Wow!!! How we have been deceived, by men of corrupt minds who have turned the grace of God into an excuse for sinful living; in our pride, others have worked very hard to earn the right to stand before God and to receive his divine favor. Today, the majority of churchgoers are deceived!! Counting on a spiritual counterfeit!!!! Trusting in an altered gospel, and believing in an Eternal Security [once saved, always saved] that does not line up with the testimony of the Holy Writ. The bible does present us [the believer] with Eternal Security, but this **security** is found in Christ alone!! The bible teaches that God will **preserve** [hold in safekeeping] the believer unto the end [for He will never leave us, nor forsake us]; but the proof of this guarantee is found in our [the believer's] **sanctification**. Sanctification is the proof [evidence] that God is in there [and present] and is working within, "if ye endure chastening, God deals with you as with sons; for what son is he whom the father chastens not? But if ye be without chastisement, whereof all are partakers, then are ye bastards, and not sons" (Heb. 12:5-17). Without chastisement means, without **correction**!! THOSE WHO CONTINUE TO LIVE AND PRACTISE SINFUL LIVES ARE WITHOUT CORRECTION!!!! This is the proof [evidence] they are not living under the Grace of God. These are the many *tares* sown among the **wheat. God, help us to examine ourselves!!!** Life is found, in Christ alone; God does not put his eternal life inside of the Christian, He give us Christ. This new life [this salvation] [this eternal life] is in him [Christ]. And God gives us Christ!!! He who hath the Son hath the life; and, he who does not have the Son of God, does not have the life. Eternal Security is not found in the Christian: it is found in Christ [in us]!! He who rejects Christ, and at the same time lay claim to the gospel [who looks to the blood for the forgiveness of sins], is condemned [damned]. The **blood** can be applied only where the flesh and the bread are eaten!! The blood of JC is applied only where the flesh of the Passover lamb, and the unleavened bread are eaten; NT forgiveness is obtained only where His life is receive [only where Christ is received] [with repentance] (with unleavened bread). The blood of the atonement will not stand and remain where His life is dishonored and abandoned. This is why Jesus said, "Except you eat his flesh and drink his blood you will have no life in you [we will have no eternal life]" (Jn. 6:53). God does not give eternal life apart from His Son; eternal life is His Son. If you have and hold the Son, you have eternal life (John 1:4; 10:10; 1 John 5:11-12; Exodus 12:7-8, 12). Many believe they can live a life in contradiction to the nature and character of the Son of God and, still have eternal life. This is impossible; if you have eternal life, then you have the Son of God; if you have the Son of God, then your life will change, it must change!!! This is the inner-force of the gospel of his divine grace imparted to us and infused within all who believe. The grace of God is a power!!! A power for living the new life for righteousness!! Not a covering; a power!!! "This is the <u>record</u> [the testimony] [the divine report] [the gospel witness], that God hath given to <u>us</u> [those who believe the gospel] [the true NT Christian] eternal life, and this [eternal] life is in his Son [is found only in his Son] [who now indwells all those who believe the gospel]" (1 Jn. 5:11). The testimony of the Scriptures are quite clear; God has given us eternal life; however, this eternal life is found only in Christ [in us]; in other words, God has given Christ, and in turn Christ in us is eternal life. Eternal Security belongs [only] to Jesus Christ and, to those found in him, and he in them. The blood is applied only where his life is received [the flesh is eaten]!!!

ORIGINAL SIN, HUMAN DEPRAVITY, AND FREE WILL

The term **"Original Sin"** was first coined by St. Augustine in the 4th and 5th Centuries. This phrase has less to do with what happen to Adam in the garden and more with man's present fallen condition. Of course, man's fall began or originated in the garden the moment he and she disobeyed God in the eating of the fruit from the tree [the tree of the knowledge of good and evil]. It is commonplace to believe man is basically good. Though man will admit he is not perfect [a flawed human being], but still inherently good. Human wickedness is minimized by most if not all despite the universality of sin [among the entire human race throughout the whole world]. The reason why most see the world as not that bad, and man as inherently innately good is because the problem is seen within man's **environment**, and not seen as coming from *within* his own **fallen human nature**. This is why billions of dollars are spent every year worldwide, and thrown at the environment of man's predicament thinking that it by education will change man [his condition or station in life]. However, the problem only seems to grow worse [or seems to worsen the more man attempts to make sweeping reforms]. While reforms do, impact lives immediately but they never seem to stick. Why is it, man seems to go back to the muck and mire from which he/she was rescued? What is it about humankind that he/she wants to return to their vomit, and the degradation from which they came? It is the **condition of man's**

nature *within* him [the fallen human condition within all humanity]. The word **degradation** *means* decline to a low place, destitute, or a demoralized state. It *means* degeneration, declination, degeneracy, and deterioration. What is it in men/women that causes him/her to have that tendency to want to fall backward toward darkness, chaos, and death?? The very fact that sin is a universal problem proves that this fallen condition [this inner state of degeneration] is at the heart of man's every social, religious, moral, and ethical problem prevalent throughout the world. This is not just something man does; it is something he [man] is!! The **doctrine of Original Sin** *explains* the reason for the universality of sin. The fall [into sin] of our first parents [Adam and his wife] has subsequently caused every human being to be born into this world: **to be born with a sinful and corrupt nature**. Again, Original sin does not primarily refer to the fall of our first parents, but primarily to the results of that fall [the corruption of the human race], [it refers primarily to the fallen human condition in which we are born]. We cannot ask, "When does individuals become sinners?" For the truth is that, human beings come into existence in a state of sinfulness!!! God sees them as sinful because of their solidarity with [fallen] Adam. David said, *"Behold, I was brought forth in iniquity, and in sin did my mother conceive me"* (Ps. 51:5). Men because of the fall became spiritually dead in his sins, and wholly defiled in all the parts of his being [his spirit, the *faculties* of both his soul and body]. The guilt of Adam's sin now *imputed* [transferred to the whole human race] [set to their legal account] and the same death in/of sin, and corrupted human nature of Adam conveyed to all his posterity [to all his descendants], whereby man is now utterly indisposed, disabled, and made the opposite to all good, and wholly inclined to all evil. This is why man is not a sinner because he has sinned, or sins; the reason why man sins is because he was born a sinner from the start [in sin did my mother conceive me] (RSB Page 17).

Human depravity is thus a universal problem that stems back to the fall of Adam and the *imputation* and the *impartation* of Original sin [the fallen sinful corrupt human nature]. The bible say, "All have sinned and fallen short of the glory of God" (Rom. 3:23). The term **glory** of God *refers* to the holy and righteous character [nature] of God. Man in his sin [sinful condition] has fallen from grace [has fallen from this place of innocence before God]. The law [of God] was given [to Moses] to remind **man** [human beings] of His [God's] **holy** and righteous standard and moral will for man [for all humanity]. Man has been tainted [flawed] by sin [and the corruption of his nature], however, somehow we think sin exists on the peripheral or, rim [or edge] of our character and never penetrates the core. Not only is man spiritually dead in those trespasses and sins, he is also made to be spiritually blind by those same sins. Man is unable or incapable of true spiritual insight into his true spiritual condition!! Man in his fallen state [fallen condition] cannot see himself!! Human depravity runs so deep within his nature that true knowledge of oneself is unattainable. Despite all the self-efforts of man to help himself, he is groping in the dark. All the so-called *wisdom* of the ancients and the many different *systems* and **schools of thought** coming from both ancient and modern man **is nothing more than spiritual blindness**. All the different moral systems and religious rigor [the ritual disciplines of men] is at best just man attempting to reform himself from the outside [a reconditioning of his mind and body]. All these things will not and cannot touch the true spiritual problem and fallen condition *within* [his sinful and corrupt human nature]. Only the Cross-can change this *hopeless* situation [posture, status] within man. The bible teaches the total depravity of the human race!! What total depravity *means* is radical corruption!! This does not mean utter depravity, which *means* to be as wicked as possible. Man is not as bad and as wicked **as he could be as his fallen nature** portends [indicates, signifies]. If men were left to his own devices [without the help of God through His divine grace], he would reach his maximum capacity for evil **[which his inner fallen condition demands]**. The bible indicates that during the last 3½ years of the [great] tribulation [period] just prior to the return of Jesus Christ to the earth, **man will experience his/her most evil and wicked days of his fallen corrupt human condition [nature] upon planet earth.** God will make every effort to impress [to pull out all the stops], and allow man to fully experience the seriousness of his fallen corrupt human condition. Man has rebelled against God and the *revelation* of His holy Word, and the *revelation* of the **true status of man** upon this earth, and the *remedy* He **provided in the gospel of His Grace for their total and complete redemption**. This total depravity [though not as bad as we could be if left to ourselves] *means* that I and everyone else are sinful [depraved] corrupted in the totality of our inner and outer being [the total man: his spirit, soul, and body]. **There is not one part of man that is left untouched by sin** [this spiritual and moral corruption]. Our mind, our will, our hearts, and our bodies are all affected by evil. We speak sinful and evil words; we do sinful deeds, have impure thoughts, all because of this fallen inner state of being *within*. Our **very bodies suffer from the ravages of** sin, sickness, disease, poverty, and physical death. The problem with sin today is that it is <u>rooted</u> and **grounded** in the very core of our being!! Many, even most of those who claim the gospel for salvation see sins as only an exterior condition in their lives, **this is why so many still try to earn their sanctification through works of the flesh** [the religious works of one's own self effort], which the bible calls **dead works**. "Are you so foolish? Having begun in the spirit, are ye now made perfect by the flesh" (Gal. 3:3)? **The same justifying grace that saves [delivers from sin] is the same sanctifying grace that now brings forth the fruits of His righteousness.** Man is totally and utterly dependent upon God for the entire Redemption process for his **spiritual regeneration**, as well for his **sanctification** and *transformation*, and finally for his **glorification [the resurrection of his body]**. For the bible says, "None are righteous, no, not one; none understands; no one seeks God. All have turned aside [gone astray]; all together they have become worthless [unprofitable]; **no one does good** [does what is right by nature], not even one" (Rom. 3:1-12). We are all [every human being] **sold under sin**, and are **held captive to the law of sin** (Rom. 7:14, 23). It is only God, who **makes us alive** by his own power [according to his own] purpose and grace: by His own quickening power [and spiritual regeneration] of the Holy Spirit are we brought out of this spiritual death and darkness, and brought into the light [eternal life] (Eph. 2:1-10). It is only in the **new birth** [the new creation] are we **circumcised in the spirit *within* our own human nature**, and now made partakers of his divine nature. This old man Adam *within* is both crucified [put to death] with Christ, **and circumcised** [or rather, **cut out and removed from our very inner being**]. Thanks be to God through JC that he in his death on the Cross-has delivered me from this body of death. Now [me] I, can delight in God and his will according to [in agreement with] a new nature [a new creation within] [RSB Page 889]. Only the true born again believer is delivered out from under this bondage to sin and death!!! For the Christian all these old things of the fallen human condition [that which belongs to the fallen adamic nature] are passed. Thanks be to God!!!

One of the most difficult and controversial subject matters in all of Christian theology [soteriology: the doctrine of Salvation] is this question of FREE WILL. **Free Will** according to the scriptures is the **moral** responsibility and the moral **accountability** of man's own choices. Is man a <u>free</u> moral agency?? It is true; man will [and must] give an account for all of his/her own choices in thought, word, and deed. This is why the bible says, *"...that every idle word that men shall speak, they shall give account thereof in the day of judgement"* (Matt. 12:39), "For it is appointed unto men once to die, after this the judgement" (Heb. 9:27). The very *essence* of free will itself <u>is to choose</u> according to one's **own desires** [according to one's own inner impulses]. The real question **is not the freedom of the will**; but rather, the <u>source</u> of all our human **desires**. Human free will is *based upon* and *influenced* by the <u>desires</u> of the human heart. If those desires are evil, and not good, then the **freedom** [of the will] is only *free* to choose those **specific desires** [coming from the true condition within]. Man is definitely free to choose; but only free to choose according to **those specific desires** inherent *within* [the fallen condition]. Without God acting directly upon man for salvation, man could not and would not repent; and, believe on the gospel. Salvation is a work of divine grace!! Man's responses to this grace of God for salvation then as well becomes an act of divine grace. WOW!!! This is why we are called of God to pray without ceasing: for God to move upon the hearts of men for saving faith. Without this work of the Holy Spirit, men would not be saved. Without this continued work of the Holy Spirit in the life of the believer, men would remain unchanged. The fall left the **human will** [the human volition] intact insofar as **we still have the faculty of choice** [the power to choose]. However, **our minds have been darkened by sin** [and the sinful condition], and **our desires** bound up by wicked impulses. Nevertheless, **we still think, choose, and act!!!!** Despite this freedom [of the will] to choose for ourselves, **we have lost all good impulses** [all good desires] to choose God [His righteousness], and rather have the continued compunction to do evil [to rebel and disobey the will/law of God]. **This is the continued state of our fallen inner status** [the true inner-condition of the heart]. *By nature* we are children of wrath because of this inner condition of rebellion now at work in the heart [and spirit] of those called by the bible, **the children of disobedience** (Eph. 2:1-3). The testimony of the scriptures say of fallen men, **"The thoughts of his heart [self] are only evil continually"** (Gen. 6:5). **The freedom of the will because of the fall of man has become for us a curse, because men choose only according to what he desires,** and what he continually chooses is sin thus he becomes accountable to the judgement of God. St. Augustine stated, that, we still have **free will**; but, we have **lost our liberty** to choose God **[what is right: righteous]** because of this fallen inner-condition of man's sinful and corrupted human nature. We are still free to desire and to choose but no longer have the liberty to choose **the good** [according to the righteous standards of God's Law]. We are free to choose as long as it is in keeping with our true inner station!!! This is the bondage of the Will to the fallen inner corruption of the sinful human nature within the human heart. We desire, and we think, and speak, and choose, and act [take action] all according to the true inner condition of the heart. This is why Jesus said, "A **good** tree cannot bring forth *evil* fruit, neither can a **corrupt** tree bring forth *good* fruit," "Either make the tree good, and his fruit good; or else, make the tree corrupt, and his fruit corrupt:

for the tree is known by its fruit" (Matt. 7:18, 12:33). What is in the **heart** of man is *known* by the things he produces [by his mind, words, choices, and actions]. Jonathan Edwards, the great Theologian of the 18th century once said, Fallen human beings retain their natural freedoms [the power to act according to their desires] but have lost all moral freedom. This is why Paul the Apostle when speaking of his own personal struggle with sin from within [before his conversion to the gospel] said, "For that which I do, I allow not: for what I would, that I do not; but what I hate, that I do" (Rom. 7:15). Paul here is saying, the will, [choice], the desire I have to obey the law is present with me [as a child it was something taught him from the outside], but how to finish, or carry this choice out in service to God I am at a loss [I am unable to obey God in keeping with His moral standard] (Rom. 7:18). Paul discovered he did not have the **inner strength** or, the inner *capacity* for obedience to God. The best Paul could do was to attempt **to reform** [to conform] his every outward thought, word, and action in compliance with the Law's demand. This is the best he could do under the circumstances. He could not get inside of himself and change his own human heart, from all those many **sinful desires** that warred *within*, and the *compunction* for **self-centeredness**. I am well aware [of] [realize] and understand very well the dismal picture the scriptures paint concerning man's present state of existence. This is why it is so hard for men to believe the word of God. No one wants to [have to] admit his or her own sin and sinfulness. All of our choices are determined from *within*; they are not coerced, nor forced. Even when men are forced or coerced this still does not change the choices they would make on their own if left to themselves. Yes, it is true our choices are and can be influenced by external things; but, this still does not change the true nature within. Every choice and action of man is ultimately determined from *within* by what he or she already is, **within, inside**, and by what he or she **already desires** coming from who he/she is within the fallen nature. This is self-determination; a self, determined by that fallen sinful and corrupted inner character. This is why in the <u>new birth</u> [that spiritual regeneration] God must **change the inner nature of man**

from within. He [God] **roots out** [cuts out] **the old stony heart** [of unbelief, and spiritual indifference and death] and **replaces it with a heart of flesh** [being renewed and now pliable (agreeable) to the will of God]. This is a spiritual regeneration!!!!! **"But those things which proceeds out of the mouth come forth from the heart [the inner nature]; and they defile the man. For out of the heart proceed evil thoughts, murders, adulteries, fornications, thefts, false witness, and blasphemies: these are the things which defile a man"** (Matt. 15:19-20). Until **this heart** [his inner nature] is changed, men cannot and will not be saved (RSB Page 1293). These *choices* and *actions* are coming out from *within* from the *heart* and human nature. When Jesus says, Out of the human heart proceeds all these evil things that prove a man's inner defilement, he means, out of this inner fallen human nature all these evil things are brought forth [from within]. Only the Cross, can set us free!!!

WHY DO MEN DENY THE EXISTENCE OF GOD?

Before I close this part of the book, I think it is necessary to say a little bit about, why people refuse to believe in God. On the other hand; or, even why do people deny His existence? The Lord spoke to me directly about this some time ago, and made it very clear to me: **God is not intellectually unreasonable, but rather, morally undesirable.** This is the important aspect [significant part] concerning why people refuse to believe in [on] God and even deny His personal existence. Notice I said, personal existence, because many are willing to make Him [God] some abstract idea or some concept [or an impersonal force]. There is no need to be concerned with moral accountability to an impersonal force, or to some abstract idea. The word <u>abstract</u> *means* disassociated, impersonal, and detached from any involvement in this world in any real and personal way. A God who is too difficult to understand or relate to, unreasonable and far removed from man and his life here [existence, here on earth]. So many who are willing to believe there is a God see him as aloof, cold, dry, unsociable, standoffish, and uninvolved [indifferent toward man]. Because of this mindset and the outright rejection of the God of the Bible, we find our world teeter-tottering on the brink of total chaos [destruction]. Chaos and utter meaninglessness!!! This word **chaos** *means* the loss of all order and meaning [the state of utter confusion]. When we look at the <u>Cosmos,</u> we see and find ORDER, the total Harmony of nature and creation: **but man has rejected the testimony of nature, itself, and opted for utter chaos, meaninglessness,** and **nothingness.** The word <u>Cosmos</u> *means*, **a complex and orderly self-**

inclusive system of existence, and harmony [by design], a **universe**. Universe is the whole body of things, existence, or phenomena organized and structured by design. The Cosmos our universe is by design that begs a designer!!! The Cosmos is by design, ordered, structured, and organized and demands a designer. So why do men ignore the obvious truth about God that is all around us in **nature** and in **life** itself. Why? MORAL ACCOUNTABILITY!!! In Romans 1:20 Paul said, "For the invisible things of him [the very existence of Him] from the creation of the world are clearly seen, being understood by the things that are made, even his eternal power and Godhead; so that they are without excuse." Paul said, the things that are not seen, those things that are invisible to the eye, ear, mind, will, and heart [understanding] of man is seen [or can be seen] by those things that are made [the visible things help reveal to us the true meaning of those invisible things]. Invisible things can be seen and/or **perceived from the heart** [one's mind's eye] [the testimony of the Conscience] when visible things are rightly understood. Paul wrote, and said, "Because that which may be known of God is manifest *in* them [revealed in them] [made known within them]; for God hath shewed it unto them" (Rom. 1:19). Here, Paul is saying, the right way to understand all of these visible things all around us is made clearly evident to them from *within* them [from within the conscience], "Because that, when they knew God, they glorified him not as God, neither were thankful; but became *vain* in their imagination, and their foolish heart was darkened. Because of their outright rejection of God: the truth about the facts of nature and life itself is now obscured, concealed, and hidden from view. "And [now have] changed the glory of the incorruptible God into an image made like [and compared to] corruptible man, and to birds, and four-footed beasts, and creeping things" (Rom. 1:23). Because of this, Paul said, they were turned over to their own blindness [unbelief] and immorality, and uncleanness. Why would man change the image of God, from God, to beasts of the field and fowls of the air, etc., **because man was bringing God down to his level in order to remove himself from moral accountability.** It is not that God himself is unbelievable; He [God], is just undesirable!! Fallen men, hate God!!! Why??? It is not a question of believability, but, moral accountability!! It is not that they cannot believe there is a God; they do not want to believe there is a God. They do not want him to exist. Why?? MORAL ACCOUNTABLIITY!! Jesus said, "For every one that does evil hates the light, neither does he come to the light, lest his deeds should be <u>reproved</u> [exposed and corrected]" (Jn. 3:20). There is no doubt; men hate God because they love their sin and sinning, and refuse to be reproved [exposed and corrected]. Men willingly blind themselves and tell themselves there is no God, so they do not have to consider the consequences of their actions. They profess themselves **to be wise**, and yet they have become <u>fools</u> (Rom. 1:22). The bible says, the *fool* says in own his heart there is no God. The wisdom of this world is based upon a belief system that attempts to disprove the existence of God. The so many different religious and philosophical systems of belief and practice is man's attempt to be wise without God. To create a God or belief system [or school of thought] **that coincides with their own personal moral choices** [their own distinctive personal value system] makes them their own God [or the captain of their own beliefs/fate]. It is the **fallen adamic nature** *within* that has rebelled in the beginning that lives on in the hearts and minds of those who refuse [and reject] God [and have rejected the gospel]. Men are willing to lie to themselves rather than face the facts of their own moral corruption [immorality; fallen human condition]. I am a good person; I haven't done anything very bad or worthy of judgement!! God doesn't exist, so what I think, or do, or say, or choose, does not matter. Everyone can do what is right in his/her own eyes (Judges 21:25). Do you see it; **no one has anything to lose over the question of the existence of God from a purely philosophical viewpoint**. However, from a moral standpoint, men have absolutely everything to lose if God exists [is real]. The question of the existence of God is not really a philosophical exercise; *within*, men know God exists, even though they block him out of their mind and heart every day. This is why men drink, take drugs, give themselves over to all kinds of vice, etc., if just to **drown out the noise**

of their conscience. Men stay busy, busying themselves with every possible distraction just to stay one-step ahead of the voice of their own Conscience. Nevertheless, once men stop, and have time to reflect, their voice of conscience comes screaming through [who is God reminding them from *within* that He exists and that he holds all men morally accountable]. The sound can be quite deafening!!!!!!!! We will create and put in place anything and everything designed to distract from this deafening [devastating] voice of conscience!! God help us all not to resist this voice of Conscience. "For when the Gentiles, which have not the law, do by nature the things contained in the law, these, having not the law, are a law unto themselves: which show the work of the law written in their hearts, **their conscience also bearing witness**, and **their thoughts** the mean while *accusing* or else *excusing* one another: **in the day when God shall judge** the secrets of men by JC according to my gospel" (Rom. 2:14-16). The conscience will bear *witness* or testify from *within* either accepting or rejecting the reasoning faculty of man. The word thoughts here in the GK *means* to reason or **reasoning** [imagination: what one believes]. The conscience from *within* will judge men's thoughts or reasons, or reasoning's [imagination and beliefs]. Man may be able to drown out the voice of his conscience, but, he will never be able to silence its testimony!!!! Paul tied the testimony of the Conscience, to the day of Judgement. Man may be able to reject the testimony given to him through the voice of conscience but, **he will never be able to erase its memory**!! Everything God has ever said to man He will play back to him through the testimony of his own Conscience. The fool who says in his heart there is no God, and, has rejected the testimony of their conscience, He will judge. On the day of judgement: God will judge men by that same conscience bearing witness against them; this is part of Paul's meaning of God judging the secrets of men. All the secrets that the conscience holds will be laid to bare on the day of judgement. All men will give an account on the day of judgement concerning everything they said and did in agreement with and in rejection of the voice of conscience, [the testimony it brings]. These who refused to retain God in their knowledge [here, in the context of what Paul is saying would make it the voice of conscience], God gave them over to a closed <u>reprobate</u> mind [a worthless intellect no longer useful to God] (Rom. 1:28). Here, Paul is saying, these who have rejected the voice of their own conscience [and the testimony it brings], are those who refused to retain God in their knowledge. As a result, their mind is now blinded and their hearts are now darkened (Rom. 1:21; Eph. 4:17-19). In Ephesians 4:19, Paul spoke of those who **were past feeling**: as those who no longer had the use of their own conscience [were no longer open to its correction] [having a seared conscience] (1 Tim. 4:2). This is why Paul said, we are to bear the truth [the word of God] to every man's conscience, because God by His word will hold all men morally responsible [accountable] (2 Cor. 4:2). I personally believe Romans 2:14-16 is speaking of a believing [born again] Gentile [internal evidence within the text, I believe, bears this out]. Notwithstanding; it is important to realize a general application can be made to all human being concerning the inner-workings of the Conscience, and its role in the conviction of sin. Men have hardened their hearts against God, to silence that inner voice of conscience; however, men who reject the voice of their conscience will not ever escape it scathing rebuke nor its moral accusation and final judgement. God, help us not to rebel against you, and refuse to hear!!

When looking at Romans 1:20, the Lord drew my attention to what He said, "Understood by the things that are made." The bible says, all creation are the works of His hands or, they are His handy work. The bible says, all of creation declares his glory or, advertise His own existence. There is no doubt; God has designed nature, life, and all of creation on earth and in the heavens to display His own personal glory [power and existence]. Paul said, "Even his eternal **power** and Godhead; so that [all men] are without excuse [having no defense; rebuttal, argument on the day of judgement]. The GK word here is <u>dunamis</u>, which means, the ability, force, and miracles. No creation is a force of nature in and of itself; but it is, the force, and the power, might, and ability of God on display for all to see [to fear] and believe [and to obey]. God designed all of what He created, and that includes man himself **to be a witness and testimony to God's own personal power**, might, rule, and majesty. "The heavens declare His glory [splendor]." "Let us make man in our image, and after our likeness: and let them have dominion" (Gen. 1:26). God made man to be an image bearer!! To bear the *image* of the invisible God, and to **represent** His *likeness* that would demonstrate the **nature** of the true God, *from* the invisible. This is what Adam failed to do in the beginning, and what Christ came to do, and then He died to restore mankind back to their original purpose as God's image bearers (Rom. 5:12-17; Heb. 1:2-3). When Paul spoke of the things that are made [created], he was speaking of the world of natural things [nature]. Today, because of the sophistication of science and man's technical abilities to traverse [or to go beyond the surface of things] [and examine] natural things, the discovery of the micro-world as it fits into the macro-world, has forced men to see his/her Creator face to face [to look into the very underpinnings of nature, itself, is to look at the very signature of God Himself]. The complexity and sophistication of natural things, with its multiple and diverse life forms begs a designer!! To this day, men still have not, under their own power, created anything as more complex than the simple living cell. The biggest and most sophisticated super computer pale in comparison to the simple living cell. Wow!!! This demands and **commands** [forces men to admit there has to be] a designer!! This is how the Lord showed it to me. Remember, man is made [created] in the *image* of God and, having his *likeness*: man will partially share in some of those attributes. God is a Creator God; so man will have *within* himself the inherent ability to create. In the spirit, God took me [through a sanctified imagination] to a big city made by the hands of mortal men. He ask me, what do you see? I said a city, brick and mortar, wood and steel. He said, how did all of these things come about? I said, by the mind and will of men, they are the works of man's hands. He said, if all you see was made by the mind, will, and hands of mortal men, and that nothing man made, that came into existence, of its own will, under its own power, was made, apart from his own personal skill, imagination, and intervention, then look around you and see the glory and majesty of your God. What I understood God *to mean* was, if man had to plan, think, and choose to act, and work with his own hands to cause to happen, or, bring into existence all that we see, without exception, how much more the God of all heaven and earth created, all that we see and enjoy [experience] here and now. If this is the way the world works, in which we all live, that, only when we use our mind, and our will, and work with our own hands, will anything exist and find a place in this world, then nothing happens by chance, or by accident, in this world of men, who work with their hands, choose with their hearts, and plan everything with their own mind. Everything we see in the world today, begs [demands] a designer!!! No one ever wakes up to a world [within the systems of men] that works and operates under its own power without a **cause [without a prime mover]** [without being acted upon]. The **effect** [or result] of the world around us [the systems of men and everything built therein] [proves] demands a **cause**!! The word cause *means* a reason for an action or condition: something that brings about an effect or a result. We cannot have an **effect** without a **cause** [without a mover] this is the true condition of the world [something **essential** for the *occurrence* of something else]. This is why the bible say, **"While the earth remains, seedtime and harvest…shall not cease"** (Gen.8:22). If the world works this way, all it [the world] is doing is reflecting and demonstrating itself as a creation. We are living in a created world by a holy God who is its Creator. He is a Moral God by Nature and Will, holy, sanctified, and set apart from everything He created. He has put a demand on holiness!!!!!! He commands men, his highest creation in this world to be holy, set apart, and consecrated to do his work [to do His will as an image bearer]. However, men have rebelled against his maker, and has chosen rather to call himself, god, [or has chosen to make himself his own god] or, he has chosen to create other gods to worship [to worship them as god]. The question of the existence of God is not just an intellectual one: an intellectual rationality [reasonability] [meaning a matter of the intellect] but as well, a matter of moral accountability [God is morally undesirable]. God help!!

When we look at the first chapter of Romans, many scholars believe Paul was referencing the ancient world of Genesis [the world before the great flood]. This looks at the human race prior to the time of Abraham. This was the time when the world was influenced by the Watchers [or, by fallen angels upon the earth]. This was a time of the beginning of sin, and rebellion against God, and *both* a time of moral and spiritual degeneration. God judged this first world based on three main reasons: **1.** For suppressing the Truth [about the existence of God] **2.** For rejecting God's revelation of Himself [given through all created things] **3.** Moreover, for perverting God's *glory* [as Creator God] and, changing it [He and His power] into things that were made [into things that belong to the created order]. The truth about God; and, the true knowledge of His existence as Creator, is revealed to us and made known to the entire created world so that all men are without excuse [so the entire universe is held accountable]. Men worshipped gods, who were not God!! Men worshipped demons [devils] who posed as God [as gods]. The bible calls this Idolatry: the first great sin of the collective world before the great flood. This led to senseless thinking, and to moral insensitivity!! WE BECOME JUST LIKE THE GODS WE SERVE [WORSHIP]. Romans chapter 1 teaches a specific judgement that comes upon all men who refuse to believe in God and who work hard **to deny His existence as Creator**. God will first give them up [to vice] to moral corruption, degradation, and degeneration [to vile affections, and to all forms of uncleanness, and unrighteousness]. Second, because man [men] did not want to retain God [the Creator] in their own personal knowledge [having rejected the voice of their personal conscience], God gave them up and over to a reprobate mind [a mind void of the truth and **plunged into moral and spiritual degeneration**]. These vile persons are turned over to devils [demons] to worship those gods that are not the true God [Defending Your Faith by R. C. Sproul; Book of Romans by Chuck Missler chapter 1-2]. God, help us all to repent of all these things and turn too you alone, by faith through the gospel of our Lord JC. I am not ashamed of this gospel of JC, for it is the POWER to save!!! The judgment of God against sinners who reject the gospel of our salvation is, to turn <u>their minds</u> over to spiritual blindness; and, to give **their bodies** over to sinful lustful evil **wicked practices!!**

REVELATION OF THE MYSTERY

"Now to him that is **of power** to stablish you according to **my** gospel, and the preaching of Jesus Christ, *according to the revelation of the mystery,* which was kept secret since the world began, but now is **made manifest**…" (Rom. 16:25-26). The word power here in the text is the GK word *dunamis* that pertains to God's ability to establish the church in Christ Jesus. Now unto Him **who is able,** in whom all things are possible, to stablish you (to set in place, strengthen, and resolutely fix in a certain direction) *according* to **my gospel,** and *according* to the **revelation** of the mystery, which is *now* (at this present time) made manifest (to make known or open to view). Notice, what was once kept secret and hidden from view, is, now, made plain for all to see, and understand. This Paul says, concerns the gospel of our Lord and Savior Jesus Christ. Paul calls it **"my gospel,"** which, simply means, Paul's *understanding* of the mystery of Jesus Christ and his redemptive works on the Cross [in His death, burial, and resurrection]. Paul's [my] *gospel* was the preaching of the **Cross** as the **power** and **wisdom** of God, which is, the preaching of Christ, and him crucified. This is the Atonement. The Cross, in short, refers to the whole of the gospel.

The establishment of the Church in Christ Jesus, and her ability [opportunity] to access her full provision to the fulfilment of every promise is **according** to two things. It is *according* to the **gospel** of Jesus Christ, and, it is *according* to the **revelation** of this mystery. Notice, Paul wrote the word "according" twice, in the text. It is the GK word *kata* and it means, after the manner of, which connects the establishment of the NT Church, in her full provision in Christ

Jesus, to the *mystery* of the gospel, and to the ***revelation*** of that same mystery. Did you get that? Not just the gospel, but as well, the revelation of that gospel. Not just, *according* to what he did, but as well, *according* to you coming into an understanding of what this all means. **What he did, and, you understanding what this means: the Holy Spirit, works here!!** The Holy Spirit works through the Cross-and our *faith* in all that the **Cross** has provided for our full redemption: spirit, soul and body. It is impossible for you and me to believe for, what, we do not first have a knowledge of. You must first comprehend, before, you can apprehend. We comprehend in the "spirit," and, we apprehend in this "world." The word <u>revelation</u> is the GK word *apokalupsis* and means to unveil or to reveal; to uncover or to take the lid off the cover; disclosure, or to disclose. This all comes by the revelation knowledge of Jesus Christ. Paul is speaking of the unveiling of this mystery of Christ and him crucified: the unveiling of the **meaning** of the Cross [his death, and resurrection]. Paul said, the things that are freely given to us of God are revealed to us by his Holy Spirit. It is God's will to make these things known unto us [the *meaning* of **his death** and resurrection] by a spiritual illumination: the eyes of our understanding, given light (2 Cor. 2:12; Eph. 1:17-19).

"Simon Peter, a servant and an apostle of Jesus Christ, to them that **have obtained a like precious faith** with us through the ***righteousness*** of God and our ***Savior*** Jesus Christ: **grace** and peace be multiplied unto you ***through the knowledge of*** God, and of Jesus our Lord, *according as his divine power hath given unto us all things* that pertain unto life and godliness, **through the knowledge of him** that hath called us to glory and virtue: **whereby are given unto us exceeding great and precious promises:** that *by these* ye might be partakers of the divine nature..." (2 Pet. 1:1-4). Peter said, we have obtained or received a like precious faith. The word *precious* here in the GK means ***money paid***, and comes from another GK word that means **to pay a price**. There is no doubt that, this word was intended by Peter to speak to our <u>redemption</u>. Redemption *means* **to ransom in full**; **to go to market** to purchase a slave at the public auction;

atonement. Here, it is not speaking of you and me having faith, he is speaking about **"the Faith."** In Jude verse three [3-4], the writer **begins with our common salvation**, than in verse four, he continues by exhorting the believers to earnestly contend for *"the faith"* that was once delivered to the saints. What he calls **"the Faith"** in verse *four*, he calls, our **common salvation** in verse *three*. No doubt, Peter has the *gospel* of our Lord and Savior Jesus Christ in mind when writing to the saints [the churches] in 2nd Peter. The gospel [the Cross] is the foundation of **"the Faith."**

"Through the **righteousness** of God and our **Savior** Jesus Christ, what does this mean? One of the key word meanings for righteousness is **Justice**. Peter is saying our *redemption* was wrought [made possible] first by the JUSTICE of God!! The word **Savior** comes from the GK word *soter* meaning deliverer, and the GK word *sozo* meaning to save, deliver, protect, preserve, heal, and to make whole. This word meaning speaks to our *salvation* made possible by the shed *blood* of Jesus Christ on the Cross, which provided for our justification. Justification means to make just or to declare as innocent, acquittal, cleared of all guilt. This is the exact biblical meaning of the word **atonement**. It is through the **Justice** of God, and our **Justification** that, we, are redeemed. Here, Peter [through Apostolic revelation] is drawing our attention to our [my] redemption, and saying, it is through the *knowledge* of this **redemption** that his divine *grace* [his favor, gifting, generosity, joy, benefits, blessings, promises, etc.] and peace, are multiplied unto us [this grace and peace is increased, both, within, and without]. Did you get that? It is channeled *through* the knowledge of God [our/me coming into an understanding of his divine justice] and *through* [as a channel for divine grace] Jesus Christ our Savior [our justification]. This is **the atonement** made possible by the CROSS. **Justice, comes before justification**; He is *first* **the Just**, before he can be **the Justifier** (Rom. 3:26). You cannot and must not [never] *separate* the Justice of God from our Justification. Because many do not understand, or, have rejected the need for divine justice, many have turned the grace of God into a license [permission] to sin. Many today, look at grace as God just choosing to overlook sin, arbitrarily [many today, look at the breaking of God's law as unimportant]. A divine *pardon* based on nothing more than God just doing nothing about it [nothing about the breaking of His Divine Law]. Much like clemency, which means, **to show mercy**, or, to show *leniency* toward a guilty offender. This *leniency* is based on nothing more than just individual preference and/or convenience: **how one might think or feel at the time.** Atonement must *satisfy* both the sinner's **need to be forgiven**, and, to *satisfy* **the demand** for Divine Justice, all at the same time. **Atonement** means to placate God, to appease his wrath; to cancel sin; to put off judgment; to forgive, pardon, and purge the sinner: to reconcile *both* God and man. Justice and Justification *both* applied together equals biblical Redemption. The words *payment* and to *purchase* best understands **biblical redemption**. Christ [in his death] made the payment on the Cross [and satisfied Divine Justice]; His blood shed and spilt on that same Cross is what purchased the sinner's Justification [acquittal]. His death made the **payment**; his shed blood provided the Atonement [the pardon]. God, help us, to not, take lightly, divine justice!!

Do we truly understand the *meaning* of our redemption: the unveiling of the *meaning* of the mystery of Jesus Christ and him crucified. Not just, what he did for us on that Cross, but we coming into a full assurance of our redemption (salvation). Comprehension precedes or comes before apprehension!! We cannot apprehend what we do not first comprehend. The **knowledge** of our redemption, *both* his Divine *Justice* and our own *Justification* is paramount to us being established in the faith, and we as the church accessing our full provision [full benefits] in Christ Jesus. The unraveling of this *mystery* of the Cross [his death, and resurrection] is the **key** to the strength of our justification and our continued sanctification [growth in spiritual things]. This is a legal matter, and it concerns a legal process on going in the Courts of Heaven. The NC is a **legal** [a Law] document; this is why Paul said, "Being not without law to God, but, **under the law** to Christ" (1 Cor. 9:21). Paul, here, is not speaking of the law <u>of</u> Christ, which, speaks, to loving one's neighbor, "Bear ye one another's burdens, and so fulfill the law <u>of</u> Christ" (Gal. 6:2). Paul is speaking of the New Covenant [Grace] as being under Spiritual Law [not Moses, but God] and operating [and only works] by a legal process understood only by the revelation knowledge of Jesus Christ. The revelation of this *mystery* is paramount to our continued Christian victory and continued Christian emancipation [freedom] [our Christian liberty] [our Christian salvation].

"According as His <u>Divine Power</u> has given unto us all things that pertain unto **life** and godliness" (2 Pet. 1:3). Again, the GK word here is *dunamis* "But you shall receive power [dunamis] after that the Holy Ghost is come upon you" (Acts 1:8). Divine Power is capitalized in some bibles because it is clearly portraying a Person, the personality of the Holy Spirit. Again, this is revealing the Holy Spirit working *through* the <u>knowledge</u> of God and the <u>revelation</u> of this mystery. It is He, who, takes these **things** accomplished by [in] Christ on the **Cross** and *transfers* them unto us, we, who believe "[For] He shall glorify me: for he shall receive [take] of mine, and shall show it [give it] unto you" (Jn. 16:13-15). Notice, Peter, speaks of those *things* that pertain unto ET **life** and <u>godliness</u>. The GK word here is ZOE and, belongs to those things that pertain to Eternal Life. This is spiritual life, the God kind of life, or, the God quality of life. This speaks to the <u>provision</u> of his **Grace** [being in Christ], accomplished by the blood of his Cross [in his death and in his resurrection]. This Zoe life or, eternal life, is the <u>life</u> that never ends, and is a ceaseless never-ending source and supply of God, "And, he, has given unto us **all things** that pertain to **life** [to grace, favor, gifting, joy, generosity, benefits, blessings, promises, etc.] "For in Him was *life* [Zoe], and the <u>life</u> was the *light* of men [<u>truth</u> given to all men] (Jn. 1:4). The word *light* here in the text can be used interchangeably with the word *truth*. "…I am come that they might have life [Zoe] and that they might have it more abundantly (Jn. 10:10). I am come that they might receive life [receive Zoe] and to *have* and *hold* that life in abundance *through* the **knowledge** of Him [in His death, and burial, and resurrection] who called us out of darkness into the marvelous light (1 Pet. 2:9). <u>Godliness</u> *means* holiness, and means bearing its fruit or coming into a spiritual harvest [that is, the <u>maturation</u> of the bride, or the <u>maturing</u> of sons]. Can you see how important it is for you and me to come into **a clear** and **precise** understanding of our full redemption? God help us all. This new life [Zoe] is understood through the *light* of the truth; this <u>truth</u> of the gospel is only realized by the revelation knowledge of JC. God, open up to us the eyes of our understanding!!

"Whereby [thereby] are given unto us exceeding great and *precious* **promises** that **by these** [promises] you might be *partakers* of the divine nature" (2 Pet. 1:4). **Whereby** in the GK denotes the ***channel*** of an act [conduit] *through* which God accomplishes the desired transaction [that divine exchange] between himself and the sinner. <u>Conduit</u> means the *fountain* from which all spring forth [from which all blessings flow]. These great and precious promises are given [made available] to us by the action of what Christ did <u>on the Cross</u>. The Cross is the **channel** *through* which we receive all these great and precious promises; but, it is *through* the **knowledge** of God and the **revelation** of this *mystery* of Christ and him crucified [the Cross] that we are able [are enabled] to access this provision made possible in Christ Jesus. <u>Partaker</u> in the GK means to ***share in*** like kind. It is through the revelation [knowledge] of this mystery of the Cross-his death and resurrection we are able [enabled] to share in the inheritance with all the saints **in light**. How many understand that this is not automatic? It is not that these [the promises] are not already ours in Christ Jesus, "Who **hath blessed us with all spiritual blessings** in heavenly places **in Christ**" (Eph. 1:3). The problem is our right [authority] to access these spiritual blessings that come to us only by the *knowledge* of Him [a clear and precise understanding of our full redemption]. Our salvation is a Covenantal salvation!!!! This is why, Paul, spoke of the preaching of the Cross, not only as the *power* of God that redeems, but as well, the **wisdom** of God that instructs the believer in his/her full redemption. Redemption in Christ Jesus is *both* the **power** and

wisdom of God. It is a salvation that rest upon **covenantal promises** that must be invoked by us in the time of need.

Notice, Peter called it a **precious** faith, and, precious promises!! Peter used this word precious, twice. First as applied to our salvation; second, to our sanctification "(that) ye might be *partakers* of the divine nature." This word *precious* in both cases speak to the same GK word cluster, and pertains to our **redemption**. The *promises* [of God] are connected *to* and contingent *upon* our eternal redemption. The ability [right] to receive the promises [plural] is in our redemption. The ability [right] to access [tap into] what is promised [from God] is found in the *knowledge* of that promise: the ability [right] to access the provision [supply] contained within each promise is faith [confidence] in the promise itself. The legal ground or legal **right** you have to all these *precious* promises is found in your redemption. The legal ground [or, legal right] you have to access [tap into] all these great and precious promises is found in your *knowledge* of that redemption. The good fight [the contest] of faith must include *both* the **knowledge** of those promises, and, as well the **knowledge** of our full redemption. This is the **Cross [the blood]**, the **Word**, and the **Spirit**!!!

Paul said, *"Fight the good fight of faith, lay hold on eternal life…"* (1 Tim. 6:12). The word *fight* in the GK means, a struggle or it means, to struggle. The word picture given in the GK is an **athletic contest**. It means, to compete for a prize and, to contend with an enemy [to endeavor to accomplish something]. We are fighting a spiritual enemy that does not fight fair (open to view). We need to know our *rights* and our redemptive *benefits* [privileges] in Christ Jesus. We cannot always see where our enemy is fighting from; this is why, our battle, must always be based upon our ***Redemptive*** Covenant. This battle is taking place, not only in the spirit world but, as well in heaven itself. Not just on the spiritual battlefield but, as well, **in the Courts of heaven**. There is much to be gained, and even more available in Christ Jesus for our spiritual success. All of this is contingent upon our laying **hold on** [eternal] **life** [Zoe life] in Christ Jesus. This means to *seize* or to take possession, of life, to apprehend that for which we are also apprehended of Christ Jesus (Phil. 3:12). Life, has taken hold of us; now, we must take hold of that life. We **comprehend** the life we have *received* that we might **apprehend** the *life* promised. There is no doubt; the believer is called into **a spiritual warfare**, that, by this precious faith, and through **our knowledge** of this full redemption in Christ Jesus, and through the *knowledge* of these exceeding great and precious promises we become partakers of every spiritual blessing in heavenly places in Christ Jesus. We are [made] *partakers* of his divine nature, through what Christ has done for us through his **death** [on the Cross] and his **resurrection**. It is through his *sinless life* under the Law and *sin-bearing* death on the Cross-and through the *impartation* of this **new life** by the resurrection, we are made new [creatures] in Christ Jesus. May the God of our Lord Jesus Christ, the Father of glory, grant unto us [you and me] [a supply of His grace] in a spirit of wisdom [skill] and *revelation* in the knowledge [acknowledgment] of Him [in his death, burial, and resurrection]. My prayer for you.

The Cross, the gospel [the need for a Savior, or the need for salvation] is *foolishness* to them that are lost [foolishness to them who perish]. Why??? Because they see no need for a Savior!!! They say, "I am a good person [I believe in God], I have not done anything worthy of eternal judgment [punishment]. **Therefore, to them the Cross is *foolishness*.** However, the bible calls the Cross, the gospel, the wisdom and power of God. This is where the **Law** of God comes in in the plan of salvation. The **Law** of God plays a very important role in the plan of redemption. The *law* gives the knowledge of sin, brings conviction, and reveals the true status [condition] of man before a Holy God. The **Law** reveals man as a transgressor [as a lawbreaker] **now, the *wisdom* of God can be seen [found] in the need for a Savior**. Now, through the *law,* the Cross-becomes the *wisdom* of God. Now, through the *law,* the Cross [the gospel] becomes **the power of God to save!!** Now, we see the role the *law* plays in the gospel. We preach the gospel that men might be saved. However, men reject the gospel [the Cross] as *foolishness* seeing no real need [no value] for repentance and <u>salvation</u>, until, the ***law*** has done [accomplished] its job [task] in revealing man to himself a *sinner* under divine wrath [under divine judgement]. Until this happens, he will never *hear* nor *obey* the gospel call (1 Cor. 1:18, 21, 23-24; 2:14). No conflict, no conversion!!

Now, I want to say just a little bit about how all this works in our soul sanctification [or, rather, in the <u>transformation</u> of the human soul, which is our Christian sanctification]. The gospel alone is the only true source for our Christian sanctification. The HS will not work in us without you and me putting our faith [confidence] in this SAME ONE GOSPEL. The Holy Spirit will not **empower a spiritual counterfeit!!** The HS will not work through a false gospel; the HS will not work *in* and *through* those many religious things being added to the gospel by religious men. We find in 1 Corinthians 1:30, Paul, presenting Jesus Christ in the gospel as the complete redemptive process from start to finish. "But of him **are you in** Christ Jesus, who of God **is made unto us wisdom**, and righteousness, and sanctification, and redemption." Here, *righteousness* in the GK means <u>justification</u>: the forgiveness of sins, and the impartation of new life; this must include in the new life, the *promise* of eternal life and the <u>resurrection</u> of the body, which, Paul, called in his other epistles the HOPE of eternal life. Then, Paul says, Jesus Christ is as well made our <u>sanctification</u>, and our <u>redemption</u>. While **redemption** speaks to the entire Salvation process, here in the text, it should be understood as Paul applying it to **that part of the redemptive process** that completes our redemption [salvation], namely, our <u>glorification</u>, or, the redemption [the **resurrection**] of the body. **Justification** deals with our <u>spirit</u>; **sanctification** with the <u>soul</u>; and **glorification** with our body (Rom. 8:23). Peter said, "Receiving the end of your faith, even the salvation of your soul" (1 Pet. 1:9). If a person who claims the gospel of JC does not <u>secure</u> the resurrection of their body at the end of this age **they will lose their eternal soul**. This is exactly why the bible says, "But he that [that person] shall **endure** unto the end [shall cross the finish line of their faith], **the same** shall be saved" (Matt. 24:13). Jesus said, "In your <u>patience</u> [in your endurance] you will [shall] *possess* your soul [unto everlasting life]" (Lk. 21:19). This word <u>patience</u> in the GK means, in your **continuance**; and, in your constancy in your faith you will possess your soul unto eternal life. Here in the text it *speaks* of **enduring patience** [or, endurance to the end]. No doubt; the only way to guarantee the possession of your soul unto eternal life is through *securing* the <u>resurrection</u> of the body. This is the only way **the human soul can be won, possessed, and secured eternally**. <u>Sanctification</u> is the hardest part of the Salvation process, because, it requires our personal cooperation, and participation. God alone works in our justification and, in our glorification; however, while God works in our sanctification, as well, He, God, requires **participatory labor** on behalf of the Holy Spirit, which means, the Christian works [labors] in support of the HS work in our Christian sanctification [the HS, works, and then, we work]. Christian sanctification is the transformation of the human soul. **This is Christian growth in the human soul that comes by the <u>grace</u> of God *through* the <u>knowledge</u> of God**. The <u>knowledge</u> of God is the key component **in the soul's transformation in our Christian sanctification** (2 Pet. 3:18). This [human] soul's <u>transformation</u> affects [and/or impacts] **four major areas**. The *first* being the <u>renewing</u> of the MIND [and the **emotions**] [the <u>reins</u>] (Rom. 12:2; Rev. <u>2:23</u>). The <u>mind</u> here in the text is the GK word *nous* and means the **intellect** [or, the *thought* processes]: this will as well include the <u>emotions</u>. The **mind** and **emotions** [the <u>reins</u>] are on the receiving end of the 5 physical senses. It is only when these are *renewed* [are restored to their rightful and proper function within the human soul] are we able then to **retrain** the human WILL in righteousness. In the text, the word <u>renew</u> in the GK *means* **to renovate**. To <u>renovate</u> *means* to first remove all of the unwanted stuff [the bad thoughts; and the wrong ways of thinking], **and then to furnish the mind with good things** [with good thoughts that line up the thought processes of the mind with the word of God]. It is only after this has taken place can we train the human will in righteous living. Even though in the new birth [in our spiritual regeneration] **we have received a new heart** [a new <u>desire</u> and a new <u>decision</u> for God] (Rom. 7:18), it is still necessary to *retrain* this **new WILL** in how to act, walk, and in how to work righteously (Ez. 36:26-27). Only after the *renewing* [renovation] of the mind [the intellect] [and emotions, the subjugation of one's own feelings now lining up with the attitudes of the word of God], and only after the *retraining* of the human will [which takes place at the very same time the mind is being renewed], can we now BRIDLE the TONGUE [and control our speech, righteously]. It is *through* the **renewed** [retrained] human will working through the reeducation of the mind [and the transformation of the human soul, with its soulical emotions], can we now bridle the tongue. Jesus said, "**Out of the abundance of the heart** [and, out of the *exercising* of the will working and communicating through the renewed intellect], the mouth speaks" (Lk. 6:45). Only after the Mind [and emotions] are renewed, which in turn, retrains the Will, which in turn, **bridles the tongue** [which *means*, in turn, **gives us control over our speech**], can we then, and only then, subjugate the body. The body must first be subject to us, before we can **present** it [the body] to God as a *living* and *responding* human sacrifice in holy service to God: to DO HIS WILL. In 1 Cor.1:30, we find Paul presenting Jesus Christ and **him crucified** [for us] as the entire redemptive process *from* start to finish: with nothing else being added to the gospel. Nothing else being **added to our justification**, but Christ and he crucified!!! And nothing **added to our sanctification** and glorification, but Christ and he crucified. It is important to see and come to understand that, **to add anything else along the way within the [our] redemptive process** will intrude in on this Salvation process, and stifle, and hinder, and even block the HS FROM HIS WORK. Notice, in the text, Paul, mentioned WISDOM *first* before he mentions justification and then sanctification, and finally the completion of our redemption in our glorification. Why did Paul mention **wisdom** first, here, in the text?? Paul is saying, Christ and He crucified **is the wisdom** of God. Paul said, the ***preaching* of the Cross**, is, both, the power and **wisdom** of God. In other words, Christ and him crucified is *both* the power and wisdom of God (1 Cor. 1:18, 21, 23-24). This *means* **the gospel** of JC is both the **power** and **wisdom** of God. What Paul is saying here in the text is, that, **Christ, in the gospel,** [in his redemptive works on the Cross], is not only the power of God to enter into this full salvation; but, **Christ, in the gospel,** [in our redemption], is also **the <u>wisdom</u>** [and **knowledge**] of God **for this entire redemptive process for eternal life** [in our spirit, and soul, and our body] [the *gospel* of JC is *both* the Spirit and the Word] [the **gospel** of JC is *both* the KNOWLEDGE and the POWER]. It is important **we do not attempt to add** anything else to it [the gospel], it is complete all by itself from start to finish *within* this entire redemptive process for our justification, sanctification, and glorification. To add anything else to the gospel along the way *within* this **overall gospel scheme** [within this overall entire redemptive process] would end up *violating* the gospel [the **saving grace** of Christ] (Gal. 1:6), as the <u>wisdom</u> [**and knowledge**] [and power] of God that <u>redeems</u>. God, help us, not to add anything to the gospel, and, **frustrate the grace of God.** The *revelation* of **this mystery**, includes, the **gospel**, as *both* the **<u>wisdom</u>** and **<u>power</u>** of God that enables us to enter into that/this full salvation: spirit, soul and body. Help!!!

REDEMPTION IN CHRIST

"But now the *righteousness* of God without the law [revealed independently and altogether apart from] the law is manifested, being witnessed by [although actually attested] by the law and the prophets; Even the righteousness of God which is by faith of Jesus Christ unto all and upon all them that believe [by believing with personal trust and confident reliance on Christ]: for there is no difference: For all have sinned, and come short of the glory of God; Being justified freely [and now in right standing] by his grace [his unmerited favor and mercy] through the redemption that is [provided] in Christ Jesus [has liberated and freed us from the guilt, punishment, and power of sin (TPT)]: Whom God hath set forth [put forth before the eyes of all as a **mercy-seat**] to be a propitiation through faith in his blood [through the *cleansing* and **life-giving** sacrifice of atonement and reconciliation to be received through faith] to declare [show] his righteousness for the remission [forgiveness] of sins that are past, through the forbearance of God [He, God, had passed over sin, and, ignored former sins without punishment]: To declare, I say, at this time his righteousness: that he might **be just**, and **the justifier** of him which believeth in Jesus [It was to demonstrate and prove at the present time that He [Christ] Himself is righteous [just] and that He [God] justifies and accepts as righteous him who has true faith in JC]. (Rom. 3:21-26 KJ/Amp).

In this ***book***, and in the next ***two*** books [Believer's Sanctification, and Justification by Faith] [3 books altogether] [This will be a ***trilogy*** on the Gospel of JC called the **"Evangel"**], I will address some specific words that are contained in the Scriptures that will help us to understand this *revelation* of the **mystery** of Jesus Christ and Him crucified. This will not be exhaustive but it will be complete. I will explain *words* like, Substitution, identification, imputation, and to reckon. I will also explain the **Divine Exchange**, and *words* like reconciliation, restoration, and resurrection. I will attempt to explain **Water Baptism** from a redemptive perspective [how it applies to our sanctification]. I will take the time to explain the **Cross** [the blood]. I will explain the meaning of **Romans 8:2** as applied to our redemption [and sanctification]. We will take a closer look at *words* like, Atonement, Propitiation, Expiation, and Redemption. I will also spend some time explaining the words Salvation, Justification, Righteousness, and Sanctification.

In this chapter, we will attempt to paint the full picture of **redemption** as revealed in the scriptures. "And without controversy **great** is the *mystery* of godliness: God was *manifest* in the flesh [for the purpose of the Cross]; *justified* in the Spirit [this is vindicated righteousness by the resurrection], seen of angels [who watched the entire redemptive plan unfold], preached unto the Gentiles, believed on in the world [the great commission], *received up* in glory [his ascension]" (1 Tim. 3:16). Here, the Apostle Paul presents the *gospel* in a nutshell [briefly]. Here, Paul first speaks of the incarnation [when the **Word** was made *flesh*] [when God became a man] then he [Paul] pushes past His entire earthly life, ministry, and death on the Cross; he [Paul] highlights his [Christ's own] **resurrection** and **ascension** "justified in the Spirit, and received up in glory." Here, Paul, calls the gospel of our salvation [that is, the plan of eternal salvation] "**the** *mystery* **of** godliness." This word *godliness* in the GK means the **gospel scheme [plan]**; Scheme *means* to form a plan; this speaks to the **entire overall plan for Salvation**. When Paul says, "**Great is the mystery of godliness**" he is saying, **great is the overall plan for man's eternal redemption. GOD BE PRAISED!!!** Not just the Cross, but his resurrection and, his victorious ascension!!

WHAT THE GOSPEL HAS ACCOMPLISHED [THE FINISHED WORK]

The word <u>righteous</u> *means* perfect conformity to the Law of God. This Law of God points to both God's Divine Character and His Moral Will. The standard of obedience that is required by the Law of God is absolute perfection [James 2:10]. Only perfect obedience to His Righteous Standard is acceptable to God!! Christ came and fulfilled that righteous standard through his obedient life under the Law. Because of what Christ accomplished through his **sinless-life** and **sin-bearing death** a *righteousness* by faith of Jesus Christ came unto all and upon them that believe. Notice, it came to all, but, all did not believe!! This received *righteousness* is the perfect righteousness of JC [his perfect holiness] who through his **sinless-life** and **sin-bearing death** [perfect obedience to the Law of God: all three branches of the Law of Moses: Moral, Civil, and Ceremonial]: He, JC, perfectly fulfilled [kept] this righteous standard and, through his death on the Cross perfectly and completely satisfied the righteous demand for divine justice [The Cross has satisfied the entire OT redemptive economy of the blood of bull and goats; the priesthood; and everything else the OT Temple stood for]: for *both* Justice, and, justification. Thank God!!

The <u>righteousness</u> that is ***imputed*** to those who believe is a real righteousness, worked out in a real world by a real person. God [Christ/the Word] became a Man, and in his human existence [Incarnation], He lived a life of perfect obedience to God's Holy Standard. In Romans 5:1-21, Paul, clearly contrasts the **disobedience** of Adam with the **Obedience** of Jesus Christ. <u>**Sin**</u> and <u>**Righteousness**</u> are the two spiritual forces at work in the world today. Today, there is only two men or, only two types of man in the earth: fallen <u>Adam</u>, or the new-man <u>Christ</u>. All of humanity fall under these two categories/ these two men. All humanity is born into the first [Adam]; a new-birth or spiritual rebirth is required to be a part of the New Man [Christ]. When Paul writes, of a *righteousness* <u>by faith</u> of Jesus Christ that comes to all and upon them that believe he is speaking of this new-birth. This spiritual rebirth/new birth is the New-Creation in Jesus Christ. It is a real righteousness imputed/imparted [given] to all who place their trust in Jesus Christ for Salvation. Righteousness is a real living vibrant force *supplied* to the believer by the Grace of Christ. This is why Paul said, "That as Sin hath reigned [ruled] unto death, even so might Grace reign [rule] through ***righteousness*** unto Eternal Life by JC. These two forces have no choice but to [collide] confront each other in the world today. [The actions of *both* Adam and Jesus Christ affects the entire world. Death passes to all who are in Adam; life passes to all who are in Christ. Each is a corporate head of a race of people. God sees every person as, in Adam or, in Christ. Romans 5 is the contrast between Adam's sin and transgression and, Christ's Redemption [his righteousness]. Redemption, is all about these <u>two</u> men; spiritual <u>death</u> *in* Adam, and spiritual <u>life</u> *in* Jesus Christ (The Passion Translation Page 406, footnotes *f, g,*)]. God, help us to comprehend its meaning!!

Jesus Christ has perfectly fulfilled the Law of God, both in its requirements and in its penalty. He [JC] did what Adam failed to do, that is, rendered perfect obedience to His [God's] Righteous Standard. Now by his death on the Cross-he completely paid the price for sin [took the penalty] for God's broken Law. This received righteousness that comes by faith of Jesus Christ is none other than the perfect righteousness of Jesus Christ: the very same righteousness that perfectly obeyed His [God's] Righteous Standard, and as well completely satisfied the demand for Divine Justice. Wow, we hold a real righteousness!!!!! Not just any righteousness, but the very same righteousness of Jesus Christ. This Grace of Christ works *through* the very same righteousness of Jesus Christ by the **power** and *internal* working of the Holy Spirit. This righteousness or Right-Standing with God *imputed* to us is the very same **standing** Christ Himself has and holds with the Father. The believer in Christ is declared *righteous* by the very same imputed righteousness of JC. The word imputed means, **to credit to one's personal account**. The key to the believer's spiritual success is to look to that/this *imputed* righteousness: and to never take your eyes off that righteousness [provision God has made for the believer in Christ Jesus]. We have **been clothed** [endued/imbued] with His righteousness **like a garment** [cloak] (Isa. 61:10). Faith means, to put one's personal trust and self-reliance upon Him. Faith becomes **the hand** that reaches out to take hold of Jesus Christ. The **heart** must be empty [must be emptied] to be useful. It cannot be Law mingled with Grace. Faith plus Self!! One must entirely abandon themselves over to the Grace of Christ and, **to the sanctifying** and **perfecting work** of the Spirit of Christ *within* to have any real spiritual success. All efforts by the believer must be by faith. This faith must work in conjunction with [in cooperation with] the work [action/operation] of His Grace from within. God, help us to understand, your matchless Grace!! I am clothed with his righteousness; I have his righteousness like a garment!! Grace, is the first action; *followed* by the required second action, being faith.

What do we believe about Jesus Christ? He is the Son of God who was clothed in our humanity "**…born of a woman**" (Gal. 4:4), and who lived a perfect *sinless* life under the Law, "**…made under the Law**" (Gal. 4:4). Then died on the Cross-for our sins [for our justification], "To *redeem* them that were under the law, that we might receive the *adoption* of sons" (Gal. 4:5). Jesus Christ [his person] is the object of our faith!! Christianity is not a doctrine but a faith. It contains *doctrines* but it is a faith, and this **faith** [trust] is in the *person* of the Lord and Savior JC and in his redemptive *work* on the Cross. Grace saves us, through faith; it is the gift of God (Eph. 2:8-9). Grace is the first action, and *faith* is its corresponding action. It is not the second action that *saves* but the first; the second action only appropriates what the first action provides. This means, it is through the second action "faith" that men [the believer] are able to *access* what the first action [grace] provides. This means Grace is the *gift* of God!!! This **gift** of God is the ***gospel*** of his Grace!! The **Cross** of Christ is the Gospel of his Grace. What his sacrificial death [subsequent resurrection] provides [has accomplished] on the Cross-and the Grave, has become the gift of God!!!!!!! Faith is the required *response* to receive what **grace** provides: this is only possible by the *Justifying* and *Sanctifying* work of the Spirit of Grace [the Holy Spirit]. Salvation is not a work of man but a supernatural work of God on behalf of man [Lk. 18:26-27]. We are to trust [believe] in Jesus Christ alone for our Salvation [justification] and Sanctification, *"For it is not from man that we draw our life but from God as we are joined to Jesus, the Anointed One. And now he is our God-given wisdom, our virtue [righteousness], our holiness [sanctification], and our redemption"* [1 Cor. 1:30 TPT]. **The same *grace* that justifies is the same *grace* that sanctifies. The very same *power* [grace] that saves is the very same *power* [grace] that consecrates!!!** The same grace that saves is, the same grace we live by everyday of our lives *"In the same way you received Jesus our Lord and Messiah by faith [so walk ye in him] and continue your journey of faith, progressing further **into your union with him**"* (Col. 2:6 TPT), *"...the life I now live in this flesh [my body] I live by the faith of the Son of God [Christ/Grace]"* (Gal. 2:20). Paul said, **"and have no [put no] confidence in the flesh** [in one's own self-effort]" (Phil. 3:3).

My daily acceptance before God solely rests upon His Grace, and His *imputed* righteousness. My spiritual success and daily consecration as a Christian rests solely upon His Grace, and His *imputed* righteousness. Everything for my future success [our future provision] looks back to the Cross and the ***gospel*** of His Grace, and His *imputed* righteousness. Our very own success, and, the foundation for all spiritual growth, and our victory over all the forces [powers] of darkness rests solely upon His Grace, and His *imputed* righteousness.

"For by grace are you saved through faith; and that not of yourselves: it is the gift of God: not of works, lest any man should boast" (Eph. 2:8-9). "Are you so foolish?? Having begun in the Spirit, are you now **made perfect by the flesh**?? (Gal. 3:3). *"Your new life in the Anointed One began with the Holy Spirit giving you a new birth. Why then would you so foolishly turn from living in the Spirit by trying to finish by your own works?* (TPT). We are dependent on Christ [His grace] on a daily basis for our Right-Standing before [with] God. This righteousness is available to all on the very same basis for all have sinned and fallen short of God's Righteous Standard. God's plan of Salvation treats all men [persons] equally, because, all are sinners, and, all are subject to the penalty of death. Because of this truth of man's true spiritual state/condition before God, all are guilty!! All are made equal at the FOOT of the CROSS. Our victory over **sin** and **death** rests solely upon His Grace and, His imputed righteousness that comes by way of the Cross [the power and provision of the BLOOD].

All who put their trust in JC are freely justified by His Grace. To be *justified means* to be absolved [cleared] of all guilt, and declared innocent [righteous]. God, now, personally accepts us, **through the Cross of Christ, through faith in His Blood.** This Justification, from a biblical standpoint *means*, to declare [as] not guilty, and to declare as righteous. This Justification in JC [the Blood of His Cross] *means*, as if we had never sinned, and, as if we had always obeyed (Col. 1:20). A Justification based solely and entirely on the meritorious work of Jesus Christ and our co-union with Him. **This is a legal matter forever settled in the Courtrooms of Heaven.** His death on the Cross becomes our death, His [resurrection] life becomes our [NEW] life, and His righteousness becomes our right-standing with/before God. JC stood in our place as our representative both in his *sinless* life and in his **sin-bearing** death. To live by the *gospel* [the Cross] *means* to live by these truths!! Justification is a completed [finished] work [an accomplished fact] as far as God is concerned: **for the *sin* price was paid and His *justice* was satisfied.** This is what Paul *means* by, "**Holding faith,** and a good conscience" (1 Tim. 1:19). It is necessary for the Christian to hold to these truths in a good conscience [fully assured], "Let us draw near with a true heart in full assurance, having our hearts *sprinkled* from an evil conscience **[by rightly applying the atonement]**...because that the [believers] worshippers once purged [by his blood] should have no more consciousness of sins" (Heb. 10:2, 22). "There is therefore *now no condemnation* to them which are in Christ Jesus, who walk not after the flesh, but **after the Spirit [who understands and stands on these truths]**" (Rom. 8:1). This is the grace of God [and provision] through faith wherein we all **stand** [which is the same place where we all *believe* and take our stand, and overcome] (Rom. 5:1-2). Paul said, Let us draw near to God in this full assurance of our redemption; in this full assurance, God has removed from us an evil conscience of dead works; the true born again believer is once and for all purged by his blood of all dead works. The word once in the text means "onetime, conclusively," purged, or rather, once and **for all cleansed**. This *means* to expiate, which means, **to put an end to sin** [in his/her reborn spirit] (Rom. 8:10): because of this we should no longer have any consciousness of sins. This does not mean that sin is no longer present [in the body]; but, sin no longer has the power [or, the right] to dominant man [those who believe]. This means the believer no longer has to live under the constant threat of sin; nor, a constant awareness of sins. Sin is still present in the body; however, its conscious presence, it has been extinguished!! The Justified saint is no longer a conscious sinner; but a conscious saint, now having a righteousness consciousness. The Justified saint who is **blood washed** and **Spirit-filled** is now more conscious of the NEW LIFE, then he/she is of the OLD SINS, "... [because] the [human] spirit is now made alive [to God] because of justification [the forgiveness of sins and the impartation of new life] (Rom. 8:10). All of these things are a big part of the believer's victory in their Christian sanctification [and transformation]; this is you and I being **renewing in the spirit of our mind**, and having learned Christ (Eph. 4:20, 23).

This <u>redemption</u> is possible only by the Blood of His Cross. This word in the GK *means* to ransom. A purchase price had to be paid!! The blood of Jesus Christ shed on that Cross-was the price [the cost] that purchased our redemption. This purchase price [the Blood] redeemed us from God's Just and Holy Wrath!! This is why we find Paul using the word <u>propitiation</u>. This word *means* to appease wrath [to placate] in order to restore [man/the believer] [back] to divine favor. The Cross is not man placating God, but God placating His own wrath on our behalf!!!!! His Blood, sprinkled on the Mercy Seat in heaven, indicated that the righteous <u>judgment</u> of the Law of God had been executed [to impose a judicial punishment]. This changed the Judgment Seat into a Mercy Seat, and now it is a Throne of Grace and a place of/for communion [common ground and common union] between God and man [the sinner]. To **justify** is to declare that the **claims of Divine Justice** had been fully met [satisfied]. Christ on the Cross-satisfied the demand of God's Divine Standard for Justice [for our Justification and Redemption]. This is why Paul said, **"...that He [God] might be Just,** and the Justifier of him which believes in Jesus" (Rom. 3:26). His [Christ's] death on that Cross-completely and perfectly satisfied the Justice of God [the penalty and judgment for sin fully paid by him]. God presented Jesus as the *sacrifice* of <u>Atonement</u> through faith in his blood [as the One who would turn away God's wrath by taking away sin]. <u>Atonement by necessity would than include both His Divine Justice and our Justification</u>. God is the One who presented Christ as the Atoning Sacrifice, and the Father is the one who initiated the whole plan of Salvation. The Father provided the *sacrifice* of **his Son** to satisfy his divine justice and appease his own wrath. **Justice** will always come before **Justification**!!!!!!! The same Blood that satisfied Divine Justice becomes the same blood that *expiates* sin [the same blood that takes away Sin] [to <u>expiate</u> *means* to amend, and to put an end to SIN]. To <u>expiate</u> means to extinguish the guilt incurred by Sin [to atone for; to mend it or, to fix it; to redeem]. It is the blood of Christ that *cleanses* our **consciences** from sin and dead works that we might be free and consecrated to serve the living God. It is by the *blood* [of his Cross] we are **cleansed** and have **access** [have the right to enter] into the ***presence*** of a Holy God. The Blood of Christ is an Eternal Force [power] ever living to make intercession for us at the Throne of Grace. It is by the Blood of Christ, we have all obtained his mercy!! We have peace with God *through* faith in his Blood!!!!!! "...Blessed is the man, unto whom God ***imputes*** [counts] righteousness without works...Blessed are they whose iniquities are forgiven, and whose [trespasses] sins are covered...Blessed is the man to whom the Lord will not ***impute*** sin [count his transgressions (trespasses) against him]...But believes on him that justifies the ungodly, his faith is **imputed** [counted to him] for righteousness" (Rom. 4:4-8). Christ being made a curse for us: thus, he took away the curse (Gal. 3:13). God in Christ has blotted out every transgression and all our sins]; He [God], remembers those sins [transgressions] no more, "that God was in Christ, reconciling the world unto himself, not <u>imputing</u> [counting] their trespasses against them" (2 Cor. 5:17-21). The <u>Atonement</u> is the [only] basis [foundation] upon which all the *promises* of God for forgiveness and blessings are forged and founded. The Cross [of Jesus Christ] is the very <u>centerpiece for all Justice and Redemption</u>. Now that [His] Divine Justice is satisfied, God can deal with us according to His Divine Grace and Mercy. Thanks be to God for Jesus Christ, and the Cross!!!!!!! This is my prayer for you, that, you will trust in the fullness of this redemption, and adding nothing to this divine eternal work of reconciling men to God. No religious system, tradition, doctrine, and commandment of men will do.

God through Christ's death has done away with all our transgressions. Now that His Divine Justice is satisfied God can extend His Divine Mercy. It is in and through Christ's death on the Cross that *mercy* rejoices against [wins out over] judgment (James 2:13). We cannot exalt Mercy at the expense of His Justice!!! Divine Justice must be satisfied *first* before Mercy can rejoice in justifying the sinner, "...and without the shedding of [His] blood [there] is no remission [forgiveness of sins]" (Heb. 9:22; Rev. 1:5 TPT) "...*Now to the One who constantly loves us and has loosed [freed] us from our sins by his own blood.*" He has forgiven us of all our sins (Col. 2:13). "For He [God the Father] has made Him [Christ] to be sin for us [the Sin-Offering (Isa. 53:4, 10; 1 Pet. 2:24)], who knew no sin [He was not guilty; He was perfectly holy and pure]; that we might be made the Righteousness of God in Him [here at the Cross of Christ we are made acceptable to God **through our acceptance of Him** and what he did on the Cross] (2 Cor. 5:21 TENT). All forgiveness and all blessings [the benefits of his grace] flow out of the gospel of His Grace. This [the Cross] has become for us the very ground for our justification and <u>reconciliation</u> [restoration to divine favor]. "But God, Who is rich in Mercy [mercy comes to us by means of the Cross], for His great love wherewith He loved us [the love shown at Calvary], even when we were dead in sins [speaks of a state in which we could by no means help ourselves], has quickened us [made us alive] together with Christ (by grace you are saved) [this new life is imparted to us through our <u>identification</u> (in how we identify) with Christ in His Death and Resurrection]" (Eph. 2:4-5 TENT). His *imputed* righteousness [that is his, imputed life of obedience] credited to us through identification with Him. God has **exchanged** our sins [life of disobedience] for his righteousness [life of obedience]. All of this takes place in Him [Christ]. Christ is *both* **our legal representative** [*in* and *through* his sinless life and sin-bearing death] and we are in living union with Him by the indwelling presence of the Holy Spirit [He is the True Vine, and we are His many branches, Jn. 15:1-16]. The phrase "in Him" or, "in Christ" is found over 130 times in Paul's writings. This term used by Paul to *identify* the believer with Christ **is our placement** [being placed] in Him. In Him, our **sins** [life of disobedience] is *imputed* to Christ and, His righteousness [life of perfect obedience] is *imputed* to us. All that is ours [in the curse] in fallen Adam *imputed* to Christ on that Cross-and all that belongs to Christ [in his perfect righteousness and all the benefits that go with a perfect life of obedience under the Law] now belongs to us. This is all made possible through his sinless life and sin-bearing death, and subsequent resurrection. This is the Great Exchange!!! *"Listen to what the Scriptures say: Because Abraham **believed** God's words, his faith* *transferred God's righteousness into his account"* (Rom. 4:3 TPT). It is through faith alone we access all that God has made available to us in Christ Jesus. God has made **provision** in Christ for the fulfilment of every promise of God "For all the promises of God in him are yea [yes], and in him Amen...for by faith ye stand" (2 Cor. 1:20, 24). It is living daily in the *reality* of the Cross [the Great Exchange] that makes all the difference in the world. It is believing that in every instance where I have failed to obey, Christ has obeyed in my place. His death is my death. His life is my life. His righteousness is now my righteousness; his obedience is now my obedience; his favor is my favor. It is when we embrace the Cross [the gospel of His grace] on a daily basis, and looking away from ourselves [outside of ourselves] to Christ's shed blood and righteousness we prosper. God, help all of us to abandon ourselves to these truths!!! This is my prayer, that, we will all abandon ourselves to these truths.

[This section, What the Gospel has accomplished [the finished work] is supplemented by the Audiobooks, The Discipline of Grace: Chapter 3, "preach the gospel to yourself," and, The Transforming Power of the Gospel: Chapter 4-5, "the great exchange" and "a daily embracing of the gospel" authored by Jerry Bridges. I highly recommend both of these books; he did a masterful job with this material. The late Jerry Bridges was a highly respected Evangelical Christian author, speaker, and staff member of The Navigators. The Navigators is a worldwide Christian para-church organization headquartered in Colorado Springs, Colorado. Its purpose is the discipline [training] of Christians with a particular emphasis on enabling believers to share their faith with others. He will be greatly missed!! God, help us all to come into the saving knowledge of Jesus Christ. God, help us to balance our understanding of biblical salvation in keeping with Your Word. God, help us to truly commit to the gospel alone, for salvation, and Christian sanctification. God, help us, not to **mix law *with* grace**, nor, **to mingle** the religious systems, traditions, doctrines, and the commandments of men, with the gospel of Jesus Christ].

REDEMPTIVE TERMS

"**C**hrist ***hath redeemed us from*** the curse [Judgement] of the law, being made a curse for us" (Gal. 3:13). He was made a curse for us **when he went to the cross in our place**. "Who ***gave himself for us,*** that he might redeem us from all <u>iniquity</u>" (Tit. 2:14). The key word meaning for *iniquity* means **violation of the law.** His *death* on the **cross** took our violation of the law. This is the **substitutionary** work of Jesus Christ on the cross of Calvary. This is his <u>redemptive</u> work in redeeming man. This is the *key* biblical concept for man's eternal redemption. All of man's salvation and sanctification hinge on this key redemptive concept, without which ***forgiveness*** would be impossible. God is reconciling [restoring] man to his rightful place that *he* had with him before the fall of Adam, and this was made possible through the ***blood*** of his Cross. This substitutionary work includes both his death [on the Cross] and <u>resurrection</u>. This is why the preaching of the *gospel* concerns **his death** on the Cross, but as well his subsequent **resurrection** from the dead. *"Dear friends, let me give you clearly the <u>heart</u> of the **gospel** that I've preached to you–the good news that you have heartily received and **on which you stand**. For it is through <u>the revelation of the gospel</u> that you are being saved, <u>if you fasten your life firmly to the message</u> I have taught you, unless you have believed in vain [unless you have failed the grace of God]. For I have shared with you what I have received and **what is of utmost importance**: The Messiah died [on the Cross] for our sins, fulfilling the prophecies of the Scriptures. He was **buried** in the tomb and was **raised [from the dead]** after three days, as foretold in the Scriptures. Then appeared to Peter the Rock and to the twelve apostles"* (1 Cor. 15:1-4TPT). **Resurrection** *means* to make alive again [to make the body alive again]. To rouse from death; to rouse from disease; moral recovery: to excite to "new" thought and to "new" action [from inactivity; from dead works or from dead religion]. Resurrection is *both* an **event** and a present active **principle**; and, the resurrection will as well be **a future event**; while, it is actively a present principle. The resurrection of Jesus Christ must be understood in all three aspects of time. The resurrection is a **past event** [in the resurrection of JC] and, **a present active principle**, as well, a **future promise**. The future promise is the resurrection of the body; and, the resurrection power as a present active principle, is, the Holy Spirit **active in/through the gospel of JC in our salvation** and Christian sanctification. God, help us to receive the power of this gospel to save, to rescue, to heal, and to protect, preserve, and **to bring us into the fullness of the abundant life** promised us in JC.

The word **substitution** in the OE means *to take the place of another.* This word means to *replace* or a replacement: to put something or someone in the place of another. Christ's death on the Cross is a **substitutionary** work!! He did not go to the ***Cross*** to die for his own sins; he [Christ] took our place in suffering, death, and eternal punishment. **Christ died for me!!!!!!!!** Moreover, since Christ died for me, thus his death now becomes my death. Because he died, I died, and because he rose from the dead, ***with him*** I also have been raised to new life. Because he lives, I have received new life!!! I have become a new man [new creation] in Christ Jesus, through *faith* and by **identification** with his death, burial, and resurrection. This is where it all begins. It begins with his **substitutionary** work and our **identification** with that work. Without identification with Jesus Christ in his substitutionary work on the Cross: his death, burial, and resurrection *salvation* would be impossible. I must **identify** with [believe on him in] his ***death*** [on the Cross] and [His] resurrection as my own death and resurrection [as my own personal redemption]; or, salvation [deliverance and healing] on an individual basis would not be possible [this applies to every other promise of God contained in the scriptures]. His ***substitutionary*** work must come first; then our ***identification*** with that work must follow or, nothing moves and/

or nothing changes for man. We must identify with Christ in all things!! To **identify** *means* to associate or, to affiliate closely with someone and/or something [**Christ** and the **Cross**]. It is not enough just to associate with Christ, you must identify with *both* Christ, and he crucified!!!

Substitution is his redemptive work; **identification** with that redemption is ours. The word identification means taking on [receiving] what belongs to another; the act of ascribing to oneself the qualities and characteristics of another person [that which belongs to another]. This *means* to be the same as or, to come into the same [as that person]. "He that *believes* on me [looks to me] the works I do he shall do also" (Jn. 14:12). This is identification!! They are his works and his works alone; but, we can participate in [become a part of] all these things [works] when we look to him [and then, we come into the same]. This is identification. "Because [just] as he is, so [also] are we in this world" (1 Jn. 4: 17). **Identification** is to believe on Christ and become one with Christ in that place. "He [God] spared not his own Son, but ***delivered him up for us all*** [substitution] how he [God] **with him shall also freely give us all things** [identification] (Rom. 8:32). To identify **with him** [Christ] in everything will enabled [open the door for] the believer to access the provision [the spiritual blessings] made possible by the cross [which are held in Christ Jesus]. To *identify* with him [believe on him] in his death, burial, and resurrection ***means*** **to become one with him in that death** and **resurrection** "Likewise **reckon** ye also yourselves to be dead indeed to sin, but alive unto God *through* Jesus Christ our Lord" (Rom. 6:11). To **reckon** means to *think* it to be so or, to *conclude* it as such. To **count** it to be so *means* we must *consider* it done [finished; completed]. We **identify** with Christ in his death and resurrection as our own, and then, we consider it done or, we conclude it as such. To **reckon** [count it as so] *means* to consider it to be a forgone conclusion. To *reckon* yourselves dead to sin and alive to God *means* to take these things as an absolute fact. Until the believer [the Christian] takes his **stand** on the **word of God** [the promises] and fights the good fight of faith, he/she will never *endure* the battle involved in laying hold onto life [and to *have* and *hold* that life in abundance]. Faith must labor, and war; that labor is the battle or struggle for faith, and, the faith. This faith comes by hearing, and hearing, and hearing by the word of His Grace [the Covenant]. We **comprehend** the life we [the believer] have *received* that we might **apprehend** the *life* promised. The word *fight* in the GK means **a** struggle, or, it means, **to** struggle. We are fighting a spiritual enemy that does not fight fair, or, open to view. We need to know our ***rights*** and our redemptive ***benefits*** [privileges] in Christ Jesus. Our battle must always be based upon our Spiritual Covenant, the gospel of His Grace. All of this is contingent upon our [**reckoning**] laying **hold on** [eternal] *life* [Zoe life] in Christ Jesus. This means to *seize* or, to take possession of life; to apprehend that [it; that thing] for which we are also apprehended of Christ Jesus (Phil. 3:12). Life has taken hold of us [in the new birth]: now we must take hold of [and possess] that life!! Again, we **comprehend** [reason] [come to understand] the [new] life [the Zoe life] we have *received* that we might **apprehend** [take possession of] [in this world] the [Zoe] *life* promised. All these things *promised* [in the word of God] are <u>spiritually discerned</u>!!!!!!! This *means* these things must be comprehended [understood] first. [Zoe] mean spiritual life, the God quality of life received as a **treasure** [wealth] [divine deposit] [benefits] [blessings] in us in Christ Jesus. We [never] cannot and must not underestimate the need to comprehend [understand] these thing **in the spirit** in order to apprehend them **in this world**. God, help us to see and understand our place in JC. We have received this life, but, we have not yet come into the promised abundance of this new life!!! We are to be identified with him in this life, just as he is now in his ascended position; identification is me and him [Christ] as ONE: this is a spiritual UNION [He is the Head and, I am a member of his body; he is the true Vine and, I am his many branches]. The bible says, "...all things are possible to him that believes..." as a result of this, "...and nothing shall be impossible unto you" (Mk. 9:23; Matt. 17:20). "For **God, nothing is be impossible**," [for] "with God all things are possible" (Lk. 1:37; Matt. 19:26). The key to the fulfilling of all these many promises is our UNION in Christ [the secret is found in our union with him; and, in that union alone]. Thanks be to God, for JESUS CHRIST our LORD

Imputation *means* to set to the account of, or, to put to someone. "Abraham believed God and it was *imputed* unto him for righteousness" (James 2:23). His faith in God's promise *imputed* or, put to his account, righteousness. "To wit, that God was in Christ, reconciling [restoring] the world unto himself, not *imputing* [counting] their trespasses unto them" (2 Cor. 5:19). The redemptive work of Jesus Christ on the Cross *imputed* [transferred] our sins to him, and [transferred] his righteousness to us. Our sins are **imputed** to Christ, and in turn, we have received his righteousness **imputed** to us. This word *imputation* ties into the biblical concept of the <u>Divine Exchange</u>. Our sins *imputed* to Christ, his righteousness *imputed* to us. In our place, he, was **counted** a sinner [with our sin], received our punishment; we in his place was **counted** as righteous [with His righteousness] "For he [God] hath made him [Christ] to be **sin** for us [GK sinful] who knew no sin; that we might be made the righteousness of God in him [Christ]. The *imputation* of our sin [sinful] condition to Christ, and the *imputation* of his righteousness to us was possible only by the CROSS-and his subsequent resurrection [that Divine Exchange]. In the OT, we find this *concept* [imputation] in Leviticus chapter 16, on "the Day of Atonement." The High **Priest** laid his hands on the *offering* [the goat] to both <u>identify</u> with, and to <u>transfer</u> his guilt [sin], and the guilt of the nation *upon* the **sacrifice**. There were two GOATS: the *first* the Sin Offering, the *second* the Scapegoat. The *first* typifies Christ as the holy and spotless lamb, the *second*, He, being made sin for us!! This is biblical imputation. Our sin [guilt] transferred to him, His innocence [rights, and righteousness] [and every spiritual blessing and benefit of the Covenant, transferred] to us. The High Priest laid his hands on the *second* goat, and then, send it away [outside] from the camp to never to return, again [this is **our sins being removed** as far as the east is from the west]. The Cross **[the atonement]** must be understood by these two goats!!

God, help us to understand Jesus in the atonement from *both* sides of this same one gospel truth. The gospel of Jesus Christ is, **a double imputation**. Imputation means, a/to transfer, so, this is a double transfer. When we speak of Christ's redemption, we are to speak of it, in the plural. It is the redemptive works of JC that has affected our full and complete atonement. The *works* must be seen and understood as plural. These **works** by necessity must include *both* his obedient life, and, his obedient death!! Both, his **sinless life** of obedience under the law and, his **sin-bearing** death on the Cross. The gospel of Jesus Christ is called **the Great Exchange**, this is a **double imputation** or, a double transfer [our sin to his account; his righteousness to our account]. It is through his **sinless life of obedience** under the law that, he, Christ, perfectly fulfilled every *jot* and *tittle* of the Mosaic Law. It is through **his sacrificial death** that, he, Christ, perfectly fulfilled the **ceremonial branch** of the law [becoming the final required sacrifice of the OT in fulfillment of the Old Covenant redemptive economy: the OT Atonement]. When Jesus Christ came to John the Baptist, to be baptized, he said, we must do this in order to **"fulfill all righteousness."** What does this mean?? John's baptism, was, a baptism of repentance, for the confession of sins. Jesus had no sins, so, why did he need to be baptized?? To finish the **righteous requirements** of *both* the law and the prophets. In the incarnation, God, become a man; now, born of woman, and born under the law: it was required of him **as a pious Jew** to obey everything demanded of him under the Mosaic code [and the prophets]. The last thing that Jesus had to do, as a pious Jew, before his **ministry** and **Messiahship** began, was, John's Baptism. This baptism of John was the very last thing, God, the Father, was doing, before, He closed out this Old Testament Redemptive Model. John the Baptist was the last of the OT Prophets, so, what God had given him to do was the last of the Old Covenant requirements in upholding His righteous standards. After Jesus was baptized it was the final act/work necessary, to fulfill, and to finish, every requirement of the law and the prophets in preparation and for qualification for Redemptive Service. As the suffering servant, he was made ready for service *through* all the things he suffered, in his human nature, in order to be proven to be a worthy, and spotless [sinless] offering for SIN, to make reconciliation for the sins of the people [to make atonement] (Isa. 53:1-12; Heb. 2:17-18, 4:15, 5:7-9). Because Jesus had fulfilled all righteousness, he, Jesus, as a man, had earned every Covenantal blessing and benefit of the Abrahamic promises. Now, in this double imputation, he, Jesus, received all of our curse for disobedience, and now, we, receive all of his earned benefits/blessings of this Covenant. Yes! We find in *both* 2 Corinthians 5:21 and Romans 5:10, this principle of a **double imputation**. JC, who knew no sin was made to be sin for us, so, we might be made the righteousness of God, in him; we being reconciled by his death, even more, we are saved by his life [here, this speaks of more than just his resurrection life, it, as well, speaks of his **sinless life** as a man]. Thank God!!!

The bible says in Mark 10:45, Christ came to **give his life** a **ransom** for many. The word for **life** here, in the text, is, the Greek word, **psuche**. It is translated in the NT as, **soul**. It *means* the soul-life, or rather, it speaks of human life [the natural man]. God, in Christ, became a man in the **incarnation**, the Person of the Word [of God], was made flesh [was made a man], that he might dwell among us [and live a perfect obedient life], and **die** [as a redemptive price for sins]. Here, the word ransom means, redemption or, the redemptive price: **the atonement**. For God, so loved the world, he gave his only begotten Son as the **redemptive price** for sins (Jn. 3:16). Christ came to give his life **for** the world; that, he, Christ, might give his life **to** the world. Christ gave his life *for* the world on the Cross in his death, that he might give his life *to* the world in his resurrection. It is necessary to see and to understand **the atonement in two** parts or, in two equal and opposite halves. We find in Romans 3:26, God [the Godhead], is *both* the JUST, and the JUSTIFIER of those who believe on Jesus Christ, and he crucified. Just here in the text means, holy, justice and righteous. Justifier means, to render and to regard one as innocent: to set free. Listen to the way Peter states it, in 2 Peter 2:1, "...to them of like precious faith with us, through the righteousness of God and our <u>Savior</u> Jesus Christ." Faith, here, in the text, must be understand as our common salvation (Jude 3). Our Redemption is wrought by God in two ways, it is through **righteousness** and it is *through* our <u>Savior</u> Jesus Christ. What does Peter mean by, through the <u>righteousness</u> of God we have been redeemed?? Righteousness, here, must be understood as, the **holiness** and, as well, the **justice** of God [has initiated this atonement]. Not just the love of God (Jn. 3:16)!! But, the Justice [and holiness] of God has required this specific gospel [this specific atonement]. Not just the love of God, but, as well, the holiness and **justice** of God sent Jesus to the Cross, too die. <u>Savior</u> here in the GK means, to deliver or, deliverer [to save]. This salvation is biblically termed the MERCY of God; however, **before this mercy of God** [before this salvation] can be realized, God, in Christ, on the Cross, and in his death, had to SATISFY the demands **for Divine Justice**. Justice, comes before Justification. Justice comes before mercy. Mercy can and will win out over judgment, only, if Justice is first satisfied. Christ had to *first* pay the **price** for sin, before, Christ could procure forgiveness/acquittal/pardon. We understand <u>redemption</u> *through* two key words: **payment**, and **purchase**. On the Cross, a <u>payment</u> was made, for the sole purpose, that, God, he, might <u>purchase</u> us out from under Satan, death, darkness, sin, sickness and disease, poverty, and the whole curse of the Law. This is why, in Paul's understanding of the gospel, we, were **<u>bought</u>** with price, the precious **blood** of Jesus Christ; now, we are no longer our own: we belong to him.

In the Atonement there are two key words that must be applied at all times to keep this gospel of Jesus Christ from *corruption* and *distortion*. These two words are **propitiation** and **expiation**. Propitiation speaks to the Justice of God; while, expiation, speaks to the Mercy of God. The one, is toward **God**; the other, is toward **man**. **Propitiation**, is toward God; **expiation**, is toward man. Propitiation means, to placate God: to appease his wrath against sin and sinners. Expiation means to extinguish guilt [to remove sin], and to procure forgiveness. Without Justice, there can be no Mercy!!!

Christ, is *both* our Propitiation and our expiation. Christ, has *first* paid the redemptive price, on the Cross through his shed blood, thus, cancelling our moral indebtedness before God. This is the **act** of propitiating God; he, Christ, satisfied the righteous demands of God's holy law. In turn, Christ, then, after satisfying the demands of Divine Justice, turn toward man, and became the expiation for the sins of the people, meaning, he, Christ, could then take away every guilt and stain [he removed our sins from us as far as the east is from the west]. This is the OT picture of the Scapegoat as, [Christ] the **expiation** for our sins; and, the goat of the Sin Offering as [Christ] the **propitiation** to the Father for the Sin debt. Remember, even though in *both* the Old and New Testaments, it says, God, **forgives Sins**; notwithstanding, God, has never, and, will never, allow any Sin or sins to go unpunished. Technically speaking, God, does not directly forgive sins!! He, has punished all sins in the Person of his Son on the Cross, "God, in sending his own Son, in the likeness of sinful flesh, **and for sin** [God did it for this reason] [that, he, might] condemn sin in the flesh [that God might judge Sin, and, all sinning, in the body of his Son on the Cross] (Rom. 8:3). The best way to understand this is, God has punished all sins in the body of his Son, on the Cross, that, God, he, might procure [earn/gain/secure/attain] forgiveness/pardon/acquittal for the sinner. God does not truly and directly forgive sins; he, God, forgives the sinner through the atonement of Jesus Christ; and, in this atonement, he, God, judged and punished all sins in JC. It is the ONE ATONEMENT in the **two essential required parts**: the two halves of the same ONE WHOLE. Expiation was/is made possible only, through Christ who our propitiation is: where the mercy of God was made possible, only, after, Divine Justice was satisfied. **Atonement** means, to placate God: to appease his wrath against Sin, sinning, and the Sinner. It means, to **cancel debts**: to cancel Sin, and sins, and, **to put off judgement**. It means, then, after propitiation has done its job [only after propitiation has accomplished its task of satisfying justice], it procures pardon and the forgiveness of sins. It expiates Sin and, last but not least, it, **purges** the sinner and takes away **every guilt** and **stain** in order **to reconcile** *both* God and men. **Justice** and **Justification** applied together equal biblical Redemption. We cannot and must never separate the **Justice** of God from our **Justification**. Do not think, God, just overlooks sin, and sinning, NO, he punished Sin in JC.

The bible teaches, the believer, has **passed from spiritual death to new life** because of this double imputation or, this Divine Exchange. "...But now once in the end of the world hath he **appeared to put away sin** by the sacrifice of himself. And **as it is appointed** unto men once to die, but after this the judgement: **so Christ was once offered** to bear the sins of many..." (Heb. 9:26-28). Many, have missed the point that Paul was making here, in this text, "...as *it is appointed* unto men *once to die...so Christ was once* offered [and died]." Paul is speaking about Christ's death on the Cross as a Divine Appointment with Divine Justice as a substitutionary work. This *principle* [as it is appointed unto men once to die, but after this the judgement] in verse 27 is applied to the **subject matter** of verses 26-28. While it [this] is true in principle, that all men die and face the judgement; here, **this appointment with death is applied to the Cross,** "But we see Jesus, who was made a little lower than the angels [incarnation: when God became a man] for the suffering of death...that he [Christ] by the grace of God should taste death for every man" (Heb. 2:9). It was on the Cross: in his substitutionary work on the Cross: he tasted death for every man, and in his death suffered divine punishment in our place [on our behalf]. What is the fear of death, but Divine Judgement (Heb. 2:14-15; 1 Jn. 4:17-18). "O death, where is thy sting? O grave, where is thy victory? The **sting of death is sin...**" (1 Cor. 15:55-56). The sting of death is sin, and the victory of death is found **in the grave** and its subsequent **judgement**. "For the *wages* of [the reward for] sin is death [eternal separation from God] but, the gift of God is eternal life through Jesus Christ our Lord" (Rom. 6:23). Jesus not only took *our sins* but as well our **judgement**. The *sting* of death is sin, and the reward for sin [and sinning] is Divine Judgement, or, what the bible calls the Second Death. The Second Death is, spiritual death or, eternal separation from God. The bible calls [characterizes] the First Death or, physical death, as sleep [sleeping]. Death in the bible does not mean to cease to exist; rather, it means to undergo or to experience a separation. Physical death is nothing more than the *spirit* part of man separating from his physical body (James 2:26) "or ever the silver cord be loosed [that which connects the inward man to the outward man] or, the golden bowl be broken [the heart]" (Eccles. 12:6). The First Death [physical death] for the believer is **sleep** [not soul sleep, the believer will never lose consciousness, but rather, a transition from this physical plane to the eternal dimension]. "We are confident, I say, and willing rather to be ***absent*** from [out of] the body, and to be **present** [at home] with the Lord" (2 Cor. 5:8). The Christian will not suffer nor experience the Second Death. The Second Death is for the **sinner** [those who rejected the gospel], which is Eternal Judgement [eternal separation from God]. Most Christians do not understand the true biblical meaning for death. When we die, we separate temporarily from our physical bodies. However, the bible teaches a bodily resurrection for all of mankind, one, to **eternal life** with God, the other, to **eternal damnation** [and separation from God] [eternal judgement]. All of these things must be understood in the context of Romans 5-8: the believer's baptism by the Spirit into identification with Christ's death, burial, and resurrection. God, HELP US!! We have already DIED; we have already met our appointment with death; we have already met with our own personal time for/with judgement; all of this took place with and in Jesus Christ in our identification with Christ on the Cross: we being put into his death; and, being put into his burial, and subsequent resurrection, and ascension. Thank you Jesus!! Praise be to God!!

DIVINE EXCHANGE

"For I am not ashamed of the *gospel* of Jesus Christ: for it is the **power** of God unto salvation to everyone that believes; to the Jew first, and also to the Greek" (Rom. 1:16). Here, Paul is calling the **gospel** of Jesus Christ a POWER. This word power is the GK word *dunamis* where we get our English word dynamite. This speaks of explosive power. The true gospel is explosive power!!! This *power* is the mighty sanctifying and perfecting work of the Holy Spirit in the life of the believer (Acts 1:8). This **power** will both work the works of God [operate the *gifts* of the Spirit] and bring forth the *fruit* of the Spirit [reproduce the character of Jesus Christ in the life of the Christian] **[Fruit: is the character of Christ: produced by the Spirit of Christ: within the follower of Christ]**. All of this is contingent upon a right [proper] understanding and application of the gospel of JC. The Holy Spirit will not recognize nor work through a spiritual counterfeit. This is why so many are weak in spiritual things, and susceptible (in bondage) to carnal vices (things of the flesh). No power!! The power (of the Holy Spirit) will work; but, it will only work in conjunction with the preaching of the true gospel, "For the preaching of the Cross...unto us which are *saved* it is the **power** of God" (1 Cor. 1:18). Notice, for the saved, the Christian, the preaching of the **Cross** continues to be the POWER of God. This salvation where of Paul speaks means deliverance [rescue] from sin; healing from bodily sicknesses and diseases, soundness [wholeness] a complete **redemption** that will impact not only the spirit's regeneration, but the soul's total transformation, and the body's subjugation, and future resurrection (1 Thess. 5:23). This salvation [gospel of his Grace] where of Paul speaks must include *both* Justification and Sanctification. The true gospel *promises* both the **power** of God to save us, and then, through it, that same *power* will continue to keep us through sanctification and honor to God. **The grace [the gospel] of Jesus Christ is a ruling power!!** Keep in mind; a bent toward either legalism or lawless tendencies could disqualify you from accessing His sanctifying power in your own personal life and spiritual growth [this becomes a *form* (an outward appearance of the gospel) of godliness]. Most of the church today find themselves in some form/appearance of the gospel [which, is nothing more than a spiritual counterfeit]. God, help us all!!!

To *lean* toward **legalism** will quench the *power* of this gospel [grace of Christ] from performing its divine function in the life of the believer. Legalism is the tendency to lean on one's own strength and efforts in sanctification. To *lean* toward **lawlessness** will *deny* the grace of Christ the right to rule over the life of the believer, and the sanctification process, which, will in turn, very soon, plunge the Christian into even greater deception. This will cause the spiritual counterfeit to become operational in the life of that Christian, which, in turn, will create **a form of godliness** [which, will create a new form of the gospel]. This is the beginning of an **altered gospel**, if left unchecked, it, will soon grow and transform into just one of the many different strange *gospels* that often come about by men who struggle with (are bent toward) either moral corruption or ascetic tendencies. Asceticism *means* exercised or hardened; rigid; severe; austere, given to mortifications. This means given to abusive tendencies, whether self-abuse or, abusive toward others in the application of harsh and stern discipline. This will always lead to a more legalistic approach to the truth [this will always lead to a more legalistic approach to the gospel], which, Paul, called a different gospel or a spiritual counterfeit. I am taking the time at this moment to explain [reveal] the difference between these two, and their leanings, **so you can see how critical the concept of Divine Exchange really is to the preaching of the Cross.** To err to the right or, to the left of center, could be just enough for one to miss out on this sanctifying and perfecting work of the Holy Spirit in that particular area of one's life. To lean toward any human effort or on any human dependency [or, anything other than the Cross], will forfeit your right to this divine exchange within the sanctification process. To deny the *right* the *grace* of God [Christ] has, **to intervene, in, and to transform the moral character of the Christian is, to reject outright the entire principle of this Exchange.** This will encourage [will promote] the acceptance of a sinful lifestyle [instead of rejecting ungodliness]; and, it will neutralize or render powerless the sanctification process from having any true real transformative effect in that person's life: these, having rejected the true gospel, exchanging it, for another [for a different] gospel. I just want to *clarify* at this time, there is an *effort* by faith required by the believer, and, this *effort* is the **fight** [the labor and warfare] of faith [you and me struggling for the faith: Jude 3]. Fasting, prayer, and every other spiritual discipline are simply you and me <u>contending</u> for [fighting for] the faith (1 Tim. 6:12). It is necessary for the Christian to apply themselves to these spiritual disciplines, but these disciplines are only a means to an end; or, **the tools used that are necessary to help accomplish sanctification**, but, it is not sanctification itself. Fasting, prayer, mediation on God's word, and the like are only the means given [by God] to help promote [spiritual] growth. These things [these spiritual disciplines/tools] are a means to an end, they are not an end in and of themselves. God, help us to understand all these things!!!

Paul made a point of preaching the Cross as *both* the **wisdom** and **power** of God. His death on the Cross [the gospel] contains a wisdom from God, and, a power through which all who believe could enter into **victory** and **authority** that will give them the **right** to *rule* over every circumstance and in all situations. This is why Paul said, "For I determined not to know anything among you, except, Jesus Christ, **and him crucified**" (1 Cor. 2:2; 1:18, 23-24). "For if by one man's offence death reigned [ruled] by one; much more they which receive abundance of grace and of the gift of righteousness shall reign [rule] in life by one, Jesus Christ...that as sin *hath* (past tense) reigned [ruled] unto death, even so *might* (present tense) grace reign [rule] through righteousness unto eternal life by Jesus Christ our Lord" (Rom. 5:17, 21). *"And just as sin reigned [ruled] through death, so also **this sin conquering grace** will reign as king through righteousness, imparting eternal life through Jesus, our Lord and Messiah"* (Rom. 5:21 TPT). Paul spoke of the **gospel** [of His Grace] as containing [holding] and *hidden* from within *"the mystery"* of Jesus Christ. This speaks of the **grace** of Christ as a *ruler* made possible through the **gospel** of Christ. Grace is the **empowerment of a new life** of righteousness that exercises its authority through the power [ability] and wisdom [knowledge] of the CROSS. The preaching of the Cross is foolishness to them who perish, and, to them who believe not, [and, to them who do not truly understand the spiritual and legal and eternal reality of the true gospel], these, see GRACE, as just an exemption, or, as just immunity from prosecution [these, see grace, as simply a covering for a life still subject to and under the powers of sin and the fallen human condition]. Paul, revealed in his First Epistle to the Corinthians, to those who struggled under the pressures and temptations of sin, the world, and the devil, the secret [key] to true Christian emancipation: the **power** and **wisdom** of the **Cross.** To those who really [truly] know him, who came into a true and genuine saving faith and knowledge of the gospel of Jesus Christ as *both* Savior and Lord: **to them the preaching of the Cross is the very *wisdom* and *power* of God.** Paul said, "But we [who believe] preach Christ **crucified**...Christ the power of God, and the wisdom of God" (1 Cor. 1:18, 23-24). Paul is saying, Christ *crucified* [in His death on the Cross] is *both* [is understood as] the **power** and **wisdom** of God. The redemptive works of JC on the Cross, his death and burial, and subsequent resurrection, and ascension, is understood by Paul as *both* the preaching and the experiencing of both the WISDOM and POWER of God [found in/through JC alone]. God, help to understand this gospel, its **wisdom**, and, its **power**, in our sanctification!!

"For the *preaching* of the **Cross** is to them that perish foolishness; but unto us **which are saved it is the power** of God" (1 Cor. 1:18). You will notice Paul spoke this in the present tense. The *preaching* of the CROSS today [for the Christian] it continues to be the **power** [and ability] of God to all who believe. Paul said, "For I am not ashamed of the *gospel* of Christ: for **it is the power** [ability] of God unto salvation [new life] to everyone that believes" (Rom. 1:16). In both text, the GK word for power is *dunamis*. Here, Paul is referring to the very same thing, that **Divine Exchange** "For it is God which works in you both to will and to do of his good pleasure" (Phil. 2:13). This is possible in the life of the believer through the *continued* preaching of the Cross "As you *have therefore received* Christ Jesus the Lord, *so walk ye* in him" (Col. 2:6). The key to Christian sanctification [victory in the life of the believer] is this continued application of the **Divine Exchange**. We must continue to use the *Cross* as the means for that Divine Exchange. The **Cross** is a symbol of death; it means an instrument for capital punishment [to be used for those who commit a capital offense] figuratively, it means, *exposure* to **death: the atonement**. The CROSS-continues to be the **power** [and ability] of God: because the Holy Spirit continues to use it as the means of [Divine] Exchange between God and the believer [the sinner]. This is why the **gospel** of JC [or, the preaching of the Cross] continues to be the **power** [and ability] of God: because, it is the only thing God has available, or, it is the only thing God has at his disposal to draw the sinner [the believer] near to himself. The Holy Spirit works in and through the CROSS-to effect [and to apply] that **Divine Exchange**. This is why Paul said, "...For by the works [the deeds] of the law shall no flesh/shall no man be justified [be received, or forgiven, and made acceptable in his sight]" (Gal. 2:16). It is not through man's human efforts to change that will transform him [whether, that effort is coming from a sinner, or, a born again believer]: but, only when men [when people] yield themselves to God [or, it is only after we surrender ourselves to God], will He, God, exchange our weakness for His Strength: exchange our moral failings for His manifested holiness. It is not how much we can **do** [in our own strength, will power, and efforts to change] but, it is only in *trusting* in him and *yielding* to what He [God] has already done [has accomplished] for us through the ***blood*** of His **Cross** [the atonement]. This applies to both our justification and sanctification, "But of him [God] are ye in Christ Jesus, who of God is made unto us wisdom, and **righteousness**, and **sanctification**, and redemption" (1 Cor. 1:30). Christ *crucified* is the **power** [and ability] of God to redeem us from sin, but, Christ *crucified* is as well the **wisdom** [and knowledge] of God in/for our sanctification. The *power* and *wisdom* of God found in the Gospel of Christ [the Cross] is best understood through this doctrine of the atonement or, the Divine Exchange. For many this is foolishness. The **Blood** of His Cross simply refers to the *human life* of Jesus Christ poured out to make atonement [as a sacrifice for sins], "For the *life* of the flesh is in the **blood**: and I have given it to you upon **the altar** [of the Cross] to make an atonement for your souls: for it is the *blood* that makes atonement for the soul [and, it is the application of that blood that forgive sins]" (Lev. 17:11). This is understood as that Divine Exchange [the Cross]. We find the POWER of this Cross applied to our Justification; we find the WISDOM of the Cross as well applied in our Sanctification. We are growing in the GRACE of God [our justification]; and, we are growing in the Knowledge of God in our sanctification. The power of God, which is the power of his grace, **works through the knowledge of God** found in the *revelation* of Jesus Christ in this gospel: in his death, burial, and resurrection. The Spirit of God will work only *through* **revelation** and **faith** in this gospel of JC: which, is found in his death, burial, and subsequent resurrection, and his ascension. Christ is our wisdom; he, is our justification and sanctification; JC is the **completion of** our entire redemption. The POWER of this Cross has put to death the old man and the old life [the old world]; and, the WISDOM [and knowledge] of this Cross now informs the NEW LIFE *within* of its inherent/innate power and rights and benefits [in us] [in Christ] in order to empower it [and us] to bear its fruit [and, to work its works]. God, help us to see and understand this wisdom and knowledge of God found in the gospel of JC; and, God, let us truly and really fully experience all of its power and provision available to us through the Cross by the indwelling Person of the Holy Spirit, this, abundant life in JC.

Too many separate the *grace* of God from the *gospel* of Christ [the concept of that Divine Exchange]. His unearned unmerited undeserved <u>favor</u> [Grace GK *Charis* the divine influence upon the heart and its reflection in the life] is not possible apart from **the atonement** [that Divine Exchange]. There is no Grace, nor undeserved favor possible, nor, is it made available apart from the atonement [the true gospel and its Divine Exchange]. Any bent toward legalism or lawless tendencies will disqualify one from receiving its divine supply. Everything we receive from him in our **justification** and, everything he accomplishes in us through **sanctification** can only come to us through that **Divine Exchange**. There is no *grace* apart from the **gospel**; and the true gospel is the only *means* by which God will ever bestow his grace upon unredeemed humanity. There is no other Salvation!! For *both* the biblical **gospel** and the biblical **grace** is bound up in the same one Person of the Lord Jesus Christ. To deny the true gospel is to reject the grace of God!! Both the **gospel** and the **grace** of God are found in the same **one person** and **redemptive works** of our Lord and Savior Jesus Christ on that CROSS. You cannot and must never separate the grace of God from the gospel of Christ. The one [grace] depends entirely on the other [the gospel]. The *preaching* of the CROSS [that Divine Exchange] is *both* the **power** [the ability] and the **wisdom** [the knowledge] of God. God, help us to abandon all our religious systems and religious traditions of men in order to come to a clear and precise understanding of the one and only true gospel of JC and its divine exchange!!! God, have MERCY!!! God, help us to identify, and, to come into a true understanding of this GOSPEL. It is important to understand *both* the PERSON and WORKS of Jesus Christ in both **his incarnation** and, in **his redemption**. A big part of the gospel of Jesus Christ is not only his Works, but, **his Person**. Jesus Christ before **his incarnation** was and still is the Divine Word, the Divine Logos [the <u>Second</u> Person **of the Godhead**/Trinity: who is **co-essential**, and **co-eternal with the Father** and the Holy Spirit, and, faith in these things where it concerns His Person is foundational to saving faith in the gospel of Jesus Christ]. We must deny any view of Jesus Christ that reduces him in any way; or, we must deny any view of Jesus Christ that rejects his full deity, as being a true gospel faith, or, that, which, will avail in true Christian salvation, and eternal life. The deity of Jesus Christ is a vital central point in the gospel of JC. The content of the NT focuses chiefly and predominantly on *both* the <u>Person</u> and the Redemptive <u>Works</u> of JC on the Cross: in his death, burial, and resurrection, and ascension, as absolutely essential/necessary for true biblical saving faith. Even though we can distinguish between *both* his Person and his Works, we must not and never separate these two. It is the significance/importance of His Person that makes His Works, valid and effectual. It is through his redemptive works that we gain an even deeper insight into the importance of his person: there is an intimate connection between who he is, and, what he does [in what he has accomplished for us on the Cross on our behalf]. Jesus Christ is God, **who became a man**: the **Word** that was made **flesh** and, dwelt among us [his name is <u>Emmanuel</u>: being interpreted, GOD WITH US] (Jn. 1:1, 14; Matt. 1:23). We find in Paul's epistle to Timothy when speaking of this Great Gospel Scheme, he said, "... **God was manifested in the flesh**, justified in the Spirit, seen of angels, preached unto the Gentiles, believed on in the world and, received up into glory. Received up into glory, is the Ascension; he being justified in the Spirit, speaks to his resurrection; however, notwithstanding, when Paul said, **God manifested in the flesh**, here, Paul, was speaking of **Christ's personal incarnation**, when God, the Word [the Word of God] was made flesh [or, when God was made a man] (1 Tim. 3:16). For the first four centuries of Church history, the Church *labored* and *battled* over the <u>nature</u> and <u>person</u> of Jesus Christ. Who really is this person of the Lord Jesus Christ?? Is he just a man, or, is he God?? If God, then, how does that work?? If man, then, how does that work?? If, he, is the **God-man** [if he is *both* God and man], then, how does that work?? This defining the Person and Nature of the Lord Jesus Christ in the first four centuries dominated the Church's understanding of this gospel. In the first four centuries of the church, **it was not his works** that were called into question, but **his person**. It is important to understand that the gospel of Jesus Christ has everything to do with *both* his Person and his Works. This Divine Logos of God, the Word of God, is more than just the First Principle of Existence/**the first principle of all creation**: He, this Divine Logos, is God, a Person, and, He, is not a mere created thing but, the Creator Himself, the Second Person of the Godhead/the Trinity. He was with God [the First Person] in the beginning before all things, and, He is God [the Second Person], and He is the source and the reason for the creation of all created things. He is not a creature [the first creation] but, the Creator [himself]. Jesus Christ is God: co-essential, and co-eternal with the Father and the Holy Spirit (Jn. 1:1-4; Heb. 1:3; Matt. 28:19; Col. 1:14-22; 2:9; 1 Jn. 5:7). He is not, just, like God: He, Jesus Christ, the Divine Logos, the Word of God, is the same as the Father and the Holy Spirit, who, He, Jesus Christ, the Word, is ONE in essence and substance with the Father, and the Spirit. He, Christ, God the Word, from before the beginning, participates in His Divine Being with the Father and the Spirit. Jesus Christ is ONE in Divine Being with the Father and the Spirit. The Bible is quite clear; there is only ONE GOD, and yet, this ONE GOD is seen and understood as expressed in THREE DISTINCT PERSONS: the Father, the Son, and, the Holy Spirit. The Father is not the Person of the Son, and the Son is not the Person of the Spirit, and the Person of the Holy Spirit is not the Person of the Father; notwithstanding, these THREE PERSONS are ONE, and, are the ONE and only same ONE GOD [found in *both* the Old and New Testaments]. The early fourth/fifth century Church determined, that, a confession of the full deity of Jesus Christ is foundational and was essential to true NT gospel faith; in other words, it is not true and right for someone to look to Jesus Christ in a salvific way [for atonement] and, at the same time, deny his **true Person**, and to deny his **Deity** [as the Arians (Arius) did at the Council of Nicaea; and, as Jehovah Witnesses and the Mormons do, today]. Christ, is not only **pre-existent**, He is also, **eternal**: He has no beginning of days, nor, does he have any end of [His] life (Heb. 7:1-3). He, the Lord Jesus Christ, the Word of God, the Divine Logos, is the self-existent ONE [and is self-contained] with the

Father and the Person of the Holy Spirit [within this ONE GODHEAD]. Jesus Christ has *both* a **true human nature**, and, at the same time, a **true Divine Nature**: He was/is **truly man** and **truly God** [in the sense, that, he was fully a man, and, at the same time, fully God] [meaning: *within* his human nature, he, was **fully human** and, within his divine nature, he, was **fully divine**]: Jesus Christ having two natures that were clearly distinct from each other, **one human**, and the other, **Divine**. These **two natures** were not to be understood as either, **divided**, nor **mixed**; but, these **two natures** were understood to be [as] perfectly united, however, notwithstanding, they were not to be understood as mixed or confused. Christ's Person within *both* his **human** and **Divines natures** were perfectly united and yet, **not confused**. The Lord Jesus Christ is One Person **having two natures**. It is very important that we embrace *both* His Divine/human **Person** and His **redemptive Works** for true NT biblical saving faith. The Lord Jesus Christ is *both* **human** and **divine**, being only one DIVINE/HUMAN PERSON having [in] two distinct/united/unmixed/unseparated natures. Thanks be to God for our Lord Jesus Christ!! Our salvation is found in Christ [his Person] and, him crucified [his Works].

    Reconciliation *means* exchange, i.e. to **restore** to Divine Favor-atonement. The word **Restoration** *means* full recovery of man from sin and alienation/separation from God: to *restore* again to a former good state [the time of *Reformation*: Heb. 9:10] [the time before the fall of man]. **Reconciliation** *means* to make atonement; to forgive; to be merciful; to cleanse and to purge away sins; to expiate-to cancel/abolish the sin debt; **Expiation**: to atone for sins-to appease the wrath of God against sinners (propitiation); to make satisfaction for the guilt of the sinner-to procure forgiveness [to conciliate or to win the favor of an offended person]; to expiate sins is, to, extinguish and remove the guilt and stain of sin: to take away sins. There is no doubt; there is an overlap of meaning among the many different biblical terms used in the Scriptures for Atonement. The word **Exchange** *means* to lay aside [to lay down] one thing in order to take up [pick up] another thing: **to give one thing for another**. The OLD for the NEW. A **thing** received in *return* for the **thing** given. "We were reconciled to God [changed: made different] by the death of His Son…much more [to an even greater degree], being reconciled [being changed], we shall be saved by His life. The word **saved** here in the GK is *sozo* and *means* delivered, healed, and made whole [made completely well, and entirely sound]. **Life** here in the GK is *Zoe* and means receiving the God kind or the God quality of [spiritual] life. Here, Paul is referring to the *resurrection*. His *death* [on the Cross] has **changed** us by putting away the Old [Adamic] life; His *resurrection* [from the dead] has **saved** us by ushering in NEW LIFE. In this text, **life**, here, can as well be applied to Christ himself, in his **sinless life** of obedience under the law **imputed to us** as righteousness in our Christian justification. Paul goes on to say, "…by whom [Christ] we have now received the **atonement**" (Rom. 5:10-11). The word atonement here in the GK is *katallage* and *means* **exchange**, i.e. restoration to divine favor: atonement, reconciliation. In other words, we were *reconciled* "changed" by the death of His Son, much more, we being changed [this is where the old ended] we shall be **saved** and *brought* into **new life** by his resurrection; and, it is by Him [Jesus Christ] we have now received Reconciliation [the restoration] [that Divine Exchange]. Here, the new life we have received through the resurrection of Jesus Christ is, his, very own obedient life under the law of God. "For if while we were *enemies* [sinners] we were reconciled to God through the death of His Son, it is much more [certain], now that we are reconciled, that we shall be **saved** [daily delivered, and set free from sin's dominion] through His [resurrection] life [through faith in his sinless life and sin-bearing death imparted to us through the resurrection] [through the power of his righteousness bestowed upon us through faith in the gospel of his grace, made possible by the indwelling presence and power of the Person of the Holy Spirit]" (Rom. 5:10; 8:4 Amp). This is the *power* and the *wisdom* of the Cross!! God be praised!! Give God all the glory for what He has done for us in redeeming us from spiritual death and destruction. In Romans 5:11 it says, "…by whom [by him] [by the Cross] [by Christ and him crucified], we have *now* [at the present time] (have) **received** the **atonement** [*that* divine exchange]. Paul is applying these *things* **to our victory in our Christian sanctification**. We find Paul referring to **our justification** in Romans 5:8-10a, and in Romans 5:10b-11, to **our sanctification**. Paul is saying, WE HAVE RECEIVED!!! In the GK this word received *means* to TAKE or, TO GET HOLD OF; Christ has come that we might HAVE and HOLD this NEW LIFE within us **in its abundance** [in its fullness] (Jn. 10:10). We war [against the enemy of our soul] in agreement with the Spirit and, in agreement with the New Life within (2 Cor. 10:3). War here in the GK means, to serve in a military campaign; to contend with carnal/fleshly inclinations. We are pulling down strongholds of the mind, which are vain imaginations [vain thought patterns] that contradict the word of God (2 Cor. 10:3-5). The word imaginations here in the GK means, thoughts of the mind; or, mental reasoning's. The bible teaches that, we are to bring into captivity every thought of our mind to the obedience of JC [according to the scriptures]. This is how we stand against [withstand] all the *wiles* [strategies] and temptations of the devil (Eph. 6:10-18). Withstand *means* to **resist** and **to oppose** every *fiery* dart of the wicked one [in the battle ground of the mind]. **Fiery darts** *means* to be *inflamed* with passions, such as anger, grief, lust, and the like, through stirring up the **reins** [the mind and emotions] to sin. In order to overcome in our Christian sanctification and to get the victory, we must win the battle of the mind. The bible tells us to, HUMBLE OURSELVES (2 Chron. 7:14). And, to, SET THINE HEART TO UNDERSTAND, and to CHASTEN thyself before God (Dan. 10:12). According to Daniel, God said, **his words** [Daniel's prayer] **was/were heard the very moment he humbled himself through fasting's and prayer** (Dan. 9:3-4). Daniel said, "...I set my face unto the Lord God, to seek by prayer and supplications, with fasting, and **sackcloth**, and **ashes**: and I prayed unto the Lord my God, and made my confessions." Confessions here in the text, are the confession of sins; to chasten *means* to depress, **to a base oneself**; to *afflict* the soul [the self], and to submit to God. **Sackcloth** is a course garment worn under the clothes. It is here where we find

Daniel **choosing to make himself very uncomfortable**, on purpose. To wear sackcloth under the clothes **was to deliberately afflict the soul through making the body uncomfortable**. This is exactly how we should understand the phrase to HUMBLE OURSELVES before God as found in 2 Chronicles 7:14. To **humble** yourself before God is to make yourselves [to make the soul] uncomfortable [in the body] **in order to deliberately set your heart on God** [we do this to remove every distraction of the flesh: such as pleasure or, any conveniences, even the bare essentials]. It is through the use of these spiritual tools/these spiritual disciplines that will help **to humble us** [that will help to chasten us] in our Christian sanctification [and transformation] in order to ensure that we get the victory in our spiritual war [in our spiritual battles] against the enemy of our soul. Now, the only danger is, is to take this to an extreme in *both* our understanding and application *within* our Christian sanctification. The object [objective] [and focus] of our humiliation is not the body itself; but, the objective and focus is our soul-life before God. We chasten the body in order to humble the soul!! To put too much into the body [to put too much emphasis on the body], as the actual focus [and objective] of one's own personal sanctification is to miss the point entirely. This will lead to Christian Asceticism. This will lead to a harsh mistreatment of the body, which is not what Paul is saying, it is absolutely unnecessary to put the physical body under any extreme condition [to put the body under any harsh treatment] [as the objective] [and focus] in and of itself for Christian sanctification (Col. 2:16-23). We are now only simply attempting to show the value of these spiritual tools [these spiritual disciplines] as applied to our Christian sanctification. If we do not apply these spiritual disciplines correctly in afflicting the soul-life we will not benefit from their application. We do not want to apply ourselves in our Christian sanctification, PHYSICALLY, RELIGIOUSLY, but SPIRITUALLY. God help us to understand the difference!! Christian Asceticism is an unhealthy preoccupation with the physical body in/for Christian sanctification.

Atonement in the Hebrew means *to cover; fig. to expiate* which means to make satisfaction. Atonement was made to both satisfy the sinner's need to be forgiven, and, to satisfy the demand for divine justice. The **atonement** will **cancel** sin, **forgive**, pardon, and purge the sinner, **satisfy** justice, **placate** God, and **appease** His wrath, **put off** judgment, and **reconcile** God and man. The **Cross**-means the *atonement* of JC [and means *exposure* to death: was an instrument of capital punishment]. This is where satisfaction [the payment] was made to make reconciliation. This is where the *relationship* between God and man [men] was restored and brought back into fellowship and, where man was restored to divine favor. The **atonement** of JC is something **done** [is something that had to be done] to affect or to make reconciliation [in order to restore men to God]. To **atone** [the atonement] *means* to perform some act whereby His wrath is appeased and His mercy [forgiveness] procured [accomplished]: to make *payment* for a debt in order to make a*mends* or to correct for wrongdoing: to both satisfy *justice* and to *pardon* sins. In the OE the word "At-one-ment" means, to come back into agreement. Something had to be done to make this possible thus the *blood* of His Cross. Agreement is the union of minds; harmony of opinion, action, and character "Abraham *believed* God's word, and his faith transferred God's righteousness into his account" (Rom. 4:3 TPT). Here, Abraham simply came into agreement with God and His promise. Another very important redemptive term is **propitiation**, which is simply another word used for **atonement**. He [God] set forth Him [Jesus Christ] to be a propitiation through faith in his **blood** [the blood is the means through which *mercy* and *forgiveness* is procured and accomplished]. This *transaction* takes place through faith in His blood as the Expiator: the one who takes away sins [as the **atoning** victim]. The [One], he, who suffered, was punished, and died in our place as the Mercy Seat [the blood on the atonement cover: the lid on the Ark of the Covenant]. The meaning of the **mercy-seat** [the atonement cover] is, too make reconciliation for sins of the people. The **mercy seat** in heaven was sprinkled with *blood* representing that the righteous sentence of the Law had been executed, changing the

Judgement Seat into a Mercy Seat, and now a Throne of Grace and the *place* of **communion** [common union and common ground] between God and men. The mercy of God is impossible and only legal if Divine Justice is first satisfied [paid in full]. Remember, the blood upon the mercy seat provided the necessary covering for the Law of God; the Law was contained inside the Ark [making it a Judgement Seat]. [We are debtors that cannot pay our debts!! To atone is to make amends: to set things right. The **doctrine of the atonement** is *central* to all Christian theology. Luther called Christianity a theology of the Cross. The figure of a Cross is the universal symbol of Christianity. Both the Old and New Testaments make it clear that all human beings are sinners. As our sins are against an infinite, holy God who cannot even look upon sin, atonement must be made in order for us to have [to be restored to] fellowship with God. Because **sin** touches even our best acts [and efforts], we are incapable of making a sufficient sacrifice of our own. We have no gift valuable enough; no work righteous enough to atone for our own sins. In receiving the wrath of God on the Cross, Christ was able to make atonement for His people. Christ carried, and bore, the punishment for the sins of human beings. He atoned for them by accepting the just punishment due for those sins (RSB Page 1983). This atonement requires **repentance** for sins!! Repentance is a prerequisite; a necessary condition for salvation. No one who refuses to repent can ever enter the kingdom of God. In the scriptures, repentance *means* to undergo a **change** in one's mind; this will involve an entire change in one's direction, and course of action. It involves a radical change [in turning] from sin, and turning to God by faith. All true repentance will involve contrition, true and godly sorrow for sins. It is a deep remorse for having offended God; this is a godly sorrow that does not make excuses for sin. When true repentance is offered to God in a spirit of true contrition, He [God] promises to forgive us and to restore us to fellowship with Him (Ps. 51:10, 17; 1 Jn. 1:9). We will find that this attitude and action must be repeated throughout our Christian life. If we find sin in our lives, we are called upon to repent, as the Holy Spirit convicts us to do so (RSB Page 1964). To go through [to experience] true Repentance, and faith in the gospel, this will result in genuine spiritual regeneration [or, as the Reformed tradition would have it, **repentance, and genuine faith in the gospel begins with true and genuine spiritual regeneration**]; either way, repentance and faith in the gospel will propel one into a new birth [a spiritual regeneration] [a spiritual rebirth]. A spiritual rebirth is absolutely necessary for entering into the kingdom of God (Jn. 3:3; 1 Pet. 1:23). Rebirth, then, is an essential part of Christianity, without it, entrance into God's kingdom is impossible. <u>Regeneration</u> is *both* a biblical and theological way to describe rebirth. It refers to a **new genesis, a new [re] generating, and a new beginning**. It marks the new life in a radically renewed [and different] person. Regeneration is the work of the Holy Spirit upon those who are spiritually dead in trespass and sins (Eph. 2:1-10). Upon repentance, and faith in the gospel, the Spirit of God regenerates man's inner spirit, quickening it from spiritual death to new life [this happens all at the same time: simultaneously, and even instantaneously]. This is why regeneration can be seen and understood as happening *first* in our Christian justification, before true repentance, and true faith in the gospel, takes place [has occurred]. Paul called **this regeneration a new creation.** Where formerly we had no disposition and inclination toward God, but now, **we have a deep and abiding desire for the things of God**. Regeneration must be understood as that initial spiritual conception, and is not to be confused with the full experience of conversion. Our spiritual rebirth is the starting point of our spiritual life [this is justification: this is the converting of the heart; our full Christian experience with this full conversion is our sanctification: the transformation of the soul]. I would have to choose to believe, that, **regeneration** does precede true saving faith, because, true faith in God and the gospel of JC requires the ***life quickening*** power and working of the HS from *within*. God will sovereignly act upon the ***heart*** and <u>**spirit**</u> of man for true saving faith [upon the hearing of the true gospel], which in turn will lead a man to true *contrition* and **repentance** (RSB Pages 1857, and 1875)]. One final note, I would like to emphasize here is the **sinlessness** of Jesus Christ. When we speak of Christ's **perfection** or his sinlessness, we are generally referring to his humanity. The sinlessness of JC does not merely serve as an example to us [as an example to us: we who believe]. It is fundamental and necessary for our salvation!!! Christ had to be the **"lamb without blemish,"** or, he could not have secured anyone's salvation. The sacrifice on the Cross had to be made by one who was sinless!! This **perfection** [this perfect humanity] was seen in [and demonstrated by] his perfect obedient life under the Law [of Moses]. It was by His sinlessness and perfect obedience under the law that Christ qualified himself as the perfect sacrifice for our sins. But, notwithstanding, our salvation requires two aspects of redemption. This is why it is called the Redemptive Works of Jesus Christ [works are in the plural]. It was not only necessary for Jesus to be our substitute and receive the punishment due for our sins; He also had to **fulfil the Law of God perfectly to secure the merit necessary for us** to receive the blessings of God's Covenant. He [JC] lived a life of perfect obedience that was required by the law of God for our Christian salvation, and prosperity [blessings] (RSB Page 2203)]. Christ had to fulfil ***all three branches of the law**** in order to secure our **full salvation**. The gospel must be understood in terms of an EXCHANGE. The gospel is the GREAT EXCHANGE. We are found in him, as he is now found in us. We lay down our lives, and now take on his life. We relinquish our own selves to him by faith; and we now take on a new life and character [a new life with new meaning and purpose]. This is what the bible means by [to] **"believe on me."** There has to be a surrendering of oneself for there to be an EXCHANGE!! This exchange is only possible if one [who] yields to God: to his purpose, promises, and the provision God has made in JC through the gospel. The key to Christian victory, emancipation, and sanctification is this continued application of the Cross [that divine exchange]. The **power** and **wisdom** of the Cross is found in its divine exchange!! The grace of God has brought salvation to us through the redemptive works of the Cross. How does the grace of God teach us to deny ungodliness? It is by the Spirit *through* the **message** of the Cross (Tit. 2:11-12; Gal. 6:14; Phil. 3:7-14). It is through the message of the Cross, Christ and him crucified that I am crucified to this world, and this world is crucified unto to me. It is very important that we do not turn the gospel [the message of the Cross] into a license to sin. We find in Luke 24:45-47, Jesus commanding the gospel to be preached to all nations in his name. He said, "...it behooved Christ to suffer, and to rise from the dead the third day [this is the gospel]: and that REPENTANCE and REMISSION [forgiveness] of sins should be preached in his name among all nations." Notice, he called the preaching of this gospel of his grace, as, that, **repentance** and **remission** [forgiveness of sins] should be preached!! Not just forgiveness, but repentance as well!!! It is important we do not turn the gospel of his grace into the preaching of God's forgiveness alone apart from a person confessing and forsaking his/her sins in order to be forgiven and saved. The gospel of Jesus Christ is not the preaching of a gospel of forgiveness [alone] that continues to live in those same sins [that continues to promote those same sins] that one has claimed/secured forgiveness for; but, it is a gospel of JC that brings **repentance** and **remission** [pardon for, and, deliverance from sins] that leads to NEW LIFE **[that leads to a changed life]**. Luke 24 makes it very clear; faith in the gospel, and repentance of sins, brings forgiveness, and NEW LIFE. Help.

Redemption is a legal matter in the Courtroom of Heaven. All judgement in these matters is turned over to the Son [Jn. 5:22; Acts 17:31]. In the Old English to be **propitious** *means* the act of *appeasing* wrath and *conciliating* or winning the favor of an offended person [namely, God]. The offended person [God] would then in turn be gracious, merciful, forgiving, and bestowing a blessing, and restoring to divine favor. Christ **completely satisfied the just demands of a Holy God** [His Father] for **judgment** on Sin and the *sinner* by His death on the Cross. **Redemption** and the word **Atonement** are interchangeable terms [are relatively the same]: to **redeem** is to ransom or to pay in full. To redeem *means* to loosen, to free, to destroy, to dissolve, which gives [sets forth] the *idea* of someone being in captivity or in bondage, being liberated or set free [in other words, to redeem the prisoners, those who are held captive]. These who are in captivity [in bondage] and imprisoned to Sin and Satan are now liberated [set free] and points to the *warfare* of the Cross-the victory accomplished through his death. "Who hath *delivered* us from the power of darkness, and hath *translated* us into the kingdom of his dear Son: in him we have redemption through his ***blood***, even the forgiveness of sins" (Col. 1:13-14). This means, Satan no longer has control over us [mastery], and he no longer has the right [authority] to dominate us; he has no jurisdiction over my life [Eph. 120-23, 2:5-6; Col. 1:9-23, 2:14-15]. We have been ***purchased*** by His blood, and now *translated* into the kingdom of His dear Son [we have changed locations, and now moved out from under his jurisdiction]. He no longer has a right to our lives!! We have been ***reborn*** [and brought] into a new family; we no longer belong to the old family of fallen Adam. We have a *new* relationship with God; we are a part of the family of God [through faith in Christ and Him crucified]. We no longer have a *relationship* with Sin and with Satan (Acts 26:18); we have a new relationship with God and righteousness [as a new creation in JC]. To be **redeemed** *means* to be ***rescued*** [delivered] from bondage to sin and captivity to Satan. Redemption not only speaks of being brought out of something [old], but as well, being brought into something [new] "...to turn *them* from darkness to light, and from the power of Satan unto God, that they receive forgiveness of sins, and **inheritance** among them which are ***sanctified*** [set apart] by faith that is in me [Christ] (Acts 26:18; Col. 1:12-14). One of the *key* GK word *meanings* for Redemption is **"to go to market to purchase or to buy back: to pay or to ransom in full,"** "For you are **bought** [redeemed] with a price: therefore glorify God **in your body**, and in your spirit, which are God's (1 Cor. 6:20; 2 Cor. 5:15). We belong to God in redemption, spirit, soul, and body!!! The word picture here for **redemption** is clear: He [Christ] went to Market [to the slave auction] to buy slaves [those enslaved to sin and Satan]. He redeemed us [purchased us] by His Own Blood, and now we have become **his love-slaves** [bondservants]. This is where **sanctification** is understood as the *believer* now newly purchased by His redeeming blood and **set apart** to God for Holy

Service [set apart to God for holy living]. God!! Satan no longer owns me, I have been **purchased** by the **payment** of the blood of JC and, I now belong to him. "... Who hath [past tense] [already] <u>delivered</u> me [has already rescued me] from [out of] [out from under] the **powers** of darkness [the GK word here is *exousia*, which means, out from under the jurisdiction and authority of Satan]...it is **in** him [JC] we have [and hold] this **redemption** *through* his blood [through the victory of the Cross], which is the **forgiveness** of sins. Through the Cross we have been purchased: we have been set free; through the Cross we have this payment: it is through faith in the Cross we now hold this bill of sale. Satan has lost all claims on our lives; unless, we give it to him. God help us!! The key to our Christian victory is summed up in three words: The CROSS, our FAITH, and the HOLY SPIRIT.

Sanctification *means* to make holy; to separate from sin, and to set apart to God; to be dedicated to God, and consecrated for sacred service. <u>Sanctification</u> is also understood as a *process* at work in the life of the set apart believer to *prepare* him for His Divine Purposes, "...Who hath **saved** us, and **called** us...according to His own **purpose** and **grace**, which was given us in Christ Jesus" (2 Tim. 1:19). We are *saved* for God, and not for ourselves!! We are saved, according to His **purpose** and **grace**: not just His grace!! Christ was made to be my *personal* <u>sanctification</u> and <u>redemption</u>: **I was bought with a price**; I am not my own [man] (Rom. 12:1). **Salvation** in the GK means [Redemption] to deliver [to save], to rescue, to heal [it promises divine health], to protect, to preserve, to defend, to help [to come to the aid of], to keep safe, to get the victory, and to make [the Christian] whole. All these *words* are biblical **promises** tied to our Christian salvation. In short, our Christian salvation points to the <u>remission</u> [the forgiveness] of sins, and **deliverance** from all our **enemies** [it is promised victory over all the powers of darkness]. **Righteousness** *means* to declare as innocent; to be free from all guilt and debt; to be made right with God [Right-Standing]: this is our Christian <u>Justification</u>. These things are legal terms and legal matters in a Court of Law. **Justification** *means* acquittal; a not guilty verdict; to render just [**just as if you have never sinned and have always obeyed**]. To be **justified** *means* to be made **righteous** [to receive absolution: the forgiveness of sins]. It is very clear, that, all these many biblical terms that speak to our overall Christian salvation all overlap in meaning and application. God, help us to understand this full provision and emancipation!!

Salvation is a *process* that begins with justification [His Cross], then moves to sanctification and transformation [our cross], and then concludes with glorification. Justification *regenerates* the spirit; sanctification, and transformation *changes* [grows up] the soul, and last but not least glorification *resurrects* the body on the last day. The resurrection of the body is the ***completion*** of our Redemptive process. The word process in the OE *means* operations, gradual progress, and moving forward: a progressive course [a series of actions and changes in growth]. There is no doubt; this is the testimony of the Pauline Gospel [the testimony (witness) of the scriptures]. **Sanctification** is best understood as the *indwelling* work of the HS to **renew** the mind, **retrain** the will, **bridle** the tongue, and **subjugate** the body. [2 Pet. 1:1-4; Col. 1:19-23, 2:2-7, 10; Rom. 3:9-31, 16:20, 24-26; Eph. 1:15-23, 2:1-10]. This is the *process* by which God **saves** man from the gutter-most to the utter-most!! Here are the three *transactions* of the Cross: Justification [have been saved] [past tense] that takes place *first* in the man's spirit [set free from the power of guilt and the penalty of sin]. Sanctification [is you and me being saved/delivered] [in the present tense] from the power of sin, which is an on-going process and victory over sin in every area of the believers life [this affects the soul] [of course, **this victory over the power of sin** began the very moment the Christian came into new life] (the treasure of the new creation within the earthen vessel is the presence of the victory of the Lord Jesus Christ over all sin and sinning, as a divine deposit, within, within man's reborn human spirit, in the presence of sin in the body). Last but not least, Glorification [will be saved] [future] **from the presence of sin [in the body]** [the resurrection of the body, and sin's final defeat].

The *key* to our Christian victory can be summed up in *three* words: The **Cross**, Your **Faith**, and The **Holy Spirit** (TENT viii). <u>Salvation</u> is simply *believing* on Christ. This means that you believe [have faith] in what He did [on the Cross: his death and resurrection], and *accept* it for yourself on a personal [daily] basis. This means to ***accept*** Christ as <u>Savior</u>, and to **make** Him <u>Lord</u> of your life. It is through *faith* in the Cross-that saves, but it is also necessary to *continue* to put our [trust] in the Cross [the crucified Christ] on a daily basis for Christian victory. The believer must *constantly* express [put] his faith in the Cross: the Holy Spirit then provides all the help necessary, in order for victory to be had in every capacity. If we put our trust in the Cross, the HS will always guarantee victory for the believer. The *key* is the Cross, because through the Cross the HS works. The **Cross**-guarantees our victory over the Old life [of fallen Adam]. The Cross-is the only *means*, by which the sinner can be saved, and as well, the only *means* by which the Christian can walk in victory. Most of the Church understands the Cross, as it *regards* that initial salvation experience [the forgiveness of sins]; but, has very little knowledge whatsoever as it concerns the part the Cross plays in our victory over sin [you and me living and walking as an overcomer]. Every Christian must understand, that, every single solitary problem we face in this life in the body was addressed by JC at the Cross (Col. 2:14-15). This *means* that for every problem, the Christian should be directed to the Cross. He must understand that the solution is found there, and found only there. The Apostle Paul gave to us the meaning of the New Covenant, which pertains to what Jesus Christ did for us on the Cross. So, in effect, the *meaning* of the New Covenant is the *meaning* of the Cross. The **Cross**-is short for the death, burial, and resurrection of our Lord JC. The Cross without exception must always be the object of our faith as it regards the child of God. This is very, very, very important!!!!!!!!! The reason that most Christians get into trouble in some way, is because they do not understand the Cross **as the source of all their needs met**, and, that they must ever have faith [put their trust] in this accomplished fact [the Finished Redemptive Works] of JC [on the Cross]. We are **saved** and **sanctified**, through the *preaching* of the gospel [the message of the Cross] and through faith in the gospel [the Cross] [and, his subsequent resurrection], exclusively. (This paragraph within this chapter was compiled-taken out of "The Expositor's New Testament," pages 1112-1124). This *salvation* is more than just deliverance from something, but as well, you and I are being delivered into something brand new, [this is justification and sanctification]. In the OT, the Israelite's came out [of Egypt] but failed to enter in [to Canaan]. Salvation will both come ***out*** and enter ***in***!! Not just delivered **out** of something but as well delivered **into** something. This is the correct word picture given to us in the OT that best describes [that best represents] the NT *gospel* of our Salvation. God did not take us **out** to bring us back **into** what we came out of, "...having *escaped* the corruption that is in the world through lust" (2 Pet. 1:4). "For you have not received the spirit of **bondage** [slavery; servitude] again to fear [again to sin]; but you have received the Spirit of Adoption [you have received the Spirit of Son-ship], whereby we cry, Abba, Father" (Rom. 8:15-17). "Who [Christ] gave himself for our sins [on that Cross], that he might deliver us from this present evil world, according to the will of God and our Father" (Gal. 1:4). It is clear; it is the **will** of God that we be **set apart** from sin, and from our old sinful lifestyle. Praise be to God!!! Grace has taught us to live godly lives, and, to live holy [set apart] in this present evil world!!! In Romans 6:19, Paul spoke of the flesh, and its infirmities [the infirmities of the flesh]; before this, Paul spoke of the believer's positional victory in Jesus Christ in Romans 6:1-14 [and in Romans 8:2]. In Hebrews 4:14-16, Paul said, Jesus Christ is touched with the ***feelings*** of our infirmities. Paul here is saying, Christ is no longer touched by our infirmities directly, because, he already took all these things into himself on the Cross, and cancelled its power/its legal ground; now, he can no longer be touched by all these things again. In Matthew 8:17 we find a word picture that best describes *both* Hebrews 4:14-16, and Hebrews 5:7-9; this is JC, who, throughout his lifetime and, he, who under tremendous pressure in the garden of Gethsemane, before he went to the Cross [he sweat great drops of blood: Matthew 26:36-46]: where he was touched with all the feelings of our struggles in our fallen human nature [all the infirmities of the flesh: that fallen adamic **state**]. Matthew 8:17 tells us that, JC took all these *things* [the *infirmities* of the flesh] with him to the Cross and, nailed them all there, forever. He took with him to the Cross every sin, sickness and disease, poverty, death, and the whole curse of the law. Now, as a great high priest, who can be touched with the *feelings* of all our infirmities that we struggle with in this sanctification process: he understands how very painful it is to take up our Cross and to die, and, to follow after his example of death [to self] in order to follow after him daily as a disciplined follower [as a disciple]. Christ has already done away with all these infirmities of the flesh on the Cross; all that is left is for you and I to walk out this victory in our Christian sanctification by simply mortifying the flesh or, by simply putting to death the deeds of the body (Rom. 7:23-25; 8:2, 13; Col. 3:3-5). This can be a very painful process for the believer as he/she struggles in their own personal sanctification; however, JC is touched with every painful feeling in this process of our spiritual growth and transformation. Thanks be to God!!! The believer in Jesus Christ does not have to be defeated in a single battle!!!

Salvation is a theological and biblical term that means, the deliverance of the soul from sin and its present and eternal consequences. In Christianity, salvation is achieved, through the incarnation and death of Jesus Christ on the Cross, in order to make atonement for the sins of the people. The word atonement is the concept and salvific principle [that which revolves around the main idea] **of a person taking action to correct a previous wrongdoing**. This word, atonement, means "agreed," Literally, "at-one." From this definition, it is clear, that, **the work of atonement** is designed **to reconcile** and **to restore** that which is **broken** and **lost**, and, **in ill repair**. Words like, guilt, sorrow, remorse, repentance, forgiveness, pardon, and reconciliation are all seen and understood as steps on our path to redemption. Another word for salvation is redemption. This word means, deliverance from sin and its immediate consequences. It means the freedom from the captivity of sin, and **deliverance**

from its consequential bondages. The word picture here in *both* the Greek and the Hebrew is seen and understood **by the payment of a ransom**. The two key words that best describes redemption/atonement/salvation is, **payment**, and to **purchase**. We, you and me, the believer [through the payment made by our crucified Savior] through the blood of his Cross: we have been purchased out of bondage to **sin** and **death** [and, we have been delivered out from under the jurisdictional territory of the evil one/the wicked one]. These two words, **atonement**, and **redemption** [which by necessity must include the principle of salvation], are interchangeable terms. The **Cross** of Jesus Christ is the instrument of execution that, **makes atonement:** the **blood** of Jesus Christ is his human life poured out **to atone for sins** [in order to satisfy divine justice and, to procure forgiveness]. Propitiation and expiation are the two words that best describes **the two part work of the One Atonement**. Propitiation is toward God, and means, to placate God, and to turn away the wrath of God [by cancelling the sin debt: by making a redemptive payment for sins]. Expiation in the GK means, *off* and *away*, which, is that part of the same one atonement that is toward men: where, in the atonement, JC, removes the guilt, and sin stain on the people. This One Atonement effects *both* **reconciliation** and **restoration** to God. The word reconciliation in Christian theology, is an element of salvation that refers to the results of atonement. Reconciliation is the end of the hostility between God and men, caused by original sin [caused by Adam's first transgression in the Garden of Eden]. Reconciliation means, to make peace between God and men [bringing restoration and recovery to men in their fallen state]. This Christian justification [the imputation/and transfer of the righteousness of God/and the righteous earned merits of Jesus Christ under the law] given to those who believe in the gospel is, what we call that Divine Exchange. This is a double imputation or, a double transfer: where, our sins are put upon Jesus Christ on the Cross and, his earned righteousness [his perfect life of obedience] is transferred to our account, because of the resurrection, "Who was delivered [up on the Cross] for our offences [for our sins], and **was raised for** our justification [he was raised for our acquittal]" (Rom. 4:25). This salvation/atonement/redemption is a vicarious sacrifice, which means, it is a **substitutionary atonement** made by Jesus Christ on behalf of fallen men. This substitutionary work of atonement made by Jesus Christ on the Cross must as well be understood as our own personal Christian <u>sanctification</u>. The gospel is not just the justification of sinners; but, as well, the provision made for Christian sanctification. The same gospel provision that saves us in our Christian justification is, the same gospel power that empowers us in our Christian sanctification. The key to this great exchange, and, the key to all Christian victory is found, in this concept of Christian identification and the substitutionary work of the Cross. We <u>indeed</u> <u>reckon</u> ourselves to be **dead to sin** and the **old life** [which by necessity must include **the old world**] and, are now **made alive** to God *through* faith in Jesus Christ and, he crucified. <u>Indeed</u> means, to be sure that we are identified with Christ in his death, burial, and resurrection, and ascension. To <u>reckon</u> means, to count it done: to be sure that it is a foregone conclusion. I am not going to be dead: I am dead!! I am not, one day, going to be made alive to God: I am now alive to God. Thank God.

When we think of biblical salvation, it is necessary to understand the Bible's **concept of sin.** <u>Sin</u> must be understood biblically as *both* liken to a **pecuniary** debt; and is, a **penal** debt. This word <u>pecuniary</u> means, **"relating to money."** This **sin** debt is understood in terms of economic damages: damages or losses in a personal injury case. This a legal matter that must be settled in a Court of Law. In other words, **the legal problem of sin must be settled in the Court** of Heaven. Sin must be understood in terms **of something being owed** and, the failure to <u>do</u> and to <u>pay</u> what was <u>obligated</u>/owed results **in a judgement against us** [this is you and me under an obligation to pay the debt owed]. The sin debt is likened to a pecuniary debt in that we come under obligation. This sin debt is too great/vast for any man to meet its obligation, thus, the need for an atonement. For example, sin, is like owing 100 billion dollars. A man or many men can live many life-times over, and over, and over, again, and still not be able to meet this great/vast financial obligation!! He does not have the means nor the where-withal **to pay this great financial debt**. Sin is like a great financial debt that man does not have the means nor the where-withal to pay, even though through many lifetimes **he still comes up short in his financial obligation**. This is how the sin debt works; man does not have enough nor, can men do enough to meet this debt obligation. His **sin indebtedness is insurmountable apart from the Cross** of JC [apart from **this atonement**]. A penal debt is as well a legal debt; a penal debt is a **moral indebtedness**. In the very same way as a pecuniary debt: **a penal debt is a transgression of the law,** and requires **a debt to be paid**. The word penal is **punitive**, and means, involving **punishment**, and **penalties**. This speaks of sin as coming under the eternal judicial judgments of God. **All sin is punitive**, and means, inflicting or aiming at punishment. This is why, **the atonement**, must first satisfy **the demand for Divine Justice** before pardon/forgiveness can be procured. The only way the **mercy** of God can win out over the **judgment** of God is *through* a **vicarious atonement** [is through a substitute]. Man has no way nor means, to turn back time or, to undo the previous deeds done. Penal indebtedness is the demand for divine justice, which is, death!! There is no way to turn back, and, undo the sin debt: it is a moral obligation that must be paid through punitive actions of eternal punishment!! Biblically speaking, sin, is a very serious and deadly matter, something, not too trifled with!!! All sin is **penal indebtedness**, and, requires **physical death** and **eternal judgment** as payment. The Bible speaks of **three major aspects to sin**. It is a Debt; it is Enmity against God and, it is a Crime committed in the breaking of God's holy Law. Only a **penal** substitutionary **sacrifice** and **offering made in atonement to God** [and for man] would suffice [will do]. This is Jesus Christ who voluntarily submitting to the Father's plan, was punished [was penalized] in place of sinners [as a substitute], thus satisfying the demand of divine justice so God could justly forgive sins and making us at one [at peace] with God. Penal substitution teaches, that, Jesus Christ **had to suffer and die the penalty due** in order to satisfy the Father's wrath **for humanity's sins**. This means, that, God, is not willing or able to simply forgive sins without first requiring a satisfaction for it!! No Justice [first], no Justification! Sin must be understood as a <u>debt</u>; as <u>enmity</u> between God and men, and, sin is a <u>crime</u>: the violation of the law of God. We have already explained sin as a debt so, how is sin understood as enmity against God?? Enmity means, **hostility** toward God. Sin, has at its core turned men's hearts from God. This hostility is not God, toward man, but men, toward God. God did not violate the rights and persons of men, he, man, violated the rights [the law] and Person of God [when he, Adam, man, sinned in that first transgression, and beyond]. This inner fallen spirit-nature within, is, **an inborn** and **ingrained enmity/ hostility** toward God [in its inner **fallen human condition**]. Man in his fallen state, is, **a child of disobedience having a spirit of rebellion in enmity** against God [and his holy law]. This is why, men, must be born again to see and to even enter into the kingdom of God. Man must be made brand new in order to be restored to fellowship with a holy God, thus, the reason for the Atonement. There is no doubt; God is the true injured party, not man; God, **is the one who was violated** [by man] **from in the beginning**. There is no doubt; God is sorely displeased with sin, and the **sinful actions of men**. Last by not least, sin, is a Crime: here, God functions as the Governor and the Judge. God, is ultimately the Judge of all matters dealing with Justice. Remember, the Holy Righteous Standard of God is His Righteous Holy Law. Sin, as a Crime is, nothing less **than the violation** of God's holy Law. So, we can see, here, that, every time men break the Law of God, they transgress the law, and, in this **transgression they personally trespass against a holy God**. From this we can see the constant enmity and hostility of men toward God in the breaking of His Holy Law. This is why, in the NT atonement, **propitiation**, had to come before **expiation**. Jesus Christ in his Work of Atonement, he, **had to first appease the wrath** of God against sin, and the sinner, thus, making it possible to expiate sins [making it possible to take away every guilt and stain of sin upon men]. In the ONE ACT of the ATONEMENT, God, in Christ, reconciled men unto himself; how, by paying the sin **<u>debt</u>**: and no longer **counting** men's **crimes** [trespasses and transgressions] against them: having removed **the enmity** and hostility between them *through* the **blood of his Cross**. Halleluiah!!!!

I would like to say a little bit about **saving faith**. In John 3:16 it says, "For God so loved the world, that he gave his only begotten Son, that whosoever **believes** in him should not perish, but have everlasting life." The word believes, here, in the text, is *pisteuo* and means **to have faith**. It comes from another GK word *pistis* and is translated in our English Bible **as faith**, "But we are not of them who draw back unto perdition; but of them that **believe to the saving of the soul**" (Heb. 10:39). Here, the word believe is *pistis* and means, "...but of them that **have faith** in God [or rather, but of them who **have faith** in the gospel] **to the saving of the soul**. To *believe* God or, to *believe* in the gospel means, **to have faith** in the gospel, which is Christ and him crucified. Therefore being justified **by faith** *pistis* we have peace with God through our Lord Jesus Christ: by whom also we have access **by faith** *pistis* into this grace wherein we stand..." (Rom. 5:1-2). Ok, I want to draw your attention to the GK word *pisteuo* that is translated in our English Bible **as believe**. Ok, *pistis* is #4102 in Strong's and, *pisteuo* is #4100 in Strong's and is clearly a part of the same GK word cluster!! The GK word *pisteuo* in our English Bible, which is translated as believe, or believes, is a Greek **verb** and, is found in the text **in the present tense**. Here, in the New Testament, Greek present tense verbs generally refer **to continuous action**, especially those *verbs* which are present participles. In other words, **in John 3:16**, it should be translated as, he who [continually] **believes** in him should not perish, but have eternal life. In other words, it is not the one who **had believed** but, the one **who is constantly believing** that are saved, "For I am not ashamed of the gospel of Jesus Christ: for it is the power of God unto salvation to everyone that believes, or rather, to everyone who is presently still believing on the gospel [this word *believe* is a GK verb found in the present tense]. "...It pleased God by the foolishness of preaching **to save** them that **believe**" (1 Cor. 1:21). Again, this GK word for believe is *pisteuo* and means to still be presently in the faith, or rather, to presently still be believing on the gospel [or order to be saved]. There is no doubt: salvation belongs to those who are presently active in their faith in the gospel. There is a clear distinction being made in the NT between **the ongoing act of believing** and, the **simple fact of believing**, which is nothing more than what the bible calls **having faith**. Can we lose our faith?? Can someone fall away from the faith?? There is a big difference between one who **had faith** and, the one **who is believing!!** The *latter* is **present** and, the *former*, **is past!!!** There is no doubt, that, the NT writers saw continual belief as a necessary condition of salvation. The promise of salvation belongs [only] to the one [constantly] *believing* the gospel. It is only as we **keep on believing**, do we **keep on having** eternal life. Just as becoming saved is conditioned upon faith, staying saved is conditioned upon **continuing to believe** [on the gospel]. Remember, Paul said, "...it pleased God...**to save** the one [who is constantly] **believing**" (1 Cor. 1:21).

    Saving faith requires 3 main parts to its **full** and **complete conversion**. The first one, is by necessity, contingent upon **an accurate knowledge** of the true gospel itself. We must **have the content of the gospel** correct in order to believe [to be saved]. True saving faith begins with the <u>content</u> of the gospel. We cannot accurately <u>believe</u> [for] [the gospel], what we do not *first* have proper <u>knowledge</u> [of] [this gospel]. So, it first begins with having the proper content! This word <u>content</u> means, the **principle matter**, significance, or **meaning of thing**. What is the principle matter of the gospel?? What is its significance?? What is its meaning?? Therefore, we see here, that, the *first* part of **saving faith** is having an <u>accurate knowledge</u> of the gospel itself. Again, if our *knowledge* is wrong, our *faith* will be inaccurate. The *second* part of **saving faith** is our **mental assent** to [or, our mental <u>agreement</u> with] the gospel. This is our mental agreement with the facts of the Christian faith where it concerns the gospel of Jesus Christ itself. Believing by necessity requires the participation of the mind!! The bible tells us, that, it is **with the heart** that men believe [on the gospel]; however, notwithstanding, **the mind**

is used/designed to inform the **heart** [the mind is used to *inform* our faith] (Rom. 10:10; 12:2). It is absolutely impossible to believe the gospel without an accurate knowledge of this gospel in the mind. So, **saving faith** must by necessity include **mental assent** [intellectual agreement] with the content of the gospel. In other words, we cannot have **true salvation without this mental assent being a part** of that Christian conversion/Christian experience. Now, just because we have these two elements of the faith [that is, saving faith], this does not mean we have **true saving faith**. It is possible to hear an accurate message of the content of the gospel and, to come to a mental assent/agreement with the facts/truths of the Christian faith [this Christian NT gospel]; however, notwithstanding, there is still yet one more key element necessary for true saving faith. The *third* part of true saving faith is a **personal trust** and a **total reliance** upon the gospel for salvation, which is Jesus Christ and **him crucified**. This speaks to a **personal commitment to the gospel** itself: this speaks of one who has totally and completely abandoned themselves over to the overall **content** of the gospel for salvation. Of course, this is *both* an **initial acceptance** of the gospel, and then, **it grows** in commitment in our Christian sanctification and transformation. It is not enough just to claim the gospel for salvation. It is not enough just **to have** and **to hold** a *profession* of faith: there must be **a true** and genuine *possession* of the gospel faith in order to be saved. There must first be an accurate knowledge of this gospel of Jesus Christ, and then, we must come into an agreement with this Christian faith: it is at this point/place we make our commitment to the gospel by surrendering our lives to God for saving faith [in order to receive saving grace]. The Apostle John said, "Whosoever transgresses, and abides not in the doctrine of Christ, hath not God. He that abides [continues] in the doctrine of Christ, he hath *both* the Father and the Son. If there come any unto you, and bring not this doctrine, receive him not into your house, neither bid him God speed" (2 Jn. 9-10). What is the **doctrine** of Christ, but, an **accurate** and **true knowledge** and **understanding** of this **gospel** of Jesus Christ. Here, in this text, the word doctrine *means* instruction. This is exactly what we meant earlier when we said, the true **content** of the gospel. Again, what is the **principle matter** of the gospel?? What is its significance and, what is its true meaning? This is exactly how we are to understand the meaning of John, in his epistle of 2 John, where it concerns the doctrine of Jesus Christ. How can we have the true real authentic gospel, **without having the proper content** of this gospel??? How can one believe on Christ and him crucified, without having an accurate knowledge of that/his death, burial, and resurrection?? So, therefore, we can see, that, the **mind** as well as the **heart** is a very big part of **true** and **genuine** and **authentic** saving faith!! God, help us all to see, and to believe!!! Help!!

THE CROSS OF CHRIST

"*For while I was with you I was determined to be consumed with one topic-Jesus the **crucified** Messiah*" (1 Cor. 2:2 TPT). "For I determined not to know anything among you [to be conscious of nothing else] save [except] Jesus Christ and Him crucified" (KJ/Amp). The word crucify in the OE *means* to **put to death** by *nailing* the hands and feet to a Cross. To be **crucified** with Christ, is, to become dead to the law and, to become dead to sin, and, to have indwelling corruption [the sinful nature] subdued [and destroyed] (Rom. 6; and Gal. 2). We no longer look to our own obedience [under the law] for acceptance with God, and, we are no longer under sin's power. Christ and Him *crucified* is the only message Paul preached on purpose, with frequency, which will save [rescue] the sinner and, set the captives free, and give the believer perpetual victory [this victory applies only for the one who puts their total trust in him and his works for *both* justification and sanctification] (TENT Page 677). Christ and Him *crucified* is the **power** and **wisdom** of God. Christ and him crucified is the **central theme** in all the Scriptures. Everything in the New points back to it and, everything in the Old point forward toward it. The entire plan of Salvation from start to finish is the one *binding* **thread** that ties everything together in *both* the Old and New Testaments. The Cross [the plan of redemption] is the foundational doctrine [teaching] found in the entirety of the word of God "Then I said, Behold, here I am, coming to do Your will, O God-[coming to fulfill] what is **written** of Me in the volume [in roll or, in the entirety] of the book" [for it is written of me] (Heb. 10:7 Amp). The word for *foundation* here in the text means, that by which all other things [all other doctrines and truths] are supported and upheld. **The Cross [His redemptive works] is the Alpha and Omega of the Scriptures!!! Christ and he crucified [his death, burial, and resurrection, and ascension] is the wisdom and power of God.**

The plan of **redemption** through the preaching of the **Cross** is the foundational *doctrine* in all the scriptures. This means, that, every other single doctrine [every other single teaching] in all the word of God is built upon the foundation of the Cross-which means, it must be understood [and comprehended] in how it all relates to the Cross. *"To preach the message of the cross seems like sheer nonsense to those who are on their way to destruction, but to us [who believe] who are on our way to salvation, it is the mighty power of God released within us"* (1 Cor. 1:18 TPT). The preaching of the *gospel* [the cross] is the power of God. The GK word here is *dunamis* and it speaks to the **activity** of the Holy Spirit through the applied **message** of the **Cross** [Acts 1:8; Rom. 1:16]. The "message of the Cross" becomes the *ignition* point [the starting point] where God's power [and wisdom] becomes *operative* and **actualized** [toward us and, within all those who believe on him] with the ability to save, convert, and transform (TPT Page 442, *e*). The HS works through the **blood** of the Cross to *save* [to make **atonement**] [to forgive sins] and then, to bring to us victory [to make victory possible for the believer according to and in keeping with that Divine Exchange]. This is the *sanctifying* and *perfecting* work of the HS through the application of the Cross [the Divine Exchange]. Remember, to exchange means to *receive* something in return for something **given**. We must yield, and surrender it to God, and, God replaces it!!! Thanks Be To God for this Divine Exchange. This is how the true NT gospel of his grace really works in our New Covenant faith: by this divine/human transfer/imputation/exchange of us, for him. Halleluiah

Again, this is not us attempting to change, but, us simply yielding to that Divine Exchange. It is a finished work!! This redemptive work was accomplished by the blood of His Cross. The **blood** speaks of the *life* given or sacrificed on our behalf. Sacrifice means an *atoning* victim. This is a vicarious [or, a substitutional] sacrifice. The scripture says, "...Abraham *believed* God, and it was **counted** unto him for righteousness" (Rom. 4:3). All we have to do is fall in line with the gospel, and, come into *agreement* with this accomplished fact. Not work, but *yield*, "Now to him that works not, but believes on him that *justifies* the ungodly, his faith [his trust in Christ] is counted [imputed to him] for righteousness" (Rom. 4:5). In short, the "preaching of the **Cross**" speaks to his death, burial, resurrection and ascension [the whole **gospel**]. In short, *salvation* comes to us by simply believing on the gospel, by simply believing on Jesus Christ and him crucified. It is not my/our attempt at living a holy life that makes us *acceptable* to God [that wins us approval with God], but, it is by faith in JC and him crucified, and, it is by faith in his righteousness [in his perfect obedience under the Law], that makes me/us right with [acceptable to] God [and, that makes us **heirs** of God, and, now, having a **right** to access all the Covenant benefits and blessings contained in the Holy Writ]. We *simply* yield to him and to what he did for us on the Cross in his death, burial, resurrection, and ascension, and *simply* receive from him [by being placed in him] all the benefits that go with [that comes with] the Cross, and his resurrection. The bible calls this thing, *believing* on him, and, it is counted [it is imputed to us] for righteousness [for justification].

The **Cross**-typifies our **death** [with Him] to the Old Life [fallen Adam]. The Christian [must] needs to put his/her confidence in the *blood* of His Cross [His life sacrificed on our behalf]. We must not separate the blood [His life] from the Cross. We must preach Christ and Him crucified. Victory and redemption is found in the *blood* shed [or, in His life given] on the Cross. We preach Christ as an **atoning** Victim. Many preach and teach a bloodless gospel. Today, many are attempting to separate Christ, from His Cross "...without the *shedding* of his **blood** there is no release from sin and its guilt [there is no remission or forgiveness for sins, and the due (and merited) punishment for sins]" (Heb. 9:22 Amp). The biblical definition for the forgiveness of sins, is, the **pardon** for sin, and, **deliverance from sin**.

Pardon for sin [sins], and, deliverance from a sinful life and lifestyle. To *identify* with the Cross-is to identify with the death of the Old Man [that old fallen Adamic (sinful) nature] and, the putting away of the Old life [our former conversation (conduct) of this Old Man]. To identify *means* to make to be the same [to see as the same]. His death on that Cross-**becomes my death** to that Old Man!! The Cross-is the place where He died for us, and the place where all our *sins* were paid [for] by the shedding of His blood [by the giving up of His life as a **sacrifice** and **ransom**]. Ransom means *money* or the price paid for redemption. The Cross-is the place where our **forgiveness** was purchased and secured. The Cross-is the place where I was made **Right** with God. The Cross-is the place where the Old life was judged. The Cross-is the place where the Old Man was punished: the place where the Old world ended. It is at the Cross-where Satan, with all his minions, and with all their evil works, were destroyed "...For this purpose the Son of God was manifested, that he might destroy [undo all] the works of the devil" (1 Jn. 3:8). To destroy means to loosen, to break up, to dissolve, and to put off [forever] all the evil works of darkness. Satan, with all his evil *power* and evil *works* CANCELLED at the Cross!! God [Christ] be praised!!! To **undo** *means*, the Cross-reversed [and overthrew] the Curse. The curse **made void** and **set aside** [and is now *rendered* powerless]. Christ, went to the Cross-to die to take away sins, and to destroy all the evil **works** of Satan that he [Satan] **worked** [accomplished] through the sins [disobedience] of men. First John 3:8 reveals the victory of the CROSS!! At the Cross, **the old man was punished**; the old life was judged; the old world ended; and, it is where **all of Satan's evil power** and **evil works** were totally and completely **destroyed** [neutralized: rendered ineffective: annihilated].

"...He [Himself] in a similar manner partook of the same [nature], that by [going through] **death** He might bring to [nothing] **[destroy]** and [to] make of no affect *him who had the power of death-that is the devil.* And also that He might deliver and completely set free all those who through the [haunting] fear of death were held in bondage throughout the whole course of their lives" (Heb. 2:14 Amp). The two *terrors* He [Christ] set us free from was the *guilt* of **sin**, and the *fear* of **death**. Now, because of the Blood of His Cross [His death], He [Jesus] completely and totally destroyed all the works of the devil. Here, this GK word <u>destroy</u> means <u>defeated</u>, <u>broken</u>, <u>abolished</u>, and <u>abandoned</u>. Here in the GK it means to **render useless** and **entirely idle**. Satan, his demons, his dominion, and the fallen evil world he *formed* [created] [that we see all around us every day of our lives] all cancelled at the Cross. He was, cast out, ejected, expelled, and **forced out** of his *place* of authority over the earth [his dominion overthrown]; all of this took place at the [warfare of the] Cross [because of the BLOOD of His Cross]. Praise God!!! Jesus Christ came in his first advent to destroy and, to undo all the evil works of Satan [to overthrow and destroy every evil work of the dark powers] [this is *both* to undo all, and to reverse the curse] (Gal. 3:13). To <u>undo</u> *means* to make it of none [no] effect: to come open or, to come apart, and to reverse [the curse]. To <u>reverse</u> *means* to negate; to undo; loosen; to overthrow; to make void; to turn completely around in *both* position and direction. Paul said, "But is now made manifest by the appearing of our Savior Jesus Christ [through his death on the Cross], **who hath <u>abolished</u> death**, and hath [through his resurrection] brought [new] life and immortality [eternal life] to light through the <u>gospel</u> [of his grace] [it is through the redemptive works of JC on the Cross: in his death, burial, and resurrection, and ascension that the old life and the old man with his old nature ended; and, **a new eternal life in Christ** [now having a new nature] brought into existence within man, that is, in all who believe]" (2 Tim. 1:10). The **warfare** of the Cross of Christ has already ABOLISHED DEATH. Death where is your STING?? Death, where is your power to hold those who believe the gospel?? This power over death: it is found in the NEW LAW **of the new spiritual life in Christ Jesus** that has completely **set us free from the power** and **operation of SIN** and **DEATH** (Rom. 8:2). Every by product of SIN and DEATH is completely neutralized, and render entirely idle. These byproducts of Sin and Death are: sicknesses and diseases, poverty of every kind/form, death itself, and the whole entire

Curse found under the law. The word *byproduct* means a derivate or, offshoot; somethings produced through something else; a second, or, an unexpected and unintended result. Through Adam's ONE SIN [one transgression] death entered into man and entered into the world; as a result, **this curse of death spread throughout the whole world** *through* further sin, and through sicknesses and diseases, poverty, and the like. All these *things* **have now been overcome** [and overthrown] and **undone** [reversed] [canceled] by the blood [and warfare] of His Cross. The word ABOLISHED in the TEXT in the GK means, to be [rendered] entirely idle [useless]; to cease [in authority]; to be brought to nothing [by the power of the HS *through* the redemptive works of the Cross]; to destroy [all its works in the earth, and in man]; to deliver [those who believe on the gospel from its everyday active principle and operation in the body]; to loose [its grip on those who put their trust in the Cross, and the blood for atonement, and who draw/pull from JC's resurrection life and power] (Rom. 6:8-9; 1 Jn. 4:17-18; Heb. 2:14-15; Col. 2:11; James 4:7; Eph. 6:10-18; 2 Cor. 10:3-7; 2 Cor. 2:11; Eph. 2:1-3; Col. 2:14-15; Matt. 28:18; Rom. 8:2; Rom. 6:23; Jn. 12:31-32; 2 Cor. 4:3-4; Lk. 4:5-8; 1 Cor. 7:31; 2 Tim. 4:10; Gal. 1:4; 2 Pet. 1:4; Heb. 6:5; 9:10-11; Col. 3:3; 1 Tim. 4:8). God, help us all to understand the victory of the Cross!!

Satan before the cross, ruled [had dominion] [held sway] through the *power* of **sin** and **death** (Rom. 8:2). Now, all men, through the fear of death, and imprisoned by sin, were all their lifetime subject to [spiritual] bondage [under the curse]. For the wages of sin is death, which speaks of separation from God; Jesus atoned for all SINS at the Cross, thereby removing the cause [the curse] that brought spiritual death [and eternal judgment] (TENT Page 891). The fear of death, is, the fear of Eternal punishment (Heb. 2:14-15; 1 Jn. 4:17-18). "Now is the **judgment** of this world: now shall the *prince* of this world be **cast out**" (Jn. 12:31-32). Jesus spoke this in the context of the Cross!! World here in the GK *means*, the ordered arrangement of things: its décor [decorations or stage settings] it's adorning [to decorate with ornaments]. In the *context* here, it is referring to the **world** Satan brought into *being* [existence] through Adam's sin. The prince of *this* world speaks of the Old fallen world, the world he [Satan] formed [created] through [because of] Adam's fall. It is the judgment of this Old world the scriptures have in view here in the text [the old ancient systems of this fallen evil world, and, not to the world "the earth" itself]. "Who gave himself for our sins, that he might deliver me/us from this present evil world [from this present evil age]..." (Gal. 1:4). The word *now* in John 12:31 in the GK *means* "at the present time," or, the time presently after the Cross. The reality of Satan's demise is true to this **age** [of Grace]. Paul, calls this "world" of Jn. 12:31, this present world [or, at this present time] (2 Tim. 4:10), "For Demas hath forsaken me, having *loved* this present world [this present time], and is departed..." Here it is clear; Paul is speaking of the old fallen world, the world he [Satan] *formed* through Adam's fall. In Galatians 1:4, the word *might* added by the translators should read, "Who gave himself for our sins, that He delivered us *from* this present evil world [that old fallen age of **sin** and **death** before the Cross]." Again, this is speaking not of the natural world in general "the earth" but to the old ancient systems of men *formed* through demonic influences and interventions. Paul said it this way, "...for the fashion of *this* world [décor-stage settings are] passes away" (1 Cor. 7:31). Here, the word *fashion* means the *external* conditions of this world [is now departing away]. This speaks to the visual and material world of the 5 physical senses [the external realm]. This is best understood being likened to [or compared with] a hanging curtain. The world Satan *formed* and brought into being through Adam's fall is nothing more than a hanging curtain. This hanging *curtain* is now **judged** and **cancelled** at the Cross!!

The **world** he *formed* through Adam's fall is a world of sin, sickness, disease, poverty, and death: the whole **curse** of the Law. The bible tell us, "...the strength of **sin** is the **law**" (1 Cor. 15:56). "...and death [came] by sin" (Rom. 5:12). "For **sin**, taking occasion [opportunity] by the **commandment** [the law], deceived me, and by it slew me" (Rom. 7:11). It is clear from these ***principles*** that Satan used the Law of God in *reverse* to create for himself [to rule over] a fallen [cursed] world. Satan ruled and reigned through Adam's fall!! He [Satan] formed [created] [brought into being] this cursed *world* and ancient evil *systems* of fallen men through the **operations** of this **curse** [of the Law]. We are presently experiencing through our 5 physical *senses* a cursed and fallen visible and material world [which, before the warfare of the Cross, **was once deeply rooted and entrenched in a dark evil spiritual reality and "rouge" authority**]. Now, after the CROSS-the power and control of this evil dark realm and evil rule, *broken*, and banished!! **All that is left is the hanging curtain!!** Christ [because of his death and resurrection, and ascension] is now the new **ruler** [authority] in both heaven and earth (Matt. 28:18). Jesus [on the Cross] defeated Satan by his *atoning* sacrifice, leaving the Evil One with **no legal right** [no legal ground] to rule any longer over men [all humanity] [unless, men, freely give him that right; acceptance of Christ and his Cross defeats Satan and breaks his bondage as a present manifested reality in the lives of those who believe on him] (TENT Page 435). Colossians 2:14-15, tells us, that, Satan's *Armor* [defenses] and *weaponry* [wherein he trusted] is now stripped [from him] all taking place at the Cross. Now at this time [in this present age, and in the future world to come], Satan, has no legal recourse [no way to *appeal* the sentence of destruction and damnation put on him at the Cross]; he is now stripped of all authority to rule the world and men!! His rule today over this [and through this] hanging curtain is nothing more than a pretense!! When men wake up to Christ and Him crucified, and to the **victory** of the Cross-and then **resists** the devil, he has no choice but to flee [in terror] from you, and the authority of that Cross [Christ and him crucified] (James 4:7; 1 Pet. 5:8-9). This hanging curtain of Sin and Death, and all of its byproducts of sicknesses and diseases, poverty, the whole curse, and the like, represents the **former world** before the Cross, and, even the world before the great flood [the old world after the fall of Adam before the great flood and, the old world before Christ's death on the Cross]: that old period of time when Sin and Death once ruled [*through* the good law of God]: where Satan had dominion and, **held**

the title deed of the whole earth. It is *through* Christ's death on the Cross [the warfare of the Cross] where Satan's rule/authority and dominion is now put away, and rolled back by the blood of His Cross [the atonement of JC: the crucified Christ]. Satan used the principles of blessing and cursing, and, the principles of sowing and reaping to his advantage through the use of the good law of God to create for himself a kingdom [a dominion] [a domain of Sin and Death to rule over] (Deut. 28; Gal. 3:13; 6:7-8; Rom. 3:20; 5:12-14, 20; 7:11; 8:2; 1 Cor. 15:56). The curse of the good law of God brings into this world a manifested result; a manifested result of sin, and disobedience to God that brings a curse, where this curse then ushers in the consequences of sin and disobedience, being, sicknesses and disease, poverty, and finally death. Paul makes it very clear: "...**the strength of sin** [to rule in this world and, to reign over fallen men] is found in the **good law of God**" (1 Cor. 15:56). Satan used/uses the good law of God against sinners; Satan rules over fallen men *through* their **sins** and **disobedience** to God's good law. Satan has created for himself **a fallen system of Sin** and **Death** in this world *through* the **blessings** and **cursing** [and the **sowing** and **reaping**] of fallen men. Today's life and world in the visible material earth is the product of fallen men reaping the cursing of all that they have sown [all human suffering in this world is the product of (is as a result of) fallen men reaping the cursing of all that they have sown in disobedience to God's good law, either directly or, indirectly]. Christ came to destroy all the evil plots, plans, tactics, and stratagem of the devil. Not only is the god of this world [the god of this old ancient systems of fallen men we see today] deposed [he no longer holds the right to the title deed of the earth] [even though he is still presently and actively the god of this old world system that is now passing away: this present hanging curtain of sin, sickness and disease, poverty, death, and the whole curse], he, Satan, has lost all legal right/ground to rule in this earthly realm. As well, this old world of Sin and Death [this hanging curtain] is now cancelled: and stripped of its right to rule!! Satan has been conquered [and subdued] and is now under constraint [is now under the control of God's new kingdom rule in the earth] and, is under the present dominion of another, namely, Jesus Christ. Both Satan and, the present fallen creation [this world of Sin and Death] is now subdued!!

This does not *mean* Satan is without tactics and abilities; this is why Paul said, "Lest Satan should get an *advantage* of us: for we are **not ignorant** of his devices" (2 Cor. 2:11). Here the word devices *means* his plan and purposes, or, those things he is **planning** and **doing**. We are not to be ignorant of those things he has purposed and is doing. He is the father of lies!! We battle not against flesh and blood, but, against the vain philosophies [the vain imaginations] of men influenced [and promoted] by these principalities, and powers, and the rulers of the darkness of this present evil world [of the hanging curtain], and a **host** of spiritual wickedness [demonic forces] [demons] operating in the spiritual dimensions of *this* world [the high places of this earthly plain] (Eph. 6:10-18; 2 Cor. 10:3-7a). Satan will try to use *cleaver* and *crafty* devices to deceive [he will use many different deceptive methods/means in order to deceive]; he fashions himself as an angel of light [as a benevolent ruler/dictator] and [he] [Satan] **champions** the many [social, religious, economic, and political] *causes* of this present evil world system (and systems of isms): he, Satan, is behind all the many different social/economic/political [the human justice] causes of liberalism, socialism, rationalism, ritualism, humanism, and every other "ism" that is in this world that seeks to distract from the gospel and, to replace Christ and him crucified as the only true source for true spiritual and moral, physical, social, intellectual, and political emancipation [the gospel of Jesus Christ is the only true freedom for men in all these things]. The bible tells us to take our **stand** against these demonic entities, and too *resist* them: taking the victory by force. The purpose for the whole *armor* of God, is, that we **hold our ground** firmly, completely, and victoriously, by standing on His Word [his promises]. Our battle is not against people; however, we are warring against these dark entities [powers] that influences the thoughts, decisions, and actions of men. God, help us all to see and to understand the true spiritual battle that lay ahead!! (King James Bible Commentary Page 1579).

"Blotting out the *handwriting* of Ordinances against us, which was contrary to us, and took it out of the way, and **nailing** it to His Cross" (Col. 2:14). Here, the word "contrary" *means* enemy or opposed. This *speaks* of the Law of God, as the Standard for Righteousness, as the penalty and judgment that was against us. This is the Law of God as the Arrest Warrant [bench warrant] against us!! There was a [bench] WARRANT out for our ARREST!! The Law of God was our *enemy* [opposed to us] only because we could not keep its precepts and regulations no matter how hard we tried, "Therefore by the deeds of the law there shall no flesh be justified in his sight: for by the law is the knowledge of sin (Rom. 3:20, 28; Gal. 2:16, 3:11, 5:4; Tit. 3:7). The **blood atonement** on the Cross-satisfied the demand for Divine Justice [now pardoning the sinner]. The Law of God with its *decrees* and **demands** was abolished [fulfilled; satisfied] at the Cross!!! The *reason* why many do not appreciate the GOSPEL is that they do not [**sinner** and **saint** alike] [do not] loathe their sins!!!!! They are unimpressed [not impacted] by the gospel, because they are not moved [are unmoved] by their sins!! God help us all!!! When studying Church History, and finding many great **men** and **women** of faith bringing forth the fruits of righteousness, you will find a *deep* appreciation for the **gospel** of His Grace [the Cross]. What was their deep appreciation? They *felt* [was bothered by] and perceived [recognized] their sins!! They desperately *cleaved* to [clung] to the CROSS. Why?? Because, the HS had made them *sensitive* to their own personal sins!! The bible tells us, "...When He [the Holy Spirit] shall come, he will *reprove* [convict] the world of **sin**, and of righteousness, and of [eternal] judgment" (Jn. 16:7-11). This is why many of the great Reformers of the Church had such a **great** and **deep** appreciation for the *gospel* of His Grace [the message of the Cross]. These [the many great saints of old] came to *recognize* the evils of sin [their sins], thus, they came to recognize the **value** [importance] of the gospel of His Grace [the Cross]. "[Christ] having cancelled and blotted out and wiped away the *handwriting* of the note [the bond] with its **legal** decrees and demands which was in force and stood against us [that was hostile to us]. This [note with its regulations, decrees, and demands], He, set aside and cleared completely out of our way by nailing it to [His] Cross" (Amp). When the veil of the temple was **rent** [ripped from top to bottom] at Christ death on the Cross-the **legal age** was thus terminated. He [Christ] erased [blotted out] the legal ordinances that condemned us, *nailing* as it were the **certificate of debt** that was against us, to the Cross. Our DEBTS are cancelled!!! JC defeated all satanic powers that held us captive [bound] under this certificate of debt [legal obligation]. Now, in Him [Christ] we have full and complete emancipation: spirit, soul, and body (Unger's Bible Handbook Page 542). The Law of God had a valid legal claim on us [because of sin], this is why it was contrary to us [or, against us], but, **this bond of indebtedness was nailed to the Cross** and, once-for-all removed. Now, Satan, has no legal recourse against us; his accusations are all nothing but empty words!!!!!!! I do not mean to say that God has done away with the law, just put it in its proper place and function in the kingdom of God. We will say more about this in the second book of this three part series. The law of God is no longer against us; because, we are no longer under the judgment of SIN. The Law of God is not cancelled, in the sense that, it is no longer in force; notwithstanding, for the true born again Christian, the Law of God operates/works on the peripheral. We do not live by the law; we live by the new life that is in Christ, which, the law, communicates, and represents [as its standard]. The word peripheral means, relating to or situated on the edge of something; that which is of secondary or minor importance [to the Christian]. It is marginal, which means, it is **not central** to the Christian faith. The **gospel is what is central** to the Christian faith. The law of God still has a role to play in the Christian Church and in this dispensation of the Grace of God; however, notwithstanding, its role is only marginal or, of secondary importance. As important as the law of God is, it is only of minor importance/significance in comparison **to the power of God** that is inherent in the gospel of Jesus Christ. The law, is, only its shadow; the gospel of his grace is **its embodiment** [of this new life we have/hold in Jesus Christ].

"And having *spoiled* [disarmed] principalities and powers; He [Christ] made a show of them openly, triumphing [having conquered] *over* them [at the Cross]" (Col. 2:15). To show in the GK means *outspoken* and to make public!! This victory and triumph is complete; and, it was all done for us, meaning, we can now walk in power and perpetual victory due to the Cross. Satan and all of his henchmen [demons] were defeated [overcome] at the Cross by Christ's atoning sacrifice; sin was the legal **right** [the legal ground] Satan had to hold all men captive [a prisoner to sin]; with all sin atoned for, he [Satan and his dark forces] no more [no longer] have the legal **right** to hold anyone in bondage [*imprisoned* by the **guilt** and **punishment** for sin] (TENT Page 823). The *word* Principalities in the GK *means* Magistrate: these are **Seats** of Authority. The *word* Powers is the GK word *"exousia"* and *means* authorities. This is best *understood* as "Law and Order." This *speaks* to both Law Makers, and to **those** who enforce those Laws [a legal system of justice and the execution of judgment]. This *speaks* to an entire **governmental system** [to be under a system of control and subjugation] based on the Law of **Sin** and **Death** [the *curse* of the Law]. The whole *world* [and fallen men] were under the entire curse of the Law, and Satan was its enforcer [ruler] (Lk. 4:5-8). What Jesus did at the Cross was to **shut** [shoot] down Satan's entire government system [authority]. This *hanging* curtain [this **world** he *formed* through Adam's **fall**] that once had legal ground to **rule** [hold dominion] over the world of men is now **cancelled** and rendered *useless* and entirely idle. The bible says, "... and the **strength** of SIN is the LAW" (1 Cor. 15:56). "...and **death** [came] by sin; and so death [the judgement for sin] passed upon all men..." (Rom. 5:12). The bible goes on to say, "For until [before] the **law** SIN was in the world: but, **sin** is not *imputed* [counted] when there is no law [sin was counted only after the law came, and yet, it is clear that **sin** and **death** was operating in the world before the law came]" (Rom. 5:13-14). Satan used these *things* [Sin and the

Law] to create/manufacture his fallen world [his system of control and subjugation] to **rule** over all men through the *fear* of death [the fear of eternal punishment]. It is this [world] **dominion** and **rule** Jesus absolutely conquered [subdued; overcame] at the *warfare* of the Cross. This **hanging curtain** is the world of sin, sickness, disease, poverty, and death: the whole *curse* of the Law. Through this *hanging curtain*, which he forged [created, formed] through the *operation* of the CURSE [of the Law], he [Satan] held all men captive [under the authority of this curse] and in bondage too the Law of **sin** and **death**. He [Satan] *ruled* through Adam's authority [after the fall] and subjugated all men through this **curse** [of the Law]. Because of man's sin, Satan was able to use the good **Law** of God against him. Now, because of the Cross-the **power** of *sin* and *death* is now broken, and now Satan can no longer use the good law as a weapon against us. Where the law [because of sin] brought only judgement for sin, which is death, with all of its by-products of sicknesses, diseases, poverty, and the like. It is now, because of the Cross [the redemption that is found in the shed blood of JC] the curse is now reversed, and Satan is now defeated. It is not the good law of God that, **died: it is me**, the old "I" that died: it is the old man in fallen Adam that, has died!!! I died to the law; the law did not die!! The law of God is not done away with: the old man has died and, is now done away with. I died to the law, because, the old man in fallen Adam, has died. The law no longer has a hold on me, because, I am no longer under the judgment of Sin. Why?? Because, I am no longer in fallen Adam: I am now in Jesus Christ a new man. It is very important to remember, the law was added because of transgression [it was added because man sinned]; therefore, the law was given *both* to give fallen men the knowledge of sin, and, as well, to bring them under the judgement of that sin [by the giving of the good law of God]. Now, by the law, sin is defined [and exposed and counted], and now, by that same law of God, all men are now held under the power of its [the Law's] righteous demands [for Justice and Eternal Punishment]. However, it is through the gospel of Jesus Christ the execution of the good law of God in its righteous demands for divine justice is satisfied for us [on our behalf] through the **vicarious death** of JC on the Cross to make atonement. Now, Satan, and his dark forces, can no longer use the law of God against us!! Hallelujah!!!

"...But now *once* in the **end** of the world [age] has He *appeared* to put away sins by the sacrifice of Himself [on the Cross]" (Heb. 9:26). This presents to us the ONE sacrifice [for sins] *sufficient* for all time (Jn. 1:29; 1 Jn. 2:2; Heb. 10:12). This *means* in the GK the entire [whole] completion of an Era, Age, and the [old] World. At the Cross-something died [ended]; at the Resurrection, something was born [reborn] and made NEW. In Hebrews 9:10, Paul called it, "the Time of Reformation." This word reformation *means* to **restore** to a former good state [the time before the fall]. When Peter *spoke* of "...putting us in *remembrance* of these things [the gospel truths]... [That] we might be *established* in the **Present Truth**," in 2 Peter 1:12 (1-12), he was *referring* to this **restored** "Time of Reformation." When Paul wrote Hebrews 9:10, he wrote these *things* [truths] within the context of the Cross (Heb. 9:1-15). There was a World, Era, and Age, Time before the Cross-and now, after the Cross-this Era, Age, Time, and Old World has now [forever] ended!! The word here in Hebrews 9:10 for **reformation** *means* rectification: that is, the correcting, mending, and fixing-setting all things right. It also means *restauration*, which is an Old English spelling for restoration and *means* to restore to a former good state. Now [at the present time] He [God] has **cancelled** the Old World [put an **End** to sin and death] by the *warfare* of His Cross. End in the text *means* entire completion; to make an end of; to complete entirely; consummation [of an Age/Dispensation]. This *means* the Old Period of Time when Sin and Death reigned [ruled] through the good Law of God, is now [put away] cancelled, disannulled, dissolved, abolished, and rolled back [all of this taking place at the moment of/at the Cross]. This is why Paul ask the question, "What shall we say then?? **Is the law sin??** God forbid!!!! The law did not sin, but, Satan used the good law of God against us because of our sin [and sinning]. God, we thank you so very much for the gospel of your grace in the forgiveness of our sins!!! God, we thank you for the power of the shed blood of Jesus Christ that has conquered Sin and Death. The Cross of JC has put an end to the old world of SIN and DEATH: now canceled and disannulled!! Thank God!!

The bible presently speaks of **three realities** accomplished at the Cross: the <u>Time of Reformation</u> [this is the world before the fall restored through the blood of His Cross]; the Times [the periods] of the "Restitution of all things," being consummated [finished] in a **future world** to come where all things will come into an [a final] eternal state [when and where all the promises of God in the Holy Writ (the scriptures) will be fulfilled]. The word <u>restitution</u> *means* **reconstitution** and means to restore again [to constitute again or anew] (this speaks to *both* the overall process of the plan of Salvation throughout the ages <u>past</u> and <u>future</u> as well as to its final closing moments [conclusion] of the plan of Eternal Redemption [the grand finale: the new heavens and the new earth]); and, last but not least the "Times of Refreshing" [that] shall come from the *presence* of the Lord: the present day *reality* of the kingdom of God [the demonstration of God's authority] here setup in the hearts and minds of men who believe the gospel of His Grace [the message of the Cross] (Acts 3:19-21). This is a present day demonstration of power and authority [dominion] over all **natural circumstances**, and demonic supernatural powers [and, **all the by-products of sin and death**]. Praise God!!!

"The Times of Refreshing," is what Paul wrote about in Hebrews 6:4-5, "For it is impossible for those who were <u>once enlightened</u>, and have tasted of the <u>heavenly gift</u> [the New Birth], and were made *partakers* of the Holy Spirit [this speaks of *both* the <u>Baptism</u> (infilling) of the Spirit and, the Walk of the Spirit], and have tasted the good **word** of God [this *speaks* to growing in **grace** and *revelation* knowledge of JC] (2 Pet. 3:18), and the <u>powers</u> (dunamis) [forces; miracles] of the [future] world to come [*experiencing* (and walking in) the **power** of God through <u>signs</u>, <u>wonders</u>, and <u>miracles</u> impacting [affecting; changing] one's character and spiritual service all through faith in the *gospel* of His Grace: through *faith* in his death, burial, and resurrection. We live in this world, and yet, we are not of this world!! A *mature* believer is in the world, but, is not influenced nor affected by this world. Here, the GK word *dunamis* means force, miracles, ability, and strength: this is the **right** [and privilege] of every believer. Every time someone is *healed*, or receives a **break-through** [anything] from the *world* of the spirit [the kingdom of God] this is you and I *drawing* from the powers [the **provision] of the future world** to come. Abraham **believed** God, and, it [His provision] was imputed [counted] [transferred] to him as righteousness [as his legal right] [because of his faith] [and, because of our faith in the gospel of JC]. When we begin to access, by faith, this power and provision of the world to come, we are experiencing those **"times of refreshing"** coming from the very presence of our resurrected living and ascended glorified Lord and Savior [who is seated at the right hand of power making every enemy of the gospel his footstool]. God be praised for the Victory of the Cross!!! Hallelujah!!

"...But now *once* in the **end** of the world [age] has He *appeared* to put away sins by the sacrifice of Himself [at the Cross]" (Heb. 9:26). This *means* in the GK the entire completion of an Era, Age, and the [old] World. At the Cross-something died [ended]; at the Resurrection, something was born [reborn] and made NEW. "And again, when He [God] brought in the First-begotten [Firstborn from the dead] into the world..." (Heb. 1:6). This first begotten is the **firstborn** of a New Creation, bringing forth a New Life, and *ushering* in a New World through the *resurrection* of the dead [where Christ is the first-fruit]. Before the Cross, He [Christ], being the **source** and *power* that created [and upheld] all things. Christ on the Cross-is the *means* by which the Old World ended: and now, by His resurrection, has become the **source** and *power* that upholds, and [has recreated] made all things NEW. Only begotten *refers* to his Incarnation; firstborn [first begotten] *refers* to His resurrection and the New Creation [the New Man, the New Life, and the New World] "that he might be the ***firstborn*** among many brethren" (Rom. 8:29-30). This is Jesus Christ as *both* Creator and Redeemer!!! He [Christ] is the *beginning* [the origin and commencement of the Church] and the first [man] to be *raised* from the dead (to pass from [spiritual] death to [eternal] life) "... the ***firstborn*** of every [new] creature" [the **firstborn** in a brand New Age] (Col. 1:14-22). This is referring to his **resurrected** and **ascended humanity** to the highest place of authority in heaven and on earth. This is the resurrected and glorified **God-man**: the only one of his kind. However, we are [spiritually] reborn into a new kind of person that resembles the same kind [that resembles his kind]. We are not raised as new gods but, we are regenerated to new life [to eternal life] as men conformed to the image of the Son [of God]. This is God, **with us**, and, this is God **in us**. A spiritually regenerated, and soon to be resurrected and glorified triune-man [spirit, soul and body] [raised and glorified after the very same image as the resurrected and glorified God-man]. Praised God. The gospel has birthed us into the new life and new creation. All of this is a foretaste of this glory divine of the **new heaven** and the **new earth.**

"Therefore [so then] if any man be in [engrafted into] Christ, he is a **new creature**: *old things* [the previous moral and spiritual conditions] are all passed away; behold, *all things* are become **new** [the fresh and NEW has come]" (2 Cor. 5:17 KJ/Amp). "Now, if anyone is enfolded into Christ, he has become an entirely new person. **All that is related to the old order has vanished.** Behold, everything is fresh and new [behold, **a new order has come**]. And God has made all things new, and reconciled us to himself..." (2 Cor. 5:17-18a TPT). This *means* the Old is no longer *useable* and everything given to us now is New!! The Old *means* the original things [resulting from the fall], Old Time, the Old Rule, the Old Order of Things, are all passed away [have perished], behold [look on and see] all things are New [this speaks of *freshness* in respect to a New Age]. Behold [look on and see] that behind this hanging CURTAIN there is a New Age begun!!! This is why Paul said, "...We don't focus our attention on what is seen but on what is unseen. For what is seen is temporary, but the **unseen realm** is eternal [the New World Order of New Things] (2 Cor. 4:18 TPT). This includes a new *righteousness*, a new *identity*, and an entirely new *life*: this would include the **powers** of the world to come, and, the good *works* before ordained [or, prepared in advance] for us to walk into: this is a new-<u>mindset</u>. We are made completely NEW by our **union** with Christ and the *indwelling* Holy Spirit (TPT Page 493 *h*). The Old World we see today [the old fallen visible and material realm] (the hanging curtain) ended 2000 years ago when Christ died on that Cross!!!! The Old hanging curtain has lost its power and right to rule!!!! Sin, sickness, disease, poverty, and death, the <u>whole curse</u> has *lost* its power to rule. There is a New Rule, and a New Creation *introduced* into the <u>world</u> and realm of <u>men</u>. It is JC the resurrected and ascended and glorified God-man who RULES and, he, **now rules in this present world**, and in the world to come *through* this New Realm of righteousness that has [already subdued all things] and will [in the future] subdue all things. God be praised!!!

In 2 Corinthians 4:4 Paul said, "In whom the **god** <u>of this world</u> [Satan] has *blinded* the minds of them which *believe* not." When Paul said, "god of this world" he is referring to this **hanging curtain**. Satan still *rules* over this hanging curtain!! This hanging curtain is the *realm* of the fallen systems of fallen men (Lk. 4:5-8). Even though the *powers* of sin, sickness, disease, poverty, and death, the whole **curse** is broken, abolished, abandoned, and banished [at the Cross] many refuse to *believe* the **gospel** of His Grace [the record/testimony of the Cross]. "And there are Three who bear *witness* in the earth, the Spirit, and the <u>water</u> [His baptism; the Word: Eph. 5:26] and **the blood**... [His birth; the Atonement, i.e., "the Cross"] (1 Jn. 5:8). Satan is the god of this fallen world's system of men [the hanging curtain]. He and this hanging curtain is stripped of all power and authority to rule!!!!!! This is the <u>scheduled</u> [appointed] demolition [destruction] of a condemned [vacant] building [stripped of all protection]. The hanging curtain [this present evil world] is already condemn. The condemn **building** [hanging curtain] may **still be present** but it is no longer in charge [has lost its right to rule/operate] (Jn. 12:31-33). We find in the *gospels* [before the Cross], Christ already challenging its [the *fallen* world's] right to rule: it [the hanging curtain] had to bow to the words [rule] of JC. Now, it must bow to **the finished work** of the Cross, and, it must bow to the power of his resurrection. In other words, this fallen world system of fallen men is already conquered and, now, it is occupied territory under the dominion of the kingdom of God [Jesus Christ is Lord]. At the present time it is allowed to function/operate but its time is short; however, it is no longer in charge!! This is why Paul exhorts all believers everywhere to walk in the Spirit; and not to walk after the flesh or, not to walk in agreement with the physical senses that are influenced and deceived by this **hanging curtain of sin**, **sicknesses** and **diseases**, poverty, death, the whole curse. Romans 6:1-14, the believer's victory over Sin and Death, is, an accomplished fact. Romans 6:1-14 is an objective truth; Romans 7:14-25 is a subjective experience. This is where we Christians get it all wrong!!! We look at Romans 7:14-25 as the present truth; and, we look at Romans 6:1-14 as wishful thinking [a distant hope: a hope that is relegated to the future world to come]. This hanging curtain is a liar!!! Our subjective self and our subjective experiences in the body are influenced by the physical senses that are influenced and deceived by this hanging curtain of sin, sicknesses, diseases, poverty, death, the whole curse, and the like. We judge the word of God by our subjective experiences and we force it [the word of God] to bow to how we feel, and see, touch, taste, and smell: instead of judging our subjective self with its subjective experiences by the word of God, and forcing our senses to bow and to obey the word of God. Romans 7:14-25 maybe a true and genuine experience in the life and walk of most Christians; however, it is not the truth, where it concerns our true status and position in Christ Jesus [our spirit baptism into JC: into his death, burial, and resurrection] (Gal. 3:27). Romans 7:14-25 is not the normal Christian life; nor is it the true Christian experience. According to Paul, it is abnormal [Romans 7:14-25 is not a parking lot, but, a drive through]. He, God, never intended for you and me to get stuck in Romans 7:14-25 [if you do not know, Romans 7:14-25 is where Paul explained the believer's experience and struggle with personal sin and the sanctification process]. Romans 6:1-14 is not only an accomplished fact, but as well, it is *both* a past and present evaluation of man in *both* his unredeemed and redeemed state. As an unredeemed sinner: man is dominated by sin and by that fallen human condition: that fallen sinful nature. Now, born again, he has become a new man, now having a new nature, no longer is he bound by Sin and Death. The Christian is now made a ruler over all those things that once ruled him!! Romans 6:1-14 is the present truth; Romans 7:14-25 is simply Paul's failed experiences as a Christian before he came into the knowledge of this positional present truth of the gospel: **his victory in JC as an overcomer** in his own Christian sanctification. Christians will continue to fail, why, because they continue to teach that Romans 7:14-25 is the true present [reality, and genuine] Christian experience, and the normal Christian life. Romans 7:14-25 is not the truth of the gospel; rather, it is a true and genuine real subjective Christian experience for all those who do not know, nor understand the true hope and power in the gospel of JC for the overcoming Christian life [for victorious Christian living] (Rom. 1:16). Why would we ever be ashamed of this gospel? For it is power!!

This hanging curtain is the "...*course* **of this world**, according to the rule of the **prince** [Satan] and power(s) of the **air** [spiritual *wickedness* in the heavenly places [the spiritual realm]" (Eph. 2:2). This pertains to the fact, that, Satan *heads up* the systems of this fallen world. The "course of this world" refers to the fact, that, all *unredeemed* men everywhere order their lives [choices and actions] according to [and, in agreement with] [and within] this *sphere* [world] of **trespasses** and **sins** (TENT Page 785). Paul called it [this hanging curtain] in 2 Cor.10:4, the **strongholds,** arguments, theories, and reasoning's [vain imaginations], and every **proud** and *lofty* thing that sets itself up against the true knowledge of God" (Amp). All these *things* are at work within this fallen world, and are influenced by this fallen world of sin, sickness, disease, poverty, and death, the **whole curse.** "...You were once like corpses, **dead** [slain] in your sins, and offenses. "It wasn't long ago that you once *lived* in the religion [of men], [its] customs, and **values** of this world [walking habitually... following the course and *fashion* of this world, under the sway of this present age], obeying the *dark* ruler of the earthly realm who fills the **atmosphere** with his authority, and works diligently in the *hearts* of those who are disobedient to **the truth** [who have rejected the Cross]." This world [realm] and atmosphere of *sin* and *death* is both in this *present* world, and as well, **occupies** a place [of operation] within the sons of disobedience who are now *presently* in rebellion against the knowledge of the Truth [who are presently in rebellion against the message of the Cross] (Eph. 2:1-3 TPT, Amp). God, help us to see and to understand all these *things* that we might escape its deception: the deception of this hanging curtain perceived by the five physical senses within this sense realm. God, help!!

In Hebrews 2:5 Paul mentions, "...the **world** to come." In Hebrews 6:5, he calls it, "...the **powers** of the world to come." In 1 Corinthians 3:22 Paul calls it, "...or **things** to come." In Ephesians 1:21 Paul calls it, "...**that** which is to come." This speaks to the New Man, the New Life, and to the New World [Order] [the New Creation], that Christ brought into this present Age [of Grace] through His **death** and **Resurrection**. These *things* are a present reality [now here in the earth] though not *naked* to the human eye!!! This is why Paul says, "Fight the *good* fight [contest] of faith..." (1 Tim. 6:12). Paul tells all believers everywhere to lay **hold** upon this **new life**, and to *have* and *hold* it in its abundance (Jn. 10:10; Phil. 3:7-21). Ephesians 6:1-10, reveals the believer's *warfare* in the spirit against these dark forces; the vain **imaginations** [this hanging curtain] that *battles* against us [that is set against us] is the tool [vehicle] [the instrument] of their expression [demons]. The believer [the Christian] is *raised* up and **seated** with Christ in those heavenly place far above all principalities, powers, and thrones [the *rulers* of the dark world of this hanging curtain], and he [Christ] has given us all authority over all the power of the enemy (Eph. 1:17-23, 2:4-5; Lk. 10:19; Matt. 16:18-19). The bible says, "And Jesus came and spake unto them [the disciples], saying, All power [*exousia* "authority"] is given unto me in **heaven** and in **earth** (Matt. 28:18). This is the **authority** [right] Christ exercises over this *present* evil fallen world [the hanging curtain]: an authority

He [Christ] has given the Church [the believer] to *use* in His Name. It is at the Name of Jesus Christ that every knee shall bow, and every tongue shall confess Him [Christ], as Lord over all things in heaven, in earth, and under the earth (Phil. 2:9-11). The kingdom of God is here and now, just *invisible* to the carnal mind and natural man. To those individuals who are **ruled** by their *five* physical senses, this New World [of Jesus Christ] purchased at the Cross is foolishness [impossible] to them [those] who believe not [who have rejected the testimony of the Cross], and, who are in league with Satan. This New World of righteousness, healing and health, prosperity [spiritual, and material if needed], and blessings, and eternal life, and all that pertains to our **inheritance** in Christ Jesus *rules* through this New Life [New Creation] which is found in Christ Jesus [and through faith in him, and he crucified and resurrected]. All [every] spiritual heavenly blessing that are in the spiritual realm are now in Christ Jesus (Eph. 1:3). There is no doubt; this hanging curtain of sin, sickness and disease, poverty, death, which represents **the whole curse** of the law, is now, occupied territory. The kingdom of God now *rules* and *reigns* over this present evil world system of fallen men. Satan may still have a leading role in its everyday execution and operation, however, he, the devil, is a defeated foe, and is conquered, and is now under Christ's authority [is now under constraint]. It is time for you and me to begin to confront and challenge this hanging curtain of sin, sicknesses and diseases, poverty, death, the whole curse, to its right to dominate in this present world!! This is what the bible is referring to when it speaks of you and me experiencing the powers of the/this world to come (Heb. 6:5). We are given authority as the Church of the Lord Jesus Christ, to use his name in the execution of the divine will of God, in order to accomplish his eternal purposes in the earth, today, in this cursed world of sin, sickness, disease, poverty, and death. God, help!!

This **hanging curtain** is like a condemned building scheduled for final destruction!! The Bible speaks of a New Heaven and a New Earth *promised* at the finishing [of the Ages] in Revelation Chapters

21-22 [all these things were first brought forth (those things that are promised) at the resurrection of JC]. Even though its *final* destruction [its final removal] is not appointed until, the time of the end [end of this age], its demise [loss of position and status], and cancellation [loss of all authority to rule] is right now in this **present** time [the Age of Grace]. Paul said, "...God has left nothing outside of the control of his Son, even if **[now]** *presently* **we have yet to see this accomplished.** But we see Jesus... (Who) now is *crowned* with glory and honor because of what he suffered in his death [on the Cross]" (Heb. 2:8-9 TPT). It is clear; we may not **at this time** see the New World, this New Creation that gives us New Life, but we SEE Jesus who *holds* all NEW things now, and the NEW Things to Come in Himself. To God be glory in and through Christ Jesus our Lord and Savior!!! When Paul said, "...much more they which receive abundance of grace and of the gift of righteousness shall reign/rule in [this] life by one, Jesus Christ. The word life here in the GK is the word ZOE. This speaks of spiritual life/eternal life within. "He that *hath* the Son of God *hath* the life [hath the Zoe]" (1 Jn. 5:12). Christ has come that we might have this life, and that we might hold this new life *within* us in its fullness (Jn. 10:10). To have Christ is to have the life; God does not give us eternal life [this new life] apart from giving us JC. If you do not have JC you do not have the new life. This new life is in Christ in me!! We do not look within ourselves, we look away from ourselves to JC, who is in us (Rom. 8:9). We do not look to ourselves; we do not even look within ourselves; we look away from ourselves to Christ and him crucified, and resurrected, and ascended, and glorified. This new life is found in Christ in us!!! It is not in us; it is in Christ who is in us; this is why we must not look to ourselves, nor look within ourselves for the answer; however, we look to JC and what he did on that Cross for us in his death, burial, and resurrection, who is alive and resides within us. Paul called this **"...the treasure [that divine deposit] in the earthen vessel"** (2 Cor. 4:7). This is why Paul said, **"...your life is hid with Christ in God"** (Col. 3:3). Paul, in the text of Romans 5:17 is saying, we rule in this life at this time *through* the new life we have received in JC that now is alive and reside within us, which is Christ's very own obedient and victorious life *through* death and resurrection. Jesus Christ holds all these things promised and provided for us, in himself, in us [the hope of glory] (Col. 1:27). This hanging curtain is **no match** for Christ **in us** [this fallen world is no match for the **new life** *within* us]. Thanks be to God through our Lord Jesus Christ.

God has put us into Christ; this is our hope [expectation] for all those promised *things* [the provisions] that belongs to us [and are contained within us] in Christ Jesus. Through *faith* in his blood, which has redeemed us [delivered us from this present evil world], we have the **right** [privilege] to *believe* for **all** [everything] He earned on that Cross: we have the ***right*** to **receive now**, not just in the world to come. "...Having [the] ***promise*** of the ***life*** that now is [in the present], and of that which is to come" (1 Tim. 4:8). What does he mean by the Life that now is? Paul here is speaking of the **life** that is **now** hid *with* Christ in God in us (Col. 3:3) [that treasure *within* the earthen vessel]. Did not Jesus say, "and *he* that **loses** his *life* [in this world] for **my sake** shall find it" (Matt. 10:39). The promise of Christ is that we will find this life, now *hid* with Christ in God. Faith is the *living* substance [the raw material] for all those *things* we have hope for [His promises: the ***things*** we desire and have need of]; and the **action** of your faith becomes [will become] a living hope and expectation, and as well, the very *thing* [the reality of the very thing] hoped for itself (Heb. 11:1; Mk. 11:22-24). Have the faith of God!! This is the very ***promise*** [and provision] of the new **life** we now have and hold in JC. Why settle for less?? Why waste your time and your whole life on trivial matters?? **God, help us all to press into Jesus Christ!!!!** God help!!

THE MERCY SEAT

If we imagine the entire Church Age as the Book of Joshua; this entire 2000 year *battle* as the conquest of the Land of Promise. If we see this as a spiritual battle [warfare], where the enemy must be <u>dispossessed</u> and <u>removed</u> from the land [removed from all those *promises* given us in Christ Jesus], we will see, it is only a matter of just taking *possession* of all those **promises** by faith. He has no **right** to *rule* or even **occupy** those territories [promises] God has turned over to us, the Church. When Paul speaks of our warfare being against principalities and powers, and rulers of the darkness of this world, and spiritual wickedness in high places, he is calling all believers to **go** and **take** *possession* of the land [to go and take possession of all those promises] by **displacing** the enemy. The word <u>displace</u> *means* to remove from the place of, to drive out, to banish, to expel or force to flee; and, to take the place of or, **to supplant**. These [demonic forces] now occupy [hold] <u>seats</u> [places] where they have lost all authority. The Church is called of God to **teardown** these <u>High Places</u> [demonic forces]. Just as in Joshua, God has given us the victory in JC [by the *blood* of His Cross], however, most, like those who lived during the time of the book of Judges, many believers *fail* to enter in and **dispossess** [displace] the enemy in their lives because of **sin** [Carnality] and <u>unbelief</u> [the lack of knowledge]. The bible tells us to come *boldly* before the **"Throne of Grace"** (Heb. 4:16). It is here; **where the blood [rests] sits as a testimony** to our redemption, and, it is here where we receive the **mercy** necessary to obtain **His favor** in Prayer [in Spiritual Warfare]. The enemy is <u>defeated</u> and stands absolutely *helpless* and *powerless* before the **blood** of His Cross, represented here at the Throne of Grace. God has raised up the Church as a Priesthood of Believers. As Priests [warriors] we *meditate,* right here before **the blood** of Jesus Christ on the Mercy Seat. It is at the Mercy Seat we War!!! The **blood** *sprinkled* on the Mercy Seat guarantees our every Victory!!! This is why Paul when writing to the Corinthian Church said, "For I *resolved* to **know nothing** [else] (to be conscious of nothing else) among you except **JC** [the Messiah] and **Him crucified**" (1 Cor. 2:2 Amp). All these *things* here [that are now here] [those spiritual things] accomplished in the earth [the blessings] [the **promises** of God] are first won [obtained] through Prayer [at the blood on the atonement cover or, the mercy seat] [these things refer to all that Christ has already accomplished for us at the Cross-in his death, burial, and resurrection]. The blood [the payment] is His Life sacrificed [for us] on our behalf for our deliverance and victory!! His very own life offered up for us on the Cross, which becomes our very own Victory, now, here, in the earth, is now, right now, represented by the *blood* on the Atonement Cover [the Mercy Seat]. Here, we are told to come boldly, having *confidence* before God [because of the **blood** of the Covenant]; we now being *outspoken* before God [in the Court of heaven] because of the **words** of the Covenant [the promises in the Covenant] (Heb. 4:16). The blood on the mercy seat [the atonement cover] is His very own life given as a ransom [payment made] for eternal redemption. This blood [the blood of His Cross] is the atonement that satisfied divine justice and provided for divine pardon [reconciliation] [and restored man to divine favor] [just as if he the believer had never sinned, and just as if he the believer had always obeyed]. Praise God. The **mercy seat**, before the Courts of heaven, and before the Throne of God, is our seat at the table!!! Praise Be to God for his unpreceded mercy!!

The bible teaches in the first two chapters of the book Job that, Satan, came into the presence of God before His Throne. Court was in session! There is no doubt, that, when and where God is seated on His Throne [the God who sits in judgement], court is in session. It is safe to assume [I believe all would agree] that, the first two chapters of Job was a courtroom setting. The **accuser** of the brethren had come into court [after having traversed the earth back and forth], to give a report of all his findings about the children of men [for he is the *accuser* of the brethren...which <u>accused them before our God day and night</u>. The word **accused** *means* in the GK, **against one** in the assembly, i.e. a <u>complainant</u> at law (Rev. 12:10). This word here *means* the litigant, which is the one who brings a legal action against another person. The person in a legal proceeding who makes a charge of wrongdoing against another]. There is no doubt; the bible reveals that Satan is called the <u>accuser</u> that is his role, and the <u>devil</u>, which *means* enemy, an adversary, revealing he was and is the enemy of all of humanity [mankind]. His task of going back and forth [to and fro] throughout the earth was his assignment [his task] as the plaintiff [the litigant]. Notice his job [his task] was to **investigate** men and bring them up on *charges* before the Court of heaven [at any time, day and night]. As the god of this world [the ruler over the fallen realm], <u>he had</u> the authority [power over men] [the right] to bring charges and to prosecute them as he saw fit. Some believe Satan no longer has this right [position] to come before God and his throne to accuse the brethren any longer since the Cross. I do not believe this; while it is true, he [Satan], has lost his power [and position] [the right to] as a prosecuting attorney, *meaning*, he [Satan], no longer has the right [power] [authority] **to condemn those [the believers] who are under the blood.** However, he [Satan], still holds the <u>title</u> and the <u>task</u> **as the accuser**; so he [Satan], still comes before the Court in heaven to lay blame. **He has lost his power as a prosecutor, but, he can still accuse and lay blame.** Remember, God, loves men, and Satan hates humankind, so every chance he gets Satan tries to stick it to man!! Why? In order to stick it to God [in order to hurt God]. Satan was competing with God in the book of Job, and, is now still competing with/against God for the right to rule. God, help us to believe!!

The bible says, "Now there was a day when the Sons of God <u>came to present themselves before the Lord</u>, and Satan came also among them [court was now in session]. The word <u>present</u> in the Heb. *means* to come and <u>stand before</u> the Lord [the righteous judge]. He came <u>to</u>

give an account of all his activities upon all the earth; this is why God [the Judge] asked the question, "Where are you coming from? Then Satan began to give an account of all his dealings with the sons of men upon the earth [remember, this accuser is also the **tempter**]. It appears that all the sons of God [the angels] were presenting themselves before the Throne of God [the Courtroom] **to give an account of all their activities** [they were *reporting* to the Court]. The reason why God called Job an **upright** man is that he was justified or, innocent before the Court. He, Satan, had **examined** him [and, **tempted** him] [and examined him again] and could not get Job to sin or compromise his standing before the Court [his faith in God]. Did you hear what I just said?? Satan had no legal recourse, or, found no legal course of action against him!!! Wow!!! However, as the story goes, there was a legal course of action that Satan could not see [he was blind to it], until, God himself, had to tell the truth when addressing Satan [the litigant] in a court of Law [God is always under Oath]. The rest of the story is all ancient history. Thank God, that, in the end *both* God and Job **won out in the courtroom of Heaven.** Job was **exonerated [cleared from all accusation and blame]**; and all that was legally taken from him [that was at first sanctioned] [allowed] [made legal] by the court, now, overturned, by that same court, and Job, was fully restored [acquitted, and declared innocent, and was paid back all that was lost with **punitive** damages; full restitution; he got double for his trouble]. It is God who vindicates!!! When heaven speaks [when heaven commands] the earth and all therein obeys!!! Thanks Be to God!!!

Everyone in the courtroom was **under oath to tell the whole truth** and nothing but the truth so help me God [the very presence of God Himself in the courtroom automatically puts everyone in the courtroom under Oath demanding the whole truth]. Moreover, because God had asked the question, "What about my servant Job? Is he not perfect and upright in *all* his ways? He [God] just legally obligated himself to tell the whole of the matter [the whole truth]. Now, even though Satan after examining Job found no fault in him, and then, began to complain and accuse God of foul play [that the playing field was not even or fair]; God, had no choice, under Oath, but to tell the whole truth about Job's true legal standing before the Court **[that only God was privy to]**. Remember, God said, **he was perfect**, when in fact, he was *guilty* in his heart. Job had a **hidden flaw** that no one could see but him who sat in Judgement upon the Throne. Even though Job did everything right, fear was his constant struggle, "For the thing **which I greatly feared** is come upon me. I was not in safety, neither had I rest, neither was I quiet; yet trouble came" (Job 3:25-26) [he worked very hard religiously before God in obedience to him, and as well in generosity toward his neighbor]. However, despite all this effort of living right [righteous], and being very gracious toward his fellow man, **calamity had befallen him that he himself was hoping to avoid** [the motive behind most of his good works was fear, in the hope of avoiding any if not all calamity]. He was serving not for the love of God, alone, nor even love for his neighbor [alone], but, for the *fear of self-preservation*. This is why none of us is perfect before God; having a **divided heart**, between our trust [confidence] in God [our commitment to God] and, self-preservation [our commitment to ourselves and our own personal survival] [our own personal needs]. Job was actually standing on the outside of the hedge, and the devil could not see it!! So, God just opened the devil's eyes and allowed him to see that Job was already given into his hands. However, God, put the devil under strict discipline, and strict instructions were giving concerning Job's testing. The devil is not **omniscient** [all-knowing], he cannot [see] judge the hearts of men, he [Satan] can only judge [see] men **by their works** [words, deeds, actions, and responses]. You will notice in Job 1:8 that God described Job by four words: Job is **perfect**, **upright**, **fears** God, and **eschewed** evil. The word **upright** is a legal <u>term</u> [word] that *means* **righteous** and pertains to [is used in] a Court of Law. A careful study of the book of Job proves Job to be a very committed [faithful] worshiper. Animal sacrifices were a part of his daily devotions. His *righteousness* before God and the Court in Heaven was based on the *blood* of the atonement [that covered his sins]. No doubt, the hedge of protection Job enjoyed was his legal right [under the Law] [because of the atonement]. He had the legal right to expect the legal protection of the Court [of heaven] because the blood had made him righteous [in good standing with the Court]. The words <u>feared</u> God and <u>eschewed</u> evil in the Hebrew simply *means* he <u>morally obeyed</u> God by <u>removing himself from</u> all evil [things]. The real problem comes in [is] when God introduced Job to the Court as one who was **perfect**!!! This word in the text simply *means* **complete**. Was Job complete? No! Only God Himself knew this. Now under Oath in a courtroom setting the whole truth had to be told. **God now had to allow the devil to see the true condition of Job's faith.** All along Job because of his fear had stepped out from under God's divine protection, for some time now. **The devil did not have the eyes to see it!!!** Now, in the courtroom of heaven the whole truth was out!! The devil immediately took action; but, he, [Satan] **was under divine constraint** [the state of being checked or restricted] [he was now limited]: he was now under the [strict] ORDER of the Court. Why would God, the Lord of Glory, the Righteous Judge of all Creation allow this to happen to Job?? Here, the title LORD in the text is *Yhovah* (yeh-ho-vaw), and it *means* the Eternal and Self-Existent ONE. In Hebrews 12:5-29 the bible says, **"For whom the Lord loves he chastens [or corrects] [brings under discipline]"** (Heb. 12:6). There is no doubt, that, God [the Lord] for some **greater purpose** [or for some **higher good**] that is beyond our immediate understanding, He, God, **was putting Job under discipline.** Just as a loving heavenly Father would do **in training up his child** in the way, he ought to go [remember, **fear is not** the will of God, so God had no choice but to bring the **right** and **proper** correction to His believing son]. The bible says, "For what son is he whom the father chastens not?? But if you are without correction, whereof all are partakers, then are ye **bastards** [illegitimate as sons]" (Heb. 12:7-8). We may not fully understand all that took place in the book of Job, but one thing we do know for sure, all that Job **encountered [experienced]** was under *both* God's **divine providence**, and as well, under God's [the Lord's] loving hand [**loving guidance**]. All of this despite the devil's treachery!!! What *he* [Satan] had **purposed for evil**, God, will work it out for our good (Rom. 8:28; Gen. 50:20). "*...A man whose way is hid [from him], and whom God hath hedged in*" (Job 3:23). Everything Job was going through [the reason why] was hidden from him; but, despite all that the devil was given permission to do [by the Courts], **God hedged Job in** [which means to fence in; to cover over; to come to his defense, and to defend; to shut up and hedge in]. Even though Job was exposed to the enemies attack, God had hedged [fenced] Job in limiting Satan's access to His person. When we look at the restrictions given to Satan limiting his access to Job [his person and his possessions], this is God hedging Job in under His divine protection!!! We know that Job is an extreme case, but, he is the test case for all others being tested [or, is the scriptural example given for all believers experiencing God's divine discipline]. He [Satan] serves God's purposes, and is under the [strict] order of the Court [the Courts of Heaven]. Satan was/is under constraint!!! Satan, has no power and position, today, to operate outside of the Court of heaven. Keep that in mind!!!

The point being made here is the legal proceedings taking place in heaven that will impact, affect, and influence all that goes on in the earth [with men]. Nothing happens on the earth that does not first take place in the Court of Heaven. This is where the Throne of Grace and the **blood** on the Mercy seat [the atonement cover] comes in [Heb. 4:16]. We are told to come boldly before this throne, to find grace and to obtain his mercy in the time of need [not just in our time of need on the earth; but as well, in the time when the Court is in session]. Do not just pray when you go through something, or, just, when you have a need: we need to pray every day because, Court is in session every day. One of the GK word meanings for *boldly* [outspokenness] is to have confidence before God; this confidence is found **in the *blood* of his Cross**-on the atonement cover [the mercy seat]. This blood is the payment made and price paid in the Atonement [of Jesus Christ on the Cross]. Here, God, in Christ Jesus, **has taken away our every guilt and stain** from all our trespasses and sins [transgressions]. All that **we do** and **say**, in prayer [in supplication] before God, this Judgement

Seat, now turned into a Throne of Grace and Mercy Seat because of the **blood** of His Cross: we *do* and *say* all according to and in agreement with the blood [all that the Cross, His Redemptive Works accomplished for us (on our behalf) to make atonement]. We, because of the blood of His Cross are declared **innocent** and are made just [made righteous] [in right standing] before God and before this Court [of Law] [the courtroom in heaven]. The Church [the Christian] is given [and now has] the privilege [the right] to participate in all that happens in heaven in this courtroom setting that will affect all the earth [and all of humanity]. We now have the right to challenge every plot, plan, and plea [and case the devil may bring before this court], to cast it down by bringing into the courtroom the plea of the **blood** [the cry for mercy], that the will of God for the earth and all of mankind might be accomplished and as well established in all the earth, which is His mercy!! This is all made possible by the blood of His Cross [It is in and through Christ's death that *mercy* rejoices against [wins out over] judgment (James 2:13). Divine Justice is now satisfied [finished; fulfilled], now, the Mercy of God can **rejoice** [throw a celebration] in *justifying* the sinner. Our job is to remind the Court of the **blood** that has justified the sinner [and has restored men and the earth back into divine favor]. We are living in the day [time] of salvation; so, we have the right [the authority] to plead for mercy on behalf of the guilty (Rom. 4:13, 16, 23-24; 2 Cor. 6:2; Jn. 3:17). We are a priesthood of believers raised up [and assigned] [tasked] with the responsibility to pray [to make intercession] on behalf of all men and all that happens in the earth. In prayer [in supplication to God] the Church is supposed to come to man's defense [for mercy], in the same way the devil has his task [his assignment] to bring accusations against men. "Who hath reconciled us to himself by JC, and hath given to us the ministry of reconciliation; to wit, that God was in Christ, reconciling the world unto himself, not [imputing, not] counting their sins [trespasses] against them; and hath committed unto us the word [message] of reconciliation [the gospel of our salvation]" (2 Cor. 5:18-20). The ministry of reconciliation is the task of restoring men back to God in the **place of prevailing prayer**, before this Throne of Grace [the Mercy Seat]. The Church is given *both* the **word** [the message] and the **ministry** [service] of reconciliation. This is *prayer* and the *preaching* of the gospel of our Lord Jesus Christ. God help us to pray!! To pray!!! To pray!!!! TO PRAY!!!!! And, to do the work of the Evangelist!!!

"The *effectual* fervent prayer of a righteous man *avails* much" (James 5:16). He is righteous because of the *blood* that has made him **just** [justified] [right standing before God]; his prayer is effectual because he understands how the blood of Christ has bought [purchased] [secured] his right [the power and authority] to stand in this Courtroom in heaven and pled his case for Mercy. This is why [all] everything that comes to pass in *both* heaven and earth takes place where pray is the key to it!! This *means* what happens in heaven and on earth results from our prayers, and as well, what happens in heaven and on the earth is because of our praylessness. Why is this so important, because JC is the Apostle and High Priest of our **profession [confession]**. The word profession here in Hebrews 3:1 *means*, acknowledgement-confession. It comes from another GK word that *means* to confess [or profess], it means, that a confession is made, the giving of thanks, and speaking the promises; to assent to [which means to agree to or to approve of something, to concur or to acquiesce]. He is the Apostle [the one sent for our confession]; the gospel is called the great confession; He is the High Priest, the one who represents our [confession of] faith. Christ is *present* in the courtroom [as our defense attorney, advocate], the one who *represents* our case before the Court [in heaven]. To represent *means* the one who manages, [handles our] legal and business affairs before the Court. He presents his/our case before the Court based on our confession of faith [profession of the Covenant, the promises]; **and based on how we stand on the blood that has made atonement** [that made us just]. The will of God for the NC **priest** is to make intercession for the **mercy** of God to prevail over judgement!!!! "Blessed are the merciful: for they shall obtain mercy," "**Therefore seeing we have this ministry**, as we have received mercy, **we faint not** [GK-we do not fail, in heart]" (Matt. 5:7; 2 Cor. 4:1; James 2:13). The text just before 2 Corinthians 4:1, puts the believer right before God in His presence. No doubt, the mercy of God [the blood] has brought us right into the presence of God, so, we having obtained [received] mercy can be used by God in the place of prevailing prayer to secure that same mercy for others. **Christ is the one who ever lives to make intercession for us right there at the Throne of Grace**. Now, that, we know God has done all of this so we can participate with him [Christ] in His high priestly intercession why would we not be bold to enter in with confidence. This is the *ministry* of reconciliation given to all believers, the place of believing and prevailing prayer!! The throne of Grace is our seat at the table before this court [of heaven, which is in the presence of God, before His Throne]. Thanks be to be to God for Jesus Christ, and he crucified.

In Hebrews 4:16, Paul told us to come *boldly*, this word in the GK *means* we are to have confidence before God, and it as well *means* being outspoken before His Throne. The reason why we can be confident is the **blood** of the Covenant; the reason why we can be outspoken is because of the **words** of the Covenant. Hebrews 10:19 tells us to have **boldness** to enter into the *holiest* [the very presence of God] by the very **blood** of JC. This word boldness is the same GK word as in Hebrews 4:16; we are to enter into God's very own presence having *confidence* because we are trusting in the **blood**, and we are to be *outspoken* [straightforward; freehearted] *meaning* we are to come before God freely using the **words** of the Covenant [we are to **speak the promises and provisions of this Covenant**]. The word *holiest* speaks to the OT Holy of Holies; this is where the Ark of the Covenant was placed in the Old Testament tabernacle [sanctuary]. The Ark of the Covenant is a Throne Seat!! Contained *within* was the two tablets of stone, the Ten Commandments. This made the Ark not just a throne seat, but as well, a judgement seat. Now, in heaven, because of the blood of Jesus Christ sprinkled on the **Judgement seat**, this judgement *seat* is transformed from a place of judgement now **to a place of mercy**. Now, not only do we have legal representation in heaven [through our High Priest JC] but as well we now have **legal access** into the very presence of God [the Courtroom in heaven] *through* the Throne of Grace: we kneeling in prayer right before our Lord seated on the Throne [of his mercy] [the very atonement cover that is situated and placed over the Law of God]: this is the **place** for believing prayer (Eph. 2:4-8). This is the **ministry** of reconciliation, and this **is the place where we participate** in His high priestly intercession. The **shed blood covers** the Law, and now, that same **blood** *covers* the sinner. "Wherefore, holy brethren, partakers of the heavenly calling, consider the Apostle and High Priest of our profession, JC" (Heb. 3:1). *Holy* here speaks to our sanctification [consecration by the blood] into sacred service. This *service* is the call to prevailing prayer. Here, as *priests* of the New Covenant, we **share** in or, we **participate** in [**partner** with] his High Priestly function. The word partaker *means* in the GK to share, participate, and to partner. This is the *heavenly* **calling** that we all participate and share in at the **place** of the Throne of His Grace. The *ministry* of reconciliation is a *heavenly* calling; or rather, **it is a call heavenward to participate in His High Priestly intercession** at the place of believing and prevailing prayer. When looking at the story of Job on the day when Court was in session, we see [find] the **sons** of God [the angels] gathering together to come into His presence before His Throne. You will find according to the testimony of the Apostle Paul in his *epistles* that the Christian [the Church] is called the **sons** of God, and now heirs, and joint-heirs with JC (Gal. 4:5-7; Phil. 2:15; Rom. 8:17). There is no doubt; just as in the days of old when the **sons** of God gathered in one place **to present** themselves before God, today, all Christians are called of God to **present** themselves before the Lord [before the Court in heaven] at the Throne of Grace [at the **place** for *believing* and *prevailing* prayer]. Before the time of the Cross, man had no legal help or representation in the Court of heaven; he had no **legal access** to this Court. Now, through Christ's High Priestly intercession [function] we all now have legal help [representation in the Court of heaven]. Now, because of the **blood** on the Mercy Seat we *now* have **legal access** to heaven by [and through] this Throne of

Grace. It is here, at the Throne of Grace, where *both* His Holiness and His Eternal Redemption is **present** [fixed] in **one place** and in **one person** all at the same time, *forever* [this is Christ our ONE mediator in heaven as our great heavenly high priest]. Thanks be to God *through* JC our LORD!! Christ is *both* the Person of His holiness and the Person of His mercy, meet, [met], in one place, and found in only one person: Christ seated on his throne of glory, as a throne of mercy, and, as a place for securing the grace of God for every need and endeavor of life. Thank be to God for Jesus Christ.

Who qualifies to participate at the Throne of Grace? All who trust in the blood for atonement!! The bible says, "For we have not an high priest which cannot be touched with the ***feelings*** of our **infirmities**" (Heb. 4:15). Then, in the very next text Paul said, "Let us therefore come boldly unto the throne of grace, that we may obtain mercy, and find grace to help in the time of need" (Heb. 4:16). To help who?? Both ourselves and others [those being prayed for] (Heb. 5:1-4). It is while in our **infirmities** [weaknesses] we are to come boldly before the blood on the Mercy Seat. In the GK infirmities mean, weaknesses of both **mind** and **body**; sicknesses [diseases]; malady [physical ailments]; moral frailty; or rather, moral failings. It comes from another GK word that means, strengthlessness, or, without strength; impotent, sick, and weak. The one who qualifies to come boldly before God at the Throne of Grace are the weak, and the sick, and diseased [both physically and emotionally], and those without moral and spiritual strength: who suffer under moral failings!!! All that is needed [necessary] to approach God at the Court [of Heaven] is confidence in the BLOOD. Not only is our great HP JC touched with all our weaknesses and infirmities, the bible says, He [Christ], even *feels* all the pain and sufferings we go through, as we grow through all these struggles. Here in the text, the word feelings mean, to feel sympathy with, i.e. to have compassion for the one who struggles under the weight of his/her infirmity (Matt. 9:36-39). We are to boldly come before the Throne of Grace that we may obtain his mercy, and find the grace [and favor] needed to help us in our time of need. We do this *both* for ourselves, and for others, "[For] the harvest is truly great [plenteous], but the **labors** [the workers] are few [in prayer and evangelism]; Pray ye therefore the Lord of the harvest, that he will send forth labors [workers] into the harvest." This is both the **word** [message/evangelism] and **ministry** [service/prayer] of reconciliation (2 Cor. 5:18-19). It starts in prayer, continues in evangelism, and continues and ends in miracles. When I say, he [JC] is touched with all our weaknesses and infirmities, I mean, he is touched by all the things we are going through as the body of Christ; however, he is no longer personally [or, in his person] touched by infirmities, sins, sicknesses and diseases, poverty, death, the whole curse, and the like. He [Christ] already took all of these things into himself, and with him to the Cross, to cancel and to destroy every evil work of darkness [and to overcome every evil infirmity of the flesh]. In Christ there is only victory; he, in us, only awaits our faith in him, and in his redemptive works on the Cross that has overcome every enemy of our soul. Yes, Jesus Christ, as our great High Priest, is touched in his person with the feelings of all our infirmities; however, in his person, he, Christ, is no longer touched personally and directly by these actual infirmities: he destroyed them!!!

There is absolutely no grounds whatsoever for God to hear our prayers apart from the blood. Whenever we pray to God, we are brought before [the blood] the Throne of Grace. Here, we make our case, and here, we speak the Covenant [we speak the promises], and here, we remind the Court of the blood that **sanctifies** [makes holy]. The bible is not a religious book of do's and don'ts it is a Covenant book; even though it contains principles it is not a religious book of instruction; and, even though the bible gives us many instructions it must be understood and approached as a Covenant book. A Covenant is based on an agreement between two parties that have agreed to equally share what belongs to the other, this is why it is based on promises made one to another. God through Christ has bought us, our very own lives [our very own selves]; this is why he [God] has the right to ask anything of us and from us. We are promised Christ's very own life [all that he is, and all that he has]: everything he earned that now belongs to him through the conquest of the Cross: we have the legal right to ask. This is why, "No man is justified by the deeds of the Law," "For if the inheritance be of the Law [if the blessings came by keeping rules], it is no more of promise: but God gave it to Abraham by the word of promise" (Rom. 3:20; Gal. 3:18). Do you see? Abraham was received not because he kept a rule or obeyed some instruction, he was received because he believed the word of promise, which God could not and would not lie: He would keep His word and do what He said he would do, under the agreement/promise of his word [under the promise of this Covenant]. This is why for Abraham it was **imputed** [counted] to him for righteousness, which was according to his faith [Abraham put his trust in God, and the promise of His Covenant: all his promises]. I want to make this very clear; there is nothing wrong with calling the Bible a religious book of instruction because, it contains principles for instruction. However, notwithstanding, the Bible is a Covenant Book of the highest order, and, must be approach as such **to receive its greatest benefits!!**

HOW MUCH MORE SHALL THE BLOOD OF CHRIST

Jesus Christ is the fulfillment of the Old Covenant redemptive economy; He has come and has fulfilled every *jot* and *tittle* of the Old Covenant Rule of Law. The Blood of JC has put *into* effect forever the Everlasting Covenant that has now restored all creation making all things NEW [perfect]. It is in the person of Jesus Christ we find both *humanity* and *deity* converge!! God and man hanging together on the Cross shedding human blood and pouring out His divine and human life in order to put into effect forever this Everlasting Covenant between God and men. It is a valid Covenant because Jesus Christ is human; it is an Eternal Covenant because Jesus Christ is Divine. The **human** blood of Christ *mingled* with the **Life** of the Everlasting God!! The New Covenant is *signed* and **sealed** in the blood of the God-man who bridged the gap between God and all creation. It is in this unique **union** of the **redemptive action** of the God-man that made reconciliation possible. This New and Better Covenant is between the Eternal God and a resurrected eternal glorified immortal **man** no longer touchable by death!! The blood Covenant we have with God through JC has delivered us out of the hands of the merciless rule of a spiritual outlaw!! The shedding of the *blood* of Jesus Christ has put into effect forever the Everlasting Covenant that has now made all things perfect. The NC between God and Jesus cannot ever be broken this is why there is no longer any curse attached; this explains why this NC is a better covenant based on better promises. We have this hope from God as an anchor for our souls *both* true, sure, and steadfast. We who have fled to him for refuge can take new courage, for we can **hold onto his promises with confidence** and beholding the blood of this New Covenant upon the Mercy Seat [where Jesus Christ is enthrone in heaven]. God Be Praised!!!

The High Priest of that day unwittingly offered up the author of life the Lamb of God on the altar of the Cross: and the blood of the divine-human, God-man flowed purging our sins. The cut of the New Covenant was *both* the **body** of JC and the **heart** of the Father. The covenant that man has with God is a spiritual operation; and the qualification into this New Covenant is the New Birth!! We are made *righteous* in Christ, heirs of the kingdom, and a joint-heir with JC. Now signed and sealed in the **circumcision** of my own heart [the new birth]. There is absolutely without a doubt no curse attached to this New Covenant, because, Jesus Christ bore that curse for me/us on the Cross. When we use the name of Jesus Christ, we are invoking and enforcing our blood covenant rights and privileges with God in and through Jesus Christ. All heaven and earth, and the angels in heaven, are operating in the light of this blood covenant. Nothing is going on in heaven and earth except that this Covenant is the key to it!! This is why we find in the Scriptures that God has magnified His word even above His own name. God's word [covenant] is His bond (Ps.138:2). This has never happened before and will never ever happen again; there can only be one God-man, "There is salvation in no one else! There is no other name under heaven for people to call upon to be saved" (Acts 4:12). The Holy Spirit is come to <u>enforce</u> and to fulfill the New Covenant, every Jot and tittle!! The Holy Spirit will watch-over every **word** [of this Covenant] to perform it!! God will send forth His *angels* to watch over the **words** of this Covenant. Jesus Christ has redeemed us from the curse of the Law [from all the *curses* contained in the Covenant]. The resurrection of the Lord Jesus Christ has become the <u>new pattern</u> that all redeemed men will follow to *newness* **of life** [life eternal] [The Blood Covenant by Kenneth Copland 1980]. We find the same ONE **person** of the Lord Jesus Christ himself *identified* in the ONE Ark of the Covenant. All, or at least most would agree that the Ark in the OT tabernacle *represents* the **person** of Jesus Christ himself. He is both the **Grace** of God [the person of His Grace] [the **blood** on the atonement cover] as well He is seen as the **Law** of God [the **person** of the Word of God] *represented* by the **two tablets of stone**, the Ten Commandments contained *within* the Ark of the Covenant. Here, both the Law and Grace of God are put together **to coexist** [to occupy the same space/place at the same time] at the same one location of the Ark of God that *pictures* both his **Person** [the Law/Word] and **ministry** of JC [the blood] [His Atonement on the Cross]. Christ is both the Law of God and the Grace of God together **personified** [and **embodied** in the ONE person] as seen [pictured; prefigured] in the **ONE** consolidated Ark of the Covenant [to be joined together into a coherent, compact, and unified whole]. The Ark of the Covenant is **one** piece of furniture that represents Christ. In this same one location of the Ark, we find both the Law of God and the Grace of God [the blood] intertwined. This is why right here at the very Throne of Grace where the believer is called of God to make intercession we find both the *presence* of the Holy and Mercies of God. This is why we said, it is here where *both* His Holiness and His Eternal Redemption is **present** [fixed] in **one place** all at the same time, *forever* [this is Christ our ONE mediator] [the Throne of Grace]. It is here, where, we apply the blood for the mercy of God that, we might obtain and attained to His Holy and Righteous character manifested *in* and *through* our lives as true Christians: in our Justification and, in our Christian sanctification. It is here, again, where, *both* the **Law** and **Grace** of God are put together **to coexist** in the same One Person of the Lord Jesus Christ. Praise God!!!

    We said early that, the *key* to our Christian victory can be summed up in *three* words: The **Cross**, Your **Faith**, and The **Holy Spirit**. Salvation is simply *believing* on Christ and looking to the blood that makes atonement. This means that you and I must believe [have faith] in what He did [on the Cross: in his death and resurrection], and we must *accept* it for ourselves on a personal [daily] basis. This means to *accept* Christ as Savior, and to **make** Him Lord of your life. He, Jesus Christ, is the great High Priest that ever lives to make intercession for us right there at the Throne of Grace. It is right there at the Throne of Grace which is **the place for believing** and **prevailing prayer** that we make intercession on behalf of ourselves and others. It is through *faith* in the Cross-that saves, but, it is also necessary to *continue* to put our [trust] in the Cross [the crucified Christ] on a daily basis for Christian victory. This is necessary *both* in our walk with God, and when we pray to God. In order to *live* and *walk* as an overcomer as a believer in and out of prayer we must on a consistent basis trust in the blood of His Cross, and look to that blood on the mercy seat in heaven before the Court [and before the throne of God]. The believer must *constantly* express [put] his faith in the Cross: the Holy Spirit will then provide all the help necessary, in order for victory to be had in every capacity. If we put our trust in the Cross, the HS will always guarantee victory for the believer. The *key* is the Cross, because through the Cross the HS works. The **Cross**-guarantees our victory over the Old life [of fallen Adam]. The Cross guarantees our victory over all the powers of darkness: sin, sicknesses, diseases, poverty, death, the whole curse, and the like. The Cross-is the only *means*, by which the sinner can be saved, and as well, the only *means* by which the Christian can walk in victory; and, it is the only means by which the Christian will ever prevail in believing prayer. Most of the Church understands the Cross, as it *regards* the initial salvation experience [the forgiveness of sins]; but, most Christians have very little knowledge whatsoever as it concerns the part the Cross plays in our victory over sin [living and walking as an overcomer]. Many as well fail to understand the part the Cross plays [the part the blood plays] in prevailing overcoming victorious prayer. Every Christian must understand, that, every single solitary problem we face in this life in the body was addressed by JC at the Cross (Col. 2:14-15). This *means* that for every problem, the Christian should be directed to the Cross. He must understand that the solution is found there and, is found only there. This is what the blood on the mercy seat in heaven represents: the victory of the Cross!!! We come boldly before the throne of grace that we might obtain the mercy of God in our time of need, that which was won at the warfare of the Cross!! The Apostle Paul gave to us the meaning of the New Covenant, which pertains to what Christ did for us on the Cross. So in effect, the *meaning* of the New Covenant is the *meaning* of the Cross. The blood on the atonement cover in heaven points back to the blood of His Cross [and, it points back to the warfare of the Cross] [it points back to the battles fought, and to the battles won, by our Lord and Savior Jesus Christ on the Cross: in his death, burial, and resurrection, and ascension]. The **Cross**-is short for the death, burial, and resurrection of our Lord and Savior Jesus Christ. The Cross without exception must always be the object of our faith as it regards the child of God. The blood on the atonement cover in heaven, which represents and is his blood shed on the Cross, without exception, must always be the object of our faith as it regards believing and prevailing prayer. This is very, very, very important!!!!!!!!!! For the blood is the only basis upon which we are to expect an answer to our prayers!!! The reason that most Christians get into trouble in some way, is, because, they do not understand the Cross **as the source of all their needs met**, and that they must ever have faith [put their trust] in this accomplished fact [the Finished Works] of JC. We are **saved** and **sanctified**, through the *preaching* of the gospel [the message of the Cross] and through faith in the gospel [the Cross], exclusively. The reason why most Christians fail to overcome in the place for believing and prevailing prayer is because they do not place a high enough value on the blood on the mercy seat while in prayer. This *salvation* **of the Cross** is more than just deliverance from sin, and the powers of darkness, but as well, you and I being delivered into something brand new: the full provision of the gospel of JC purchased for us through the blood of His Cross. We have not, because we ask not; and if we do ask, we fail to receive, because we fail to ask *through* faith in His blood on the mercy seat, and *through* faith in the words of the Covenant. In the OT, the Israelite's came out [of Egypt] but failed to enter in [to Canaan]. Salvation will both come *out* and enter *in*!! Not just delivered **out** of something but as well delivered **into** something. This is the correct word picture given to us in the OT that best describes [represents] the NT *gospel* of our Salvation. God did not take us **out** to bring us back **into** what we came out of, "...having *escaped* the corruption that is in the world through lust" (2 Pet. 1:4). "For you have not received the spirit of **bondage** [of slavery; of servitude] again to fear [again to sin]; but you have received the Spirit of Adoption [Son-ship], whereby we cry, Abba, Father" (Rom. 8:15-17). "Who [Christ] gave himself for our sins [on that Cross], that he *might* deliver us from this present evil world, according to the will of God and our Father" (Gal. 1:4). Notice Paul said, "...according to the will of God and our Father." The **mercy seat** as the place for **believing** and **prevailing prayer** is the will of our God, and Father in heaven. How many of us are not present in prayer [missing in action everyday] at the throne of grace, on a daily basis. It is clear; it is the **will** of God that we be **set apart** from sin, and from our old sinful lifestyle. Praise be to God!!! However, it is at the throne of grace [at the mercy seat in prayer] we exercise our faith in the blood that makes atonement on a daily basis. Grace has taught us to live godly, and holy, [set apart] in this present evil world!!! It is at the throne of grace, the mercy seat in heaven, where the blood is sprinkled upon the atonement cover: where we meet God!!! The **mercy seat** is the place of communion [common ground between God and man] [it is the place of/for common union] with God for answered prayer. The blood/the Cross is the **power of this union** between God and men. It is at this place of believing and prevailing prayer [the Throne of Grace], where the blood is set upon the mercy seat, we PRAY, and, PREVAIL with God. God help us to press into Jesus Christ!! God, help us to press into the victory that is our in Christ Jesus!!! Which, the blood on the MC represents.

In Romans 6:19, Paul spoke of the flesh, and its infirmities [the infirmities of the flesh]; before this, Paul spoke of the believer's positional victory in JC in Romans 6:1-14, and Romans 8:2. In Hebrews 4:14-16, Paul said, Jesus Christ is touched with the *feelings* of our infirmities. Paul here is saying, Christ is no longer touched by our actual infirmities directly, because, he already took all these things into himself on the Cross; now, he can no longer be touched by all these things again. In Matthew 8:17, we find a word picture that best describes *both* Hebrews 4:14-16, and Hebrews 5:7-9, this is Jesus Christ, who, under tremendous pressure in the garden before and on the Cross [he sweat great drops of blood: Matthew 26:36-46]: this where he, Christ, was touched with all the actual sins, and struggles, and sufferings in our fallen human nature [all the infirmities of the flesh: the fallen adamic nature]. Matthew 8:17 tells us that, JC took all these things [the infirmities of the flesh] with him to the Cross and, nailed them all there, forever. He took with him to the Cross every sin, sickness and disease, poverty, death, and the whole curse of the law. Now, as a great high priest, who can be touched with the ***feelings*** of all our infirmities that we struggle with in this sanctification process: he understands how very painful it is to take up your Cross, and die; and, to follow this example of death to self in order to follow after him daily as a disciplined follower [as a disciple]. Christ has already done away with all these infirmities of the flesh on the Cross; all that is left for you and I to do is to walk out this victory in our Christian sanctification by simply mortifying or, putting to death the deeds of the flesh. This can be a very painful process for the believer as he/she struggles in their own personal sanctification; however, JC is touched with every painful feeling in this process of our spiritual growth and transformation. Thank God!!!! It is right here at the throne of grace that we petition God for the Spirit's help and power in our own personal sanctification process for spiritual growth and transformation. This blood upon the mercy seat represents the full work of the Cross in our lives, spirit, soul and body. This blood upon the mercy represents our full redemption: our justification, sanctification, and glorification (1 Cor. 1:30). This blood upon the mercy seat represents our full victory over SIN and DEATH; it represents our full victory over everything this fallen human condition has brought into our lives after the fall of Adam. This blood upon the atonement cover in heaven [the mercy seat] represents our full victory over sin, sicknesses and diseases, poverty, death, the whole curse, and the like. This blood upon the mercy seat represents the crucified Christ in his death, burial, and resurrection. It is very clear from the Pauline revelation: THERE IS POWER IN THE BLOOD OF JESUS CHRIST. This same blood upon the mercy seat is the same power of God found in the gospel of JC (Rom. 1:16). This is the same blood that the power of God Himself [the Spirit] works *through* in redeeming, and, in the sanctification of men. To cry out to God on behalf of others upon this mercy seat is to cry out to God for the salvation of sinners; to cry out to God on one's own behalf upon this mercy seat is to cry out to God for one's own personal sanctification [consecration] before God. This same blood of the atonement here, present, upon the mercy seat, has not only **cleansed us** [the believer] from all unrighteousness, it as well purges us from all ungodliness [in our Christian sanctification]. Praise be to God!!! This same blood upon the mercy seat has broken the devils back; it [the blood] [here present upon the mercy seat] has conquered every evil work of Satan upon this planet [planet earth]. Spending time here at this place of common ground between God and men will totally transform the heart [and lives] of all those who believe [and pray] (Lk. 18:1). Hallelujah!! Hallelujah!! God help us to understand this most sacred place: the precious presence of the blood. The mercy seat in heaven where the blood is sprinkled upon the atonement cover is the secret place of the Most High God. This is where we shall abide under the shadow of the Almighty: this is our secret prayer closet [the place for believing and prevailing prayer] (Ps. 91:1-2; James 5:16). The throne of Grace where we find the blood sprinkled upon the mercy seat is where we [will] meet God, and, pray to the Father in secret [and, the Father will hear in secret, and answer] (Matt. 6:6). God, help us to stop, **and pray.**

"...He [Himself] in a similar manner partook of the same [nature], that by [going through] **death** He might bring to [nothing] **[destroy]** and [to] make of no affect *him who had the power of death-that is the devil.* And also that He might deliver and completely set free all those who through the [haunting] fear of death were held in bondage throughout the whole course of their lives" (Heb. 2:14 Amp). The two *terrors* He [Christ] set us free from was the *guilt* of **sin**, and the *fear* of **death**. Now, because of the Blood of His Cross [His death], He [Jesus] completely and totally destroyed all the works of the devil. Here, this GK word destroy means defeated, broken, abolished, and abandoned. Here in the GK it means to **render useless** and **entirely idle**. Satan, his demons, his dominion, and the fallen evil world he *formed* [created] [that we see all around us every day of our lives] all cancelled at the Cross. He was, cast out, ejected, expelled, and **forced out** of his *place* of authority over the earth [his dominion overthrown]; all of this took place at the [warfare of the] Cross [because of the BLOOD of His Cross]. Praise God!!! Jesus Christ came in his first advent to destroy and, to undo all the evil works of Satan [to overthrow and destroy every evil work of the dark powers] [this is *both* to undo all, and, to reverse the curse] (Gal. 3:13). To undo *means* to make it of none [no] effect: to come open or, to come apart, and to reverse [the curse]. To reverse *means* to negate; to undo; loosen; to overthrow; to make void; to turn completely around in *both* position and direction. Paul said, "But is now made manifest by the appearing of our Savior Jesus Christ [through his death on the Cross], **who hath abolished death**, and hath [through his resurrection] brought [new] life and immortality [eternal life] to light through the gospel [it is through the redemptive works of JC on the Cross: in his death, burial, and resurrection, and ascension that the old life and the old man with his old nature ended; and, **a new eternal life in Christ** brought into existence within man, that is, in all who believe]" (2 Tim. 1:10). The warfare of the Cross has already ABOLISHED DEATH. Death where is your STING?? Death, where is your power to hold those who believe the gospel?? Death and Sin have no power over the Christian!! This victory that belongs to the Christian is found in this NEW **LAW of the new spiritual life in Christ Jesus** that has completely **set us free from the power** and operation of SIN and DEATH (Rom. 8:2). Every by product of SIN and DEATH is completely neutralized, and render entirely idle. These byproducts of Sin and Death are, sicknesses and diseases, poverty of every kind, death itself, and the whole Curse of the law. The word *byproduct* means a derivate or, offshoot; something produced through something else; a second, or an unexpected and unintended result. Through Adam's ONE SIN [one transgression] death entered into man and entered into the world; as a result, **this curse of death spread throughout the whole world** *through* further sin, and through sicknesses and diseases, poverty, and the like. All these *things* **have now been overcome** [overthrown] and **undone** [reversed] [canceled] by the blood [and warfare] of His Cross. The word ABOLISHED in the TEXT in the GK means, to be [rendered] entirely idle [useless]; to cease [in authority]; to be brought to nothing [by the power of the HS *through* the redemptive work of the Cross]; to destroy [its works in the earth, and in man]; to deliver [those who believe on the gospel from its everyday active principle and operation in the body]; to loose [its grip on those who put their trust in the Cross and, in the blood for atonement, and who draw from JC's resurrection life and power]. It is here at the throne of grace, because of the presence of the blood upon the mercy seat, we are reminded again, and again, and over, and over, and over again, the warfare of the Cross, and the victory wrought and won by JC in his death, burial, and resurrection, and ascension, over all the powers of darkness [and, over all the evil works of Satan]. In prayer we meet God in this place of victory at the throne of grace, where upon the mercy seat, where the precious blood is sprinkled upon the atonement cover, **we overcome** and, **prevail with God.** This **mercy seat** is the place for making intercession [because of the *presence* of the **blood**] [it is the place for believing and prevailing prayer] for the manifestation of His power and victory in the earth!! Thanks be to God!!!

Even though the *powers* of sin, sickness, disease, poverty, and death, the whole **curse** is broken, abolished, abandoned, and banished [at the Cross] many refuse to *believe* the **gospel** of His Grace [the record/testimony of the Cross]. He [Satan] and this hanging curtain is stripped of all power and authority to rule!!!!!! The hanging curtain [this present evil world] is already condemn. This condemn **building** [the hanging curtain] may **still be present** but it is no longer in charge [it has lost its right to rule/operate] (Jn. 12:31-33). We find in the ***gospels*** [before the Cross], Christ already challenging its [the ***fallen*** world's] right to rule: it [the hanging curtain] had to bow to the words [rule] of JC. Now, it must bow to the finished work of the Cross, and the power of his resurrection. In other words, this fallen world system of fallen men is already conquered and, now it is occupied territory under the dominion of the kingdom of God [Jesus Christ is Lord]. At the present time it is allowed to function/operate but its time is short; however, it is no longer in charge!! This is why Paul exhorts all believers everywhere to walk in the Spirit; and not to walk after the flesh or, in agreement with the physical senses that are influenced and deceived by this **hanging curtain of sin**, **sicknesses** and **disease**, poverty, death, the whole curse. Romans 6:1-14, the believers victory over Sin and Death; is, an accomplished fact. Romans 6:1-14 is an objective truth; Romans 7:14-25 is a subjective experience. This is where we Christians get it all wrong!!! We look at Romans 7:14-25 as the truth; and, we look at Romans 6:1-14 as wishful thinking [a distant hope]. This hanging curtain is a liar!!! Our subjective self and experiences in the body are influenced by the physical senses that are influenced and deceived by this hanging curtain of sin, sicknesses, diseases, poverty, death, the whole curse, and the like. We judge the word of God by our experiences; instead of judging our subjective experiences by the word of God. Romans 7:14-25 maybe a true and genuine experience in the life and walk of most Christians; however, it is not the truth, where it concerns our true status and position in Christ Jesus [our spirit baptism into JC: into his death, burial, and resurrection] (Gal. 3:27). Romans 7:14-25 is not the normal Christian life; or, the true Christian experience. According to Paul, it is abnormal. Romans 6:1-14 is not only an accomplished fact; but as well, it is *both* a past and present evaluation of man in *both* his unredeemed and redeemed state. As an unredeemed sinner; man is dominated by sin and by that fallen human condition: that fallen sinful nature. Now, born again, he has become a new man, now, having a new nature, no longer bound by Sin and Death. The Christian is now made a ruler over all those things that once ruled him!!! Romans 6:1-14 is the truth; Romans

7:14-25 is simply Paul's failed experiences as a Christian before he came to the knowledge of this positional truth of the gospel: **his victory in JC as an overcomer** in his own Christian sanctification. Christians will continue to fail, why, because they continue to teach that Romans 7:14-25 is the true Christian experience, and, the normal Christian life. Romans 7:14-25 is not the truth of the gospel; rather, it is a true real subjective Christian experience for all those who do not know, nor understand, the true hope and power in the gospel of JC (Rom. 1:16). It is impossible to walk after the Spirit apart from time spent here at the throne of grace!!! It is in prayer where we meet God in this place of victory at the throne of grace, where upon the mercy seat, where the precious blood is sprinkled upon the atonement cover, **is where we overcome** and, **prevail with God**. The mercy seat where the blood of JC is sprinkled upon the atonement cover is the place of victory for *believing* and *prevailing* prayer. It is in prayer we prevail and, bring forth into the earth what we have wrought [won] [accomplished] in secret before God at this throne of grace [here, in the presence of the blood]. It is here in prayer, in the presence of the blood, where we are made a ruler over all those things that once ruled us!!!!!! For it is here where we pray in secret; and, it is here where our heavenly Father will reward us openly for all to see [reward us openly in the earth] (Matt. 6:6). The reason why so many live defeated lives in this world is because of *both* the lack of time spent here in the presence of the blood in heaven at the throne of grace and, a wrong understanding and application of the meaning of the gospel. It is here at the throne of grace, in prayer, in the presence of blood, is where **we exchange** this objective truth of our positional status in Christ Jesus as an overcomer, into a subjective reality [experience] in our everyday lives in the here and now!!! It is in secret, in prayer, in the presence of the blood in heaven before his throne, where, we believe God for every promise and, we prevail *through* faith, in secret, that we might be rewarded openly. It is in prayer, in this place of victory, in the presence of the blood, in heaven, we believe, war, press, and supplicate God, worship, and rest: that makes all these things promised by God in his word a reality in the earth. God, help us all to see the connection between the **blood** shed on the Cross and, the **blood** sprinkled upon the mercy seat!! God, help us to see this most precious connection between these gospel works wrought by Christ on the Cross and, the throne of grace where the blood is sprinkled upon the mercy seat in heaven as that place for *believing* and *prevailing* prayer. Help. It is very important to maintain that perfect balance between objective truth and, personal and victorious experiences with that truth.

When Paul said, "…much more they which receive abundance of grace and of the gift of righteousness shall reign/rule in [this] life by one, Jesus Christ. The word <u>life</u> here in the GK is the word ZOE. This speaks of spiritual life/eternal life within. "He that *hath* the Son of God *hath* the life [the Zoe]" (1 Jn. 5:12). Christ has come that we might have this life, and that we might hold this new life *within* us in its fullness (Jn. 10:10). To have Christ is to have the life; God does not give us eternal life [this new life] apart from giving us JC. This new life is in Christ in me!! We do not look to ourselves; we do not even look within ourselves; we look away from ourselves to Christ and to him crucified, and resurrected, and ascended, and glorified. This new life is found in Christ Jesus, in us!!! It is not in us; it is in Christ who is in us; this is why we must not look to ourselves, nor, look within ourselves for the answer; however, we look to JC and what he did on that Cross for us in his death, burial, and resurrection who is alive and resides within us. Paul called this **"…the treasure in the earthen vessel"** (2 Cor. 4:7). This is why Paul said, **"…your life is hid with Christ in God"** (Col. 3:3). Paul in the text of Romans 5:17 is saying, we rule in this life at this time *through* the new life we have received in JC that now is alive and reside within us, which is Christ's very own obedient and victorious life *through* death and resurrection. Jesus Christ holds all these things promised and provided for us, in himself, in us [the hope of glory] (Col. 1:27). The mercy seat is the place where we meet God. It is [the Spirit of] Christ in us that give us the access to this throne of grace in heaven whenever we pray to God. Thank you, dear Lord Jesus, for being our Mercy Seat in heaven!! For being our very own Atonement on the Cross!!! For being our own personal reconciliation with God!! Thanks. We commit ourselves to you; we surrender all to you; we love you, and, we want all of you!!!

BELIEVING AND PREVAILING PRAYER

I would like to say a little bit about spiritual warfare. Jesus stated that, [it is] because of your **unbelief**: if you have **faith**...nothing shall be impossible unto you. Moreover, this kind/type [of encounter] (with demonic forces) depart not except by [the application of] **prayer** and **fasting**. It is here in this text of scripture where we find the **two key weapons of our warfare**. Our victory over the enemy of our soul is **fought** and **won** at the place of the Throne of Grace. It is there at the mercy seat [at the place of **blood**] we war! It is here where we declare the word of God in the place of **believing** and **prevailing** prayer [it is here where we declare the words of the covenant]. It is here, where we, **speak** and **degree** the **promises** of God, and stand [and resist] [and endure]. Paul said, "For **the weapons** of our warfare **are not carnal** [of this world] [nor, of the flesh], but are mighty through God to the pulling down of strong holds (2 Cor. 10:3-6). These spiritual tools and weapons are: **prayer**; **fasting**; the words/**promises** of the covenant (Matt. 17:20-21; 4:4).

I cannot possibly begin to overestimate the value and importance **of a disciplined time of prayer**. One of the most difficult things to do as a Christian, is, **to develop and maintain** a discipline time of **prayer and fasting**. Without which, effectiveness in the place of **believing and prevailing** prayer becomes an absolute impossibility. I am not saying, **without fasting** and, a disciplined **time of prayer**, God, will not answer our prayers; notwithstanding, in order to be effective and successful in our **walk** of the Spirit and **power**, these two weapons of **fasting**, and a disciplined **time of prayer** are essential [are basic] [are necessary] [are indispensable]. In other words, it is impossible to do without **prayer** and **fasting** if you want to be successful/effective in your spiritual battles against the enemy of your soul. Paul said, we are to **pray** with ceasing; and, Jesus said to his disciples, when I am taken away from you, that is when you will **fast** (Luke 5:35 and I Thess. 5:17). To live [and practice] a disciplined life of **fasting** and, to set a specific time of **disciplined** and **persistent prayer**, is paramount [is of the utmost importance]. God, help!!!

In Matthew chapter 26, we find a very interesting and insightful narrative/story taking place in the garden of Gethsemane just before Christ was marched to the Cross. He, Christ, had come to the **place of prayer**, in the garden, asking his closest disciples to <u>watch</u>, and **to pray**. Now, what is most insightful in the text, is, the call or command, **to watch**. We already understand the importance of prayer itself where it concerns our spiritual warfare; however, many underestimate the importance of this call/command to watch, given by Jesus to his disciples in this most critical time. What does it mean, **to watch**; what was Jesus really trying to convey and communicate to his most trusted companions. The word <u>watch</u> in the OE means, **a period of night**, in which one person or one set of persons stand as sentinels. A <u>sentinel</u> is a military term that means a soldier sent to watch or to stand guard: in order to observe the approach of danger, and to give notice to it. A sentinel is a <u>watchman</u>: a person who is set to stand guard against the incoming approach of an enemy. This word <u>watch</u> in the GK means, to be vigilant, **and to stay awake** [to keep a <u>vigil</u>]. It is here, in this text of scripture, where Jesus said, "**tarry** ye here, and **watch** with me." In other words, stand here [stay here], and **stay awake**!! The word <u>vigil</u> means, surveillance: to lookout!! There is no doubt; here, in this text of scripture, Jesus, was simply asking them to stay awake and keep an eye out for anything that may happen in the night; I am going to go a little further in, and pray!! There one and only job was **to stand guard**, and **to watch**, and **to wait**. However, Peter, James, and John fell asleep. All they had to do, was, stay awake, and watch, and **wait!!** This is the key insight into developing and maintaining a disciplined time of persistent and prevailing prayer. We first start by building and maintaining a vigil. A vigil is a set period of time where we discipline ourselves to simply **stay awake**, and **wait on God**. The Prophet Habakkuk, who was a SEER in Old Testament times, said, "I will stand upon my watch, and set me upon the tower, and will watch to see what he [God] will say unto me, and what I shall answer when I am corrected". We find this very important text in Habakkuk 2:1. The word watch here in the Hebrew means, to answer the **call to duty as a sentry** and, **to station oneself upon their post** [which speaks of a specific **time** and **place**]. To stand here, means, to remain, and continue: **to tarry** [and to wait]. The word tower here in the text would suggest **an elevated place**. There is no doubt, here, the prophet was set at his post to stay awake and, to lookout [and, to wait]. The key words that best help us to understand the set goal/purpose in keeping a vigil, is, simply, to stay awake, and wait. The word tarry in Matthew 26:38, means, to stay [remain] here, **and wait**. This speaks to *both* a **place**, and **a time**. In the OE the word *tarry* means **to wait**. The most **important activity** in this time [vigil] is not prayer itself [or, is not what we are saying and doing where it concerns prayer], it this biblical concept of learning how to wait on God. This is not to say we are not praying; but, the focal point is not the pray, but the watch [this concept and principle of waiting on God]. It is important to build and to develop and maintain this disciplined time of pray [of waiting on God]. I am not trying to underestimate the importance of being **skillful in prayer** and, learning how to effectively pray. However, if we learn to develop a set time of disciplined prayer, by simply you and me keeping vigil, it will go a long way in developing the skills necessary in effective prayer.

Now, let's talk about fasting. Jesus said, "This kind goeth not out but by prayer and **fasting**". This word fasting in the GK means, **to abstain** from food. This discipline of fasting is **the twin power** that works in conjunction with prayer. Fasting and prayer together will overcome that, which prayer alone will succumb too. This word succumb means, to lose the determination to oppose something:

to yield to and to accept defeat. Fasting is like a turbo boost to our prayer!! When Jesus said, this kind does not go out except by prayer and fasting, we need to understand and apply this in two distinctive ways. One, to our unbelief; two, to our spiritual warfare. There is no doubt; fasting will directly assault the supernatural realm of dark forces in spiritual battle. It is a key weapon when engaged in spiritual conflict with the enemy of our soul [fasting is also an important spiritual discipline where it concerns every other aspects of Christian ministry]. Notice in Matthew 17:20, their failure was because of unbelief. If they just believed [if they **had faith**] absolutely nothing would be impossible to them. Fasting is not only a spiritual weapon that will directly confront the enemy: it is also a **spiritual discipline** and **tool** used to confront **unbelief!!** Jesus said, "If you can believe, all things are possible to him who believes (Mk. 9:23; Lk. 1:37). "For with God, nothing shall be impossible." Fasting is where our faith in God begins to grow!! Jesus said, "Have the faith of God or, have the God kind of faith" (Mk. 11:22-24). Jesus spoke these things in the context of believing and prevailing prayer, for, whosoever shall say unto this mountain, Be thou removed, and be cast into the sea; and shall not **doubt in his heart** [through unbelief], but shall believe [and, **have faith**], he, shall have the things which he saith. God, help. There is no doubt; fasting is a faith builder!!! Fasting is designed to deliberately and to directly confront all unbelief in our life. Fasting is an unbelief, buster!! An unbelief, destroyer!! Fasting will directly and effectively deal with the **deep seeded roots of unbelief** in the human heart: for, it is with the heart men believe (Rom. 10:10). Thank God, for the spiritual discipline of fasting!!

The fall of man came about by his carnal appetites; today, many are defeated in their spiritual lives because of these same carnal fleshly appetites of the fallen unredeemed body. The problem today, is, our bodily appetites and, our **feeding habits**. Powerlessness is as a direct result of our out-of-control bodily habits of food, drink, sex, sleep, pleasure, entertainment, the improper use of the ear and the eye gate and, improper speech, and thoughts that weaken the Christians resolve to believe, and to stand, and to war, and to resist, and to overcome. What we find in Matthew 17, is, this fundamental rule and key principle [true standard] for the overcoming Christian faith that, applies the **principles** of biblical **abstinence** to every bodily appetite (1 Cor. 9:24-27). Paul said, "[these] [those who are sense-ruled] are enemies of the Cross of Christ: whose end is destruction, whose God is their **belly** and, who **mind** earthly things [those who set their mind on material and worldly things] [those who set their heart on things that pertain to the body] (Phil. 3:19). The bible speaks of that conflict between the **law of sin**, and, the **law of the mind** (Rom. 7:23). The law of sin operates/works *within* the bodily appetites of our fallen flesh; notwithstanding, the law of the mind will either work in conjunction with this unredeemed outward man or, it will desire/choose and long for the law of God after the redeemed and renewed inward man. Fasting is a very potent force/discipline that will directly confront and subjugate/subdue every **carnal** appetite and desire of the flesh. In Romans 12:1-2, Paul said, <u>present</u> your body to God a living sacrifice, then, Paul, goes on to explain how this is to be accomplished, by, the **renewing** of the **mind**. We know that the **word of God** is the key discipline where it concerns the **renewing** of the mind; nevertheless, fasting, which is a direct assault on our carnal appetites, helps, in the presentation of our body to God. Fasting and prayer in conjunction with the word of God, will bring that body under spiritual discipline in obedience to God. Fasting has proven to be a preventative of failing faith, and, a cure for unbelief. Fasting is a faith builder and, a destroyer of unbelief!! Fasting will cause us to come face to face with our own personal unbelief. Unbelief may not seem that significant/important to those who are unacquainted with fasting; however, unbelief is a very formidable foe!! When we start to fast, little by little, the presence of unbelief is detected. Over many days of fasting, the very **presence of unbelief** *within* the life and faith of the Christian becomes **quite acute**. Acute means, perceptive, sensitive, and able to sense the slightest impressions and differences taking place within our faith. Unbelief is at war with our faith: unbelief will attack our faith. **Fasting** will attack our unbelief and, help to rebuild our faith. We must see unbelief as an evil enemy!! If we see unbelief as an evil enemy, we will endeavor to apply the principles of fasting for victory. **Fasting** has so much in common with <u>faith</u>. It [fasting] likes the very same things that faith likes; it [fasting] even disregards and entirely ignores the very same things **that faith does**. So mutual are the things they have in common, that, faith becomes far more efficient, active, and developed when this great ally comes to the assistance of faith. Faith's fight is the Spirit's fight!! Faith's fight is against the five physical senses of the carnal appetites. Fasting is faith's most powerful ally!! Fasting is such a powerful weapon against carnality and unbelief that, it actually hates our physical senses, and, seeks to overcome them in obedience to God. The **senses** oppose fasting and, **fasting** opposes the senses. When we fast for any real length of time, the flesh/the carnal appetites are arrested, then, and only then, carnality is compelled to yield and bow to faith. When this done, unbelief is destroyed!! The physical senses are the seat of all that is natural, and, is the centerpiece for unbelief. The physical senses/the carnal appetites must be brought under control!! Fasting will help you to get all these things under your control [and, **under the control of faith**]. The carnal appetites of the flesh are a major stronghold used by the enemy of our soul to subdue the Christian, and to subjugate them [and, to relegate them] to a weakened spiritual state. Fasting is a power/a force that will restore the believer to their rightful place of authority over the physical body. This is why Paul would say, "But I keep under my body [which means, I stay on top of my body in order to make it my slave], and bring it into subjection [to me] [that I might present it to God a living sacrifice in sacred service]" (1 Cor. 9:27; Rom. 12:1) [fasting by Rev. Franklin Hall chapter one and two: the book, Because of your Unbelief]. The victory of the Cross and the power of the blood that makes atonement sprinkled upon the mercy seat has secured every provision needed to succeed in this life, and to overcome every enemy of our soul. The Spiritual tools/weapons of **Prayer, fasting**, and the **words**/promises of the Covenant, are given to us to be used in this sanctification process that we might fully realize this promised overcoming life [this, victorious Christian living]. Help.

IN SUMMARY

In Conclusion, the power is found in the preaching of the Cross. In the Cross is found both the *wisdom* and *power* [ability] of God. The preaching of the Cross is the preaching of Christ, and Him crucified (1 Cor. 1:18, 24, 2:2). The preaching of the *gospel* is the preaching of the Cross. The **gospel**-Cross is His death, burial, and resurrection. The preaching of the Cross-to the **saved** [the believer] it is the power [dunamis] of God. In Romans 1:16, the *gospel* [the Cross] it is called the [dunamis] **power** of God unto **Salvation** [deliverance, healing, and wholeness] for all those who believe. The power "dunamis" here speaks of the HS at work in and through the Cross, "But ye shall receive power [dunamis] after the HS is come upon you" (Act. 1:8). Paul said, "For I determined not to know anything among you, except Jesus Christ, and him crucified...And my **speech** and my **preaching** [Christ and Him crucified] was not with enticing words of man's wisdom [strength], but in **demonstration of the Spirit and of power** [dunamis]" (1 Cor. 2:2, 4). It is clear from this text and many others that, the HS will work only through the **preaching** and **promoting** of the Cross!!!! The *power* and *wisdom* of the Cross [will bring the manifestations of the HS, and] is found in this Divine Exchange, which the bible calls Imputation. **Imputation** is a divine transfer [transaction]; which, must be reckon to be so, counted as done and concluded as such. The word **exchange** simply *means* to receive something in return for something given. The word *reckon*, or to *count* it as, or to *impute* are interchangeable terms. The bible says, "Abraham *believed* God and it was *counted* unto him for righteousness" (Rom. 4:3). James said it this way, "Abraham *believed* God and it was **imputed** unto him for righteousness" (James 2:23). In Romans 4:22-24, Paul continues with this theme of imputation, "...therefore it was **imputed** to him for righteousness. Now it was not written for his sake alone, that it was *imputed* to him; but for us also, to whom it shall be **imputed**, if we *believe* on him that raised up Jesus our Lord from the dead." Paul said in 2 Corinthians 5:18-19, "And all things are of God, who hath *reconciled* us to himself by Jesus Christ...to wit, that God was in Christ, reconciling the world unto himself, not **imputing** their trespasses unto them." We find here in each place the same GK word *logizomai* and it means, to conclude, impute, count, and to reckon. There is no doubt; **imputation** must be understood as a Divine Exchange, and reckoned [counted] as such, as a Divine transaction. The Cross [His death; the Atonement] is a Divine Transaction!! The word transaction *means* a [legal] matter, undertaking, proceeding, and action; it is the *performance* of something [some deed]. **Atonement** [His Cross] is the [work] action or performance of Eternal Redemption [Eternal Reconciliation]. To be under the *law* means to be under command [the commandments]; to be under **grace** *means* to be under [a] **promise**. A command [commandments] is what we have to do; promise [promises] is what he has done for us on our behalf [and, what he will do]. The HS will not respond to the *first*, but, he will respond to our faith in the *second* [the promise]. An example of how the New Covenants works, "For you are bought with a price, so glorify God in your *body* and spirit" (1 Cor. 6:20). Many look at this as a *command*, something we have to do, but, it is a *promise* something he has already provided for in JC. This is a fruit: not a work [labor]!! The purpose of God for the indwelling presence of the HS is to accomplish His purpose in fulfilling His promises. Bearing/producing the fruits of a changed life is the work of the HS *within* the life of the believer. It is never the works [or, the labor] of men but, the work of God that *reproduces* the life of Christ. We will say more on this subject when we get to Christian sanctification. I'm not saying we do not have anything to do, but, everything we do in the sanctification process must be a consorted [and cooperative] effort between the believer and the HS. There are *six* words that help us to see and understand the operation of His grace: **Person, purpose, provision, promise, power,** and **presence**. His grace is all about ONE Person [Jesus Christ]; he saved us according to His own purpose and grace that is found only in JC. The provision of his grace [the gospel] and all that he has accomplished for us is found in this ONE **Person** in agreement with His **divine eternal** *purposes*. All the promises of God are given to us in order to **form Christ *in* us** that we might be **conformed to the image** of his Son [his *person*; his will and purposes]. The power of God is given to us to make all these things possible; the presence of God is *both* His indwelling within, and, it is the **outward change** and **manifestation of all His** *promises* and eternal *purposes* found in the ONE Person of Jesus Christ, in us, bearing its external fruit "[For] by *him* all things exist/consist [in *both* creation and redemption], that, in all things *he* might have the preeminence [that in all things He might be both the *first* and the *last*]" (Col. 17-18). God Be Praised!!!

The Cross is both the **wisdom** and power/ability of God. The Cross/Gospel is a knowledge and understanding that must be applied by faith. We cannot believe for what we do not first have a proper knowledge and understanding of. We comprehend before we apprehend. We comprehend in the spirit, and then, we apprehend in this world. The preaching of the Cross is the power/ability of God ***unto*** us which are saved; here, in this text, we find Paul applying the Cross-in the present tense (1 Cor. 1:18, 23-24). Paul said, my speech and my *preaching* of Christ and **Him crucified** came with the demonstration and **power** of the Spirit (1 Cor. 2:2, 4). This is the same GK word *dunamis* used as well in 1 Corinthians 1:18, and in Romans 1:16; and, it *means* it is through the preaching of the Cross the HS will manifest His **presence, power,** and **provision** [in Christ]. It is clear from this text that the HS will work only through the ***promoting*** of the Cross [faith in the Cross]. Paul said, that, the gospel/the Cross-is the power [dumamis] of God ***unto*** Salvation. Here, the word unto in the GK *means* **into** or to **enter into**. What do we enter into? The word salvation comes from the same GK word cluster: *sozo, soter,* and *soteria*. Here, Paul is referring to our salvation as being, *first* deliverance, *second* healing, and *third* wholeness or, soundness. It enters into deliverance and *moves* to healing, and then, its *works* toward wholeness or soundness. You come out of where you have been, and, you move toward God and His fullness. Here it is the GK word *eis* and is pronounced *ice*. The OT word *picture* [the OT image] that best describes and helps us to see and understand what true NT salvation really is, is, found in the book of Exodus. This is the story of Moses and the Exodus. We are brought *out of* Egypt, first, and then, we are brought *into* Canaan. We go **from deliverance**, and then, we are eventually **brought into wholeness** or soundness, which means, to be filled or made full [complete]. We are delivered out, that, we might be brought in!!! He delivered us out for one purpose and one purpose alone: **to bring us into fulness**. This is why Paul said in 2 Tim. 1:9-10, "(He) who hath *saved* us, and *called* us with a **holy** calling, not according to our works, but according to his **own purpose** and *grace*, which was given us in Christ Jesus before the world began, but is now *manifest* by the appearing of our Savior Jesus Christ, he, who hath **brought life** and **immortality** to light through the gospel [the preaching of the Cross]." Notice, not just His grace, but as well, His very own purpose!! God by His **grace** *delivered* the children of Israel out of Egypt, but, it was not until it was time for them to enter into Canaan. The children of Israel waited 430 years until it was time for God to keep His promise to Abraham in Genesis 15:1-21/Exodus 12:40-42. God let them **remain** [stay] in Egypt unto it was time to enter into the promise. The whole point of salvation is you and I entering into what God has promised and provided for in Christ Jesus. God's very own *purpose* for delivering Israel out of Egypt was the Promised Land. You cannot and must never divorce His **grace** from His **purpose**!! Many want to be *free* and delivered out of the bondage of Egypt but, they do not want to leave Egypt behind. Many **want the forgiveness of/for sins**, but they do not want to come out of sin!! This is a spiritual counterfeit!!! The only reason God will ever bring us out is to bring us in!!! Or else, He will just leave us there until we are ready to enter in to what God has promised. I am not saying we arrive, immediately; that is not the point, but, the decision or commitment made, to leave behind all and abandon ourselves to God and, to what He has promised us, and, to what he has provided for us in JC: without this, ours is a counterfeit faith, a counterfeit gospel, and a counterfeit conversion. God Help!!

Faith *means* to put one's personal trust and self-reliance upon Him. Faith becomes the hand that reaches out to take hold of Christ. The *hand* must be empty to be useful! It cannot be Law mingled with Grace. Faith plus Self!! One must entirely abandon themselves over to the Grace of God [the gospel of Jesus Christ] and, the sanctifying and perfecting work of the Spirit of Christ *within* to have any real spiritual success. <u>Faith</u> [is the action of the human heart] (Rom. 10:10) [and] is when your heart *sees* the **light** even when **your natural eyes and understanding sees** only darkness. All efforts by the believer must be by faith. This faith must work in conjunction with [in cooperation with] the work [action/operation] of His Grace from within. Jesus Christ [his person] is the object of our faith. **Christianity is not a doctrine, but a <u>faith</u>!!** It contains **doctrines** but, it is a faith, and, this **faith** [this trust] is in the *person* of the Lord and Savior JC and in his redemptive *works* on the Cross. Grace saves us, through faith; it is the gift of God (Eph. 2:8-9). Grace, is the first action, and, **faith**, is its corresponding action. It is not the second action that *saves*, but the first; the second action only appropriates what the first action provides. This means, it is through the second action "faith" that men [the believer] is able to *access* what the first action [grace] provides. This means Grace is the *gift* of God!! This **gift** of God is the ***gospel*** of his Grace. The **Cross** of Christ is the <u>Gospel</u> of his <u>Grace</u>. What his sacrificial death [and, subsequent resurrection] provides [and has accomplished] on our behalf on the Cross, and in the Grave, has become the very gift of God. Faith is the required *response* to receive what **grace** provides: this is only possible by the *Justifying* and *Sanctifying* work of the Spirit of Grace [the Holy Spirit]. Salvation is not a work of man but a supernatural work of God on behalf of man [Lk. 18:26-27]. We are to trust [believe] in JC alone for our Salvation [justification] and Sanctification. **The very same** *grace* that **justifies** the sinner, is, the very same *grace* that **sanctifies the believer.** The very same *power* [and grace] that saves, is, the very same *power* [and grace] that consecrates [that sanctifies]. The same grace that saves is the same grace we live by everyday of our lives, [for] the life I now live in this flesh [my body] I [now] live by the *faith* of the Son of God [by Christ and His Grace] (Gal. 2:20). Paul said, "*… and we have [put] no confidence in the flesh* [in one's own self-efforts]" (Phil. 3:3). **Mercy** is you and I not receiving what we deserve [what we have earned through our sinning], namely, the punishment [and penalty] for our sins; **Grace** is you and I receiving what is undeserved. Grace is you and me receiving redemption/atonement [the *provision* for justification and *power* for sanctification]. If we have received something from God [by his Grace] in our salvation, then, how is it possible for men who claim the gospel for salvation **to remain** [to be left] **unchanged?** This is a spiritual counterfeit. I believe too many take all these things for granted. We simply claim the forgiveness of sins as if that is all the gospel of JC entails. We claim salvation [we claim justification], but, at the same time, **reject sanctification**, as if this is acceptable to God. God, help!!

PART ONE

ATONEMENT

*Man is a sinner who is unable to pay his <u>debts</u>. He is a criminal, and a lawbreaker!!

*The Cross is where <u>payment</u> [satisfaction] was made to make reconciliation in order to restore fellowship [communion] between God and man.

***Atonement** was made to both *satisfy* the <u>sinners</u> need for forgiven, and to *satisfy* the demand for <u>Divine Justice</u> [which requires punishment for Sin, and sins].

***Atonement** is made to satisfy divine justice, and, to pardon sins [to appease the wrath of God against sinners, "...being now *justified* by his blood, we shall be <u>saved</u> **from wrath** (eternal separation/eternal judgment) through him] (Rom. 5:9).

***Mercy** [and forgiveness] is impossible, and, is only legal [lawful] if Divine Justice is first *satisfied* [and paid in full], [this is a finished work] [*both* **Justice** and **Justification** are accomplished together in the redemptive work of the Cross].

*Our legal <u>Redemption</u> [the payment made] is *both* a **substitution** and **satisfaction.**

*This means, paid in full, to satisfy a debt, the punishment for a crime: all of this is done on behalf of another: the **Just** for the **unjust**;

the Godly for the ungodly [this is a vicarious (substitutionary) sacrifice for sins].

* <u>Substitutionary</u> work *means* substitute: to stand in the place of another [to take the place of another].

***Atonement** *means* <u>Satisfaction</u>-He satisfied the demand for Divine Justice, and at the same time, He [God] provided mercy/forgiveness for the sinner, for his/her <u>Justification</u>: to be acquitted, to be cleared of all guilt: to pardon or, to forgive sins.

*There is no <u>Justification</u> where there is no [where there is not, first,] <u>Justice</u> [divine punishment for sins].

*"...that He might be [the] ***Just*** and the ***Justifier*** of those who *believe* on him" (Rom. 3:26). It is all about the <u>Justice</u> and <u>Mercy</u> of God. God by virtue of the Cross [because of the Cross] [the Atonement], He, God, can now maintain His own divine Justice, and yet, at the same time, He can as well demonstrate His Mercy [toward the sinner for the forgiveness of his/her sins].

*On the Cross, Christ *both* **expiated** sin, and at the same time, **propitiated** God.

***Expiation** *means* to <u>remove</u> the guilt [to cancel sin], through the payment of some debt [to pay the penalty for a crime] [the blood of JC was the payment made for reconciliation between God and men].

***Propitiation** *means* to <u>appease</u> the wrath of God [Rom. 5:9]. To <u>placate</u> God in order to restore men to divine favor [which the bible calls reconciliation]. Praise be to God!!!

*To **placate** *means* to <u>conciliate</u> [which means to overcome the hostility] in order to regain the good will [and favor] of another. To **appease** the wrath of God *means* to <u>satisfy</u> God-to meet the **demand** of God **for Justice** [required for justification]. God in sending his own Son was placating His own wrath [against Sin, and Sinners].

*The gospel of Jesus Christ is the Godly dying for the ungodly, the Just dying for the unjust. God is [the] Just, and the Mediator [Christ] is Just, is the Just, and, is reconciling an unjust people back to God by the work of the/his Cross.

*His death on the Cross-is a **Ransom**: a payment made to secure the release of a hostage or [a] captive. Christ releases the captives by paying a ransom: this is called Redemption-the **Redeemer** is the one who pays the ransom. His [Christ's] very own blood is the payment!!!

*His death has taken care of my punishment; His Life has taken care of my reward.

This redemption is possible only by the Blood of His Cross. This word in the GK *means* to ransom. A purchase price had to be paid!! The blood of Jesus Christ shed on that Cross-was the price [the cost] that purchased our redemption. This purchase price [the Blood] redeemed us from God's Just and Holy Wrath. This is why we find Paul using the word propitiation. This word *means* to appease wrath [to placate] in order to restore [man/the believer] [back] to divine favor. His Blood, sprinkled on the Mercy Seat in heaven, indicated that the righteous judgment of the Law of God had been executed [to impose a judicial punishment]. This changed the Judgment Seat into a Mercy Seat, and now a Throne of Grace and a place of/for communion [common ground] between God and man [the sinner]. To justify is to declare that the claim of Divine Justice had been fully met [satisfied]. Christ on that Cross-satisfied the demand of God's Divine Standard for Justice [for Justification and Redemption]. This is why Paul said, "...that he [God] might be Just, and the Justifier of him which believes in Jesus" (Rom. 3:26). His [Christ] death on that Cross-completely and perfectly satisfied the Justice of God [the penalty and judgment for sin fully paid by him]. God presented Jesus as the *sacrifice* of Atonement through faith in his blood [as the One who would turn away God's wrath by taking away sin]. Atonement by necessity would than include both His Divine Justice and our Justification. God is the One who presented Christ as the Atoning Sacrifice, and the Father is the one who initiated the whole plan of Salvation. The Father provided the *sacrifice* of his Son to satisfy his divine justice and appease his own wrath. Justice will always come before Justification!! The very same Blood that satisfied Divine Justice becomes the very same blood that *expiates* Sin [which means, to, amend for sin, and/or, put an end to sin]. The Blood of Christ is an Eternal Force [and power] ever living to make intercession for us at the Throne of Grace. It is by the Blood of Jesus Christ, we, obtain his mercy!! We have peace with God, through faith, in his Blood!! The NT Atonement [the blood] is the basis [the foundation] upon which all the *promises* of God for forgiveness and blessings are forged and founded. The Cross [of Christ] is the very centerpiece for all Justice and Redemption. Now that [His] Divine Justice is satisfied, God, can deal with us [the sinner and believer, alike] according to His Divine Mercy, and Grace. Thanks Be To God!!!

God through Christ's death has done away with all our transgressions. Now, that His Divine Justice is satisfied, God can extend His Divine Mercy. It is in and through Christ's death that *mercy* rejoices against [wins out over] judgment (James 2:13). We cannot and must not exalt Mercy at the expense of His Justice!! Divine Justice must be satisfied *first* before Mercy can rejoice in justifying the sinner, "...and without the shedding of [His] blood there is no remission [forgiveness of/for sins]" (Heb. 9:22; Rev. 1:5 TPT). All forgiveness and all blessings [the benefits of his grace] flow out of the gospel of His Grace. This [the Cross] has become the very ground for our justification and reconciliation [restoration to divine favor]. A very brilliant man, and Scholar, once said, Socrates said, in 500BC, "It may be, that, Deity, can forgive sins, but, I cannot see how." The real question at hand, is, "how can **Justice** and **mercy** *occupy* the same **space** [and, the same place] at the same **time** and in the same relationship? This is an absolute impossibility!! If justice is rightly applied, then, **mercy** [pardon] [forgiveness] has to be utterly rejected; if mercy is applied, then, **justice** would have to be compromised [and violated]. These two concepts [these truths] cannot be applied at the same time in the same relationship. Nevertheless, notwithstanding, this impossibility is now made possible in the Atonement [in the blood of His Cross]. In Christ Jesus, and, in the atonement, *both* the Justice of God and Mercy of God *meet* [converge] and are made *to cooperate* [are made to work together] in a ministry of Reconciliation. It is in this unique union of the redemptive action of the God-man that made reconciliation possible. The New Covenant was signed and sealed in the blood of the Atoning Sacrifice [of the God-man] that [who] bridged the gap between God and the sinner. It is in Christ on the Cross-as both the *spotless* [unblemished] lamb [the sinless Christ as the perfect sin-offering] to make atonement [to reconcile sinners]; and yet, in this very same redemptive action he was made **to be sin** [a sinner] for us on the Cross in order to punish sins and to satisfy Divine Justice. Christ in the Atonement was *both* sinless and sinner!!! This sounds contradictory, but, it is rather a divine mystery!!! How could Jesus Christ in the Atonement be both **sinless** and *sinner*?? While this is true in the very same relationship [meaning, in the same one redemptive work, or, in the same one atonement], this does not take place [nor happen] at the same time. Christ in the Atonement was *first* offered up as the sinless spotless lamb of God to take away the sins of the world; then, *secondly* God the Father, then, **put his hands on Christ** [functioning like the High Priest on the Day of Atonement] to *transfer* the **sins** of the whole world upon him [Christ] for judgement [for punishment]. The Day of Atonement best *illustrates* this concept [truth] of the Atoning Victim fulfilling two important functions, where the **two Goats** *chosen* in Leviticus 16 are a *shadow* that prefigured Christ's very own work on the Cross as both **sinless** and *sinner*. "And he shall take...**two** kids of the **goats for a sin offering**... and he shall take the two goats, and present them before the Lord...and Aaron shall cast lots upon the two goats; **one lot for the Lord**, and, the **other lot for the scapegoat**. And Aaron shall bring the goat upon which the Lord's lot fell, and offer him for a sin offering. But the goat, on which the lot fell to be the scapegoat, shall be presented alive before the Lord, **to make an atonement *with* him, and let him go for a scapegoat** in the wilderness...he shall bring the live goat: and **Aaron shall lay both his hands upon the head of the live goat, and confess over him all the iniquities** of the children of Israel...**putting them upon the head of the goat**, and shall send him away...and **the goat shall bear upon him** all their iniquities...and he shall let go the goat in the wilderness" (Lev. 16:5, 7-10,). Here, in the very same relationship [the same one redemptive action of the Cross] Christ was offered up a **sinless sacrifice** where he was made to be **sin for us!!!** Christ bore the iniquities of us all.

*How does Atonement relate to our justification? Does God just overlook sins? Can or will God just gratuitously or graciously overlook our sins? For God to do this, He, [God], would have to compromise, or, **even violate His Divine Justice**. This cannot be so, and, this would never happen.

*Many think **Grace** is simply God overlooking our sins!!! Many think, to be **Under Grace** means, [these understand this to be] God, He, just overlooking sins!! For many, being Under Grace *means* God is overlooking my sinning!! Many Christians are living a very sinful lifestyle, and their reasoning behind this contradiction is, "I am Under Grace." In other words, because I am Under Grace God will not punish me for my [present, current] sinning. Yet, they fail to realize that the Grace of God is tied to the Redemptive Works of JC. **Grace** is not God just being *gracious* or <u>gratuitous</u> toward the sinner, it is God, in Christ, **paying** the redemptive *price* for Sin. Grace is intimately connected to the **works** of Christ on the Cross- in His death, burial, and resurrection, and ascension. <u>Grace</u> is [His] **works**; just, not our works, but, the <u>works</u> of someone else, namely, Jesus Christ. **Grace** of God is represented by and supported through <u>the Atonement</u> [the Redemptive Works of JC on the Cross]. Apart from these **works**, His works, Grace [and Mercy] [and forgiveness] would be impossible. You cannot separate Grace, from the Cross!!!!

The Cross is where payment [satisfaction] was made to make reconciliation [to restore to divine favor] in order to restore to fellowship [communion/relationship] between God and man. The Cross [His death], or the Atonement [His redemptive works] has accomplished two things: to both *satisfy* the sinners need for **forgiveness** and to *satisfy* the **demand** for Divine Justice [which the law requires-punishment for sins]. These are the *two* **equal** and **opposite** sides of the same one truth/atonement [the same one coin]: what *God* requires and *man* requires for reconciliation. Atonement is made to satisfy Divine Justice [to appease the wrath of God against sin and sinners], "...being now justified by his blood, we shall be saved **from wrath** [eternal separation] through him" (Rom. 5:9). The Atonement has accomplished two very important things: Justice and Mercy. Punishment for sins [judgment for the breaking of the Law; and justification: forgiveness or pardon. We find 4 words in the bible that speaks to **our estrangement**: sin, transgression, trespass, and iniquity. In both Romans 8:7 and Ephesians 2:15-17, **enmity** is used to reference the *hostility* between God and man because of sin and law breaking [transgressions]. Sin *means* in the GK to miss the mark. Paul said in Romans 3:23, "For all have sinned, and come short of the glory of God." One of the many uses of the **law** is, it *reveals* the Holy Character and nature and, moral will of God. To **sin** is to miss the mark of the glory of God, which means, to fail to uphold and live by the moral standards of God's Law. **Transgressions** *mean* to break [violate] the law of God [His commands]. A **trespass** in the scriptures should be looked upon, as, an, even more serious offense, in that, it is a willful offense and personal violation of God himself. All sin and sinning is not only a transgression of God's commands, but as well, a personal violation of God's very own Person. The word **iniquity** speaks of the wrongdoing of man that stems from his *immoral* and fallen character: the ***inner condition*** of man's **heart** behind his every transgression. Man's fallen inner condition [iniquity] is found in fallen Adam. The Cross-is where satisfaction [payment] was made to make reconciliation [restoration] between God and man. Not only to restore men back to God, but, equally imperative, to restore God back to man. The Cross-is all about *both* Justice and mercy. God and man [the sinner] sitting on opposite sides of the negotiating table, in hostility, where the Cross, between, becomes the *means* by which these two estranged parties are reconciled. The Atonement must by necessity include *both* Divine Justice, and our Justification for Reconciliation to be possible. God *demands* divine Justice and every man requires His mercy. [First] on the **one side** of the Cross- we have Justice [condemnation; punishment for sins]; [Second] on the opposite side of the Cross-we have Justification [mercy and the forgiveness of sins]. Justice will always come before Justification!! No justice, no justification!! No payment for sins, no mercy for the sinner!! There is no mercy where there is no justice. There is no forgiveness where there is no punishment for sins. These two sides of the Atonement must be maintained at all times. Always keep in mind, that, they *both* are **equal because both parties require something to enable reconciliation**; and both sides **are opposites** because both parties **are estranged** [hostel toward each other]. It is true that only God was able to bring to the negotiating table the only *means* for reconciliation. Man had nothing to offer by which he could enable or affect reconciliation. The bible is quite clear; Justice had to be satisfied *first* before justification [mercy and forgiveness] could be possible, "Who was delivered [to the Cross] for our offenses [for our sins], and raised again [from the dead: the grave] for our justification" (Rom. 4:25). The Justice of God was met [and was satisfied] at the Cross, and our justification [forgiveness for sins and the impartation of new life] came to us after the payment of the Cross and, his resurrection. Thanks be to be through JC our Lord.

"Then said one unto him, Lord, are there few that be saved? And he said unto them, Strive to enter in at the strait gate [the narrow path]: for many, I say unto you, will seek to enter in, and shall not be able" (Lk. 13:23-28). Strive here in the GK *means* to endeavor or to put forth every effort: to contend with an enemy as if you were competing for a prize. This would be the second part of Atonement: to pardon the sins of the people [to provide forgiveness for sins]. This is where his Lordship is tied to His Savior-ship. Salvation is not a casual observance but a total commitment to the gospel. Are there few that be Saved? And He answered, "Strive." This word *means* to put forth every effort in believing the gospel!! The *provision* for our salvation contained in the gospel message is received by faith alone. There is nothing for us to do, but believe. So, why did Jesus instruct his hearers to "Strive?? It is clear; what Christ had in mind was the total abandonment of the believer in their commitment to Christ, and the gospel "So likewise, whosoever he be of you that **forsakes not all** that he hath [his total self], he cannot be **my disciple** [cannot be my follower-will have no part in me] (Lk 14:33). "And that **he died** for all, that they **which live** [have received new life] should not henceforth [hereafter] live unto themselves, but unto Him [Christ] which died for them, and rose again" (2 Cor. 5:15). "...And ye are not your own. For ye are bought with a price: therefore glorify God in your body, and in your spirit, which are God's" (1 Cor. 6:19-20). We have been **redeemed** and **purchased** by His precious blood; we no longer belong to ourselves and, have no right to ourselves, any longer. At the Cross, at the same time, He, God, can maintain His Justice, and at the same time, demonstrate His mercy. It is all about [the Atonement] *both* the Justice and the Mercy of God, "that He might be [the] Just and the Justifier of those who believe on Him [Christ, and he crucified]" (Rom. 3:26). Atonement, means, in the GK, Satisfaction-He [God] satisfied the demand for Divine Justice, and at the same time, He [God] provided mercy/forgiveness for the sinner, for his/her **Justification**: acquittal, to be cleared of all guilt: to pardon sins. The Atonement is His death on the Cross. The Cross-is all about Justice and Mercy!! Our legal Redemption [the payment made] is *both* **a substitution** and **a satisfaction**: He both **took our place** in punishment, and, **satisfied** the demand for **Divine Justice** [made the payment; took the penalty; suffered the punishment for our transgressions, and our Law breaking]. Atonement by necessity would than include both His Divine Justice and our Justification. The same blood spilt that satisfied Divine Justice [on the Cross] is the same blood spilt that <u>expiates</u> sin [take away sins] [to amend for, and/or, to put an end to sin]. The Atonement is the basis [foundation] upon which all the promises of God for forgiveness and blessings are forged and founded. So, what took place at the Cross that made reconciliation possible? The Atonement, satisfaction was made that both satisfied divine Justice and extended mercy/forgiveness toward the sinner. Now that His Divine Justice is satisfied, God, can now deal with us according to His Divine Grace and Mercy. Justice will always come before Justification. No Justice, no Justification. No payment for sin, no mercy for the sinner. There is no mercy, where there is no justice!! There is no justification where there is not, first, justice [divine punishment]. There is no forgiveness where there is no punishment for sins. Mercy and forgiveness is impossible or illegal apart from justice and, only legal if Divine Justice is first satisfied. God will take away sins; but before He can and will do that, he, must, [has to] satisfy the Law's demand for Justice. We cannot and must not *exalt* **mercy** at the *expense* of His Own **Justice**. Divine Justice must be satisfied first before mercy can rejoice in justifying the sinner. "And without the shedding of [His] blood there is no remission [forgiveness] of/for sins (Heb. 9:22). It is in and through Christ's death on the Cross-that mercy is *empowered* to rejoice against [to win out over] judgment (James 2:13). We are not just saved from **our sins** [we are not just saved from a life of *bondage* to the **sin-nature**, that, fallen human condition], but as well, saved from His Wrath to come (Rom. 5:9). A man cannot murder three people, and then, <u>reform</u> his life, expecting that **his former life of crime** [his former crimes committed] to be overlooked, or, just, forgotten about. Justice does not work this way. What will happen to all those things [the crimes that were committed] before he changed his life? God must *satisfy* the **just** demand of His Holy Law. God cannot and will not just overlook nor forget about our former sins, and then just forgive the sinner [the law-breaker]. God must punish sins before justification [forgiveness] for sins is possible. Justification is the ***grounds*** for our sanctification; and, is the *means* by which our sanctification is possible. What sanctification really is, is the **fruit** and *fruits* [the harvesting] [the bringing forth] [manifestation] of our justification. God cannot and will not just forgive the sinner; He must first punish for all sins [sinning] [and satisfy divine justice] [He must satisfy the demands of a Holy Law]. Once justice is satisfied, now forgiveness [mercy] [justification] is made possible [without the Cross: justification would be impossible].

How does Atonement relate to our justification? Does God just overlook sins? Can or will God just gratuitously or graciously overlook our sins? For God to do this He would have to compromise or even violate His Divine Justice. Many think **Grace** is simply God overlooking our sins. Many think, to be **Under Grace**, means, [understand this to be] God, just overlooking our sins!!! For many, being Under Grace *means* God is overlooking my sinning. Many Christians are living a very sinful lifestyle; and, their reasoning behind this contradiction is, "I am Under Grace." In other words, because, I am Under Grace, God, will not punish me for my [present, current] sinning. Yet, they fail to realize that the Grace of God is intimately tied into the Redemptive Works of JC on that Cross. **Grace** is not God, just, being, *gracious* or <u>gratuitous</u> toward the sinner; it is God in Christ **paying** the redemptive *price* for Sin. Grace is intimately connected to the **works** of Christ on the Cross-in His death, burial, and resurrection. <u>Grace</u> are **works**, just, not our works, but, the [redemptive] <u>works</u> of someone else!!!!!! **Grace** is represented by and supported through <u>the Atonement</u> [the Redemptive Works of JC on the Cross]. Apart from these **works**, Grace, would be an absolute impossibility. The **Cross** of Christ in the Bible is understood to be the Redemptive **Works** of Jesus Christ. For God, *works* come before *grace*, as divine Justice comes before Justification. Divine Justice had to be satisfied before He, God, could demonstrate [by extending] His mercy. For man, *grace* comes before [his own] *works*, because justification comes by faith alone in Christ and, in him crucified alone [his own works here refer to his personal works in cooperation with his Christian sanctification] (Rom. 4:16). The Grace of God does not stand alone apart from His Redemptive Works!!! It is the Grace of God intimately tied to the Redemptive Works of Jesus Christ on the Cross [the Atonement] that make redemption/forgiveness possible. Grace does not stand alone apart from the redemptive works of JC. These [redemptive] **works come before Grace**, or, grace would be absolutely impossible. The Grace of God, totally, depends upon the gospel!!!! The Grace of God totally depends on the Gospel of JC. The Grace of God totally depends and waits upon the redemptive works of JC to be legal and, effective, and salvific [which means, able to save]. The Cross-is the Atonement: his death on the Cross-His redemptive works. His grace and mercy [and forgiveness] would be illegal apart from the payment made in the atonement on the Cross-to satisfy divine justice. Justice comes before mercy; justice comes before justification. God, would never extend His Grace or mercy [and forgiveness] apart from His divine justice [or, at the expense of His Justice, He, God, would never by passed His Divine Justice]. Many treat grace as something, cheap!!! However, Grace is actually quite expensive; no different from a precious jewel [or gem] or, a fine wine that had to be properly aged, "Again, the kingdom of heaven is like a merchant [jeweler], seeking a goodly [a costly and one of a kind] pearl: who when he had found one pearl of great price, went and sold all that he had, and bought it" (Matt. 13:45-46). This pearl of great price [which is very expensive] is the **grace** of God *made* possible by the **Gospel** of Jesus Christ. Jesus called the gospel [the Grace] of God a New Wine put into New Bottles [new wineskins]. The gospel of JC [the Grace of God] put into a new [holy and set apart] people reborn from above. God, help us to understand all these things!!

Double Jeopardy is a *clause* in the Fifth Amendment of the US Constitution that prohibits anyone from being prosecuted for the **same crime twice** following an acquittal [a justification] [to be cleared of all guilt]. Hebrews 10:17-18 says, "And their sins and iniquities will I remember no more. Now where remission [forgiveness; pardon] of these is, there is no more offering for sins [no more sacrifice or punishment (no penalty) for sins]. The word Remission *means* pardon, forgiveness, freedom, and deliverance. Justification [acquittal] *means* to be cleared of all guilt, that is, to be **exonerated** [absolved for wrongdoing]. Today, many in the Church treat biblical justification like **clemency**. Clemency *means* forgiveness of/for a crime and, the cancellation of the relevant punishment [penalty due]: granting leniency from punishment, such as a pardon. Often the way this applies to a man on death row, is, it becomes an underserved pardon [a pardon that suspends, either temporarily or, permanently, justice]. A man is found guilty of a Capital offense [is found guilty of a crime deserving death], then, he sentenced to death, where he awaits his execution on death row. When the day of his execution arrives, he, is taken to the place of execution; as he waits, the last hope is *clemency* made possible only by the action of the state governor. For the governor to grant clemency would mean he would have to suspend [or bypass] justice [entirely], for mercy. This is exactly what most Christians believe the gospel is all about; He, God, just, overturns Justice, for mercy. In other words, He, God, just, overlooked my sins and, extended his mercy!!!!! In other words, God, just, granted me, clemency!!! He, God, just, bypassed his divine Justice, permanently, for mercy!!! This is why most Christians understand their Christian lives to be like [or, compared to] an Owner and his dog. Every day the owner walks his dog, and picks up the poop [the mess] the dog excretes. This goes on for the next 20 years or, for the entire life of the dog. This is exactly how many see Grace, as just something that follows behind them all of their lives to just clean up their mess [to just cover their sins]. This is not biblical justification!!! God does not and will never grant anyone clemency, *meaning*, he will never just overlook our sins, and, he will never just bypass his Divine Justice. He will never violate His Divine Justice, just, to demonstrate His mercy. No Justice, no mercy!!! This is why so many Christians live such spiritually and morally sloppy and sinful lives; they think they have been granted clemency!! They imagine that Christ's death on the Cross, just, provided mercy, and, the forgiveness of sins [clemency]; that is all. Many Christians today continue to take their personal sins and sinning, lightly, why, because, they imagine God, just, arbitrarily, forgiving sins. The meaning of <u>arbitrarily</u> is, to forgive without any regard to fairness or, equity: justice. To come about randomly, or by chance, or by a <u>capricious</u> and unreasonable act of the will. The word capricious means, characterized by impulsive and unpredictable behavior. Something that is likely to change frequently, or suddenly, and unexpectedly: at random. This is exactly how many so called Christians live their so called Christian lives, at random. They obey, maybe, and they sin often!!! They ask God to forgive them, expecting clemency, regardless, of repentance, or any change of life. Therefore, they continue to sin often, and, maybe, obey, sometimes. They just do not take sin, and sinning, seriously!! I am under grace, they tout!! They may even believe they should live a better Christian life, meaning, a life of obedience to God; however, they shout/tout Christ as Savior, and, maybe one day I will make him Lord [which means, maybe one day I will choose to live a life of obedience to God]. For now, I will continue to enjoy the forgiveness of my sins, and [present] sinning. Many claim, **eternal security**, that, they cannot ever lose their salvation under any circumstances: even to the point of the abandonment of the Christian faith: they still cannot lose their Christian salvation. This is the modern day Free Grace theology of the Cross, which is, **mercy**, at the expense of **His Divine Justice**. These, look at <u>mercy</u> on the one side and, his divine <u>justice</u> on the other side and, God, just, chooses mercy, against justice!! As if **Justice** and **mercy** are at war with each other and, God, just, chooses [his] mercy to win out over [divine] [eternal] justice. Divine Justice and, His Divine Mercy are **divine attributes** of the same ONE ETERNAL Person of God. God is both, JUST, and MERCIFUL; however, **what makes it legal** [what makes it right] for him to be *both* Just [toward the law] and the Justifier of the sinner, is, the Atonement of JC on the Cross, where Justice and Mercy, meet [and find agreement, there] in Christ, Jesus, through his vicarious [substitutionary] sacrifice for sins on behalf of fallen men.

Many so called Christians [false converts; the tares among the wheat] believe, that God, just, overlooks and bypasses his divine justice, in order to demonstrate his divine mercy. As if his divine **justice** and his **mercy** are incompatible, and, can never ever ever be made compatible. And yet, it was at the Cross of Christ in the Atonement where **his divine justice** and **his mercy** were made ONE [were made compatible, and, made to come into agreement]. This is why Paul said, To declare, I say, at this time his **righteousness**: that he [God] [Christ] [God in Christ] might be **just** [might continue to be just] [that he might continue to exalt his justice], and he [at the same time] [God] [as well] [might be] the justifier of him [the sinner] [that God, **with his justice**, might as well, extend his mercy toward the sinner and pardon his transgressions] which [for all those who] believe on Jesus Christ [for all those who believe the gospel: **for justice** and **mercy**] [it is *both* in the Atonement of Jesus Christ on the Cross, where, God, was able to satisfy his divine justice and, at the same time, procure the mercy of God for the forgiveness of our sins] (Rom. 3:26). God will never ever ever, just, grant clemency!!! God will never, just, pardon sins, arbitrarily!! He judges Sin and sinning on the Cross in the body of Jesus Christ: **in his death**, burial, and **resurrection**. Without justice, there is no mercy; without the Cross, there is no redemption. Jesus Christ died, for the sins of the whole world, making it possible for men **to believe**, and be **saved**; however, if men fail to believe the gospel, they will suffering the grace of God in vain [these will fail the grace of God and, fall away from any hope of eternal life]. God, help us all to take this gospel of Jesus Christ, seriously!!! Dear heavenly Father, please, do not allow us to frustrate this grace of God in our lives, and in our Christian sanctification. God, please forgive us for disrespecting the Spirit of Grace and, trampling under foot the blood of the Covenant, wherein you have **saved** and sanctified us unto eternal life. God, by your Holy Spirit, help us to take our Christian life and walk seriously; to no longer take for granted this wonderful gospel of his divine grace. Christians who truly understand the Justice of God found in the Cross, turn from all their sins; however, those so called Christians who only see the Cross as the mercy of God, often, continue to live very sinful and corrupt lives in league with the world. God help!! Paul said, "But God forbid that I should glory [in anything else] save [except] **the Cross** of our Lord [and Savior] Jesus Christ, by whom/him [in other words, it is by him, and he crucified] the world is crucified unto me, and I unto the world [in other words, it is through [my] faith and understanding of/in this gospel of Jesus Christ, where, *both* the justice and mercy of God, meet, that I am crucified to the world and, it is crucified unto me] [in other words, when I believe and understand *both* the justice and mercy of God found in the Atonement, and yield, and trust, and come into union with him, I now know and understand I have died to the world, and, the world is as well dead to me]. Only those who truly understand the Justice of the Cross, can truly believe, and receive, and understand the mercy of the Cross. God, help us not to separate these two!!!

What really happens when true authentic biblical clemency is given, is, the governor/Christ shows up at the place of execution [the Cross] to offer himself in the place of the sinner [God will not and can never violate his justice, for mercy] [So, Christ, offers up himself on behalf of the one who committed the crime, and, take his punishment for sin, thus, satisfying justice and, procuring a true legal pardon]. This way, God in Christ, can both *maintain* his Divine Justice and at the same time *demonstrate* his Divine Mercy, "that he might be **just**, and the **justifier** of him which [that person who] believes in Jesus Christ" (Rom. 3:26). This is why the writer of Hebrews says, "Now where remission [acquittal; pardon; forgiveness] of these is [these sins, and crimes committed], there is no more offering [no more penalty nor punishment] for sins (Heb. 10:17-18). It *means*, Christ has taken our penalty and punishment for sins [he has taken our many transgressions and trespasses against God and His Law and, cancelled them on the Cross]; so now, there is no way these same sins [these same crimes committed in the breaking of God's law] can ever be tried again in a court of Law, ever again, [in the Court room of Heaven]: that would be **double jeopardy**. However, this only applies to the truly repentant and, to the truly pardoned. This is one of the key arguments for eternal security. Notwithstanding, John Calvin said, if someone who claims salvation falls [away] back into a sinful lifestyle, and abandons the faith, this proves he/she was never truly among those who were truly repentant and, truly pardoned. God will never not give justice to the victims and their families by pardoning the guilty. God has never ever in all eternity <u>ever pardoned the guilty</u> **nor forgiven sins apart from the atonement**. Technically speaking, God has never ever truly ever pardoned the guilty nor, forgiven sins; rather, he punished the guilty and his/her sins, in Christ!!!!! I understand, this is very hard to fathom for many, for many of those so called Christians who see the gospel and the Cross, as, only the **demonstration** of the Mercy of God and, not as well, the **Justice** of God. We have often believed, God, has just, forgiven our sins, as if he just overlooked my sins and, still now, just, continues to overlook my sinning. This is the error [falsehood] in the mindset and attitude of most Christians. They only understand and hold to the one side of the Atonement. They preach and promote the mercy of God [the forgiveness of <u>sins</u>] but, have neglected or simply misunderstood the Justice of God. No Justice, no justification. If sins are not punished; God, cannot and will not **extend his mercy** and, demonstrate **his grace**. God does not *pardon* sins, he **punishes** sins!!!!!!!!!! God has never ever truly pardoned sin and, he, will never ever, just, pardon sins. He can *pardon* the sinner, but, only after his/her sins are properly punished [for violating of the law of God] [of course, we cannot separate the sinner from his sins, but, this is where substitution come in]. We think God overlooks sin because of NT verses that appear to present this as the truth, "In <u>whom</u> we have <u>redemption</u> through his <u>blood</u>, **the forgiveness of sins**, <u>according to the riches of his grace</u>" (Eph. 1:7). Many interpret this to *mean*, he simply overlooked sins [or, by-passed his justice for mercy] by His grace or, undeserved favor. However, notice that it was by **his blood** [by his death on the Cross-to satisfy divine justice] He [God] was able to atone for sin. This text must be understood in the context of Roman 5:9, where the sinner **was saved** from *wrath* [saved from the eternal wrath of God] through him [Christ and Him crucified]. We have **redemption** [pardon; and deliverance from wrath: eternal judgement] through **his blood** [the Atonement: his sacrifice and the *payment* made that punished all sins, for] the forgiveness of sins according to his divine grace [which was earned by JC on the Cross, in his redemptive works]. From man's perspective [from our point of view] the bible teaches, that, we have been pardoned for sins; but, from God's perspective [from God's point of view] the bible teaches, that, the **sinner** was judged/condemned with all of his/her **sins** when punished in Christ Jesus, on the Cross. The most notable [and familiar] text in all the bible that present the gospel to fallen man, is, John 3:16, "For God so loved the world, that he gave his only begotten Son, that whosoever believes in him should not perish, but have everlasting life." The love of God gave Jesus Christ to die on the Cross-for the atonement of sins. Apart from this atonement, the love and mercy of God would not be extended toward the sinner [fallen men], for this would be an absolute impossibility!!!!!!! The love of God is seen and found in the redemptive of works of JC on the Cross. Apart from the Cross, God's grace and mercy [and the forgiveness of our sins] would be **unlawful and illegal**. It is through faith in Christ and he crucified that, the love of God for the sinner is realized [and actualized]. We have been **justified** [acquitted; cleared of all guilt; pardoned for sins] **by his blood** on the Cross [by the atonement: the satisfaction (the payment) made that satisfied divine justice for the forgiveness of sins] [as a result] we have been saved [delivered] from his wrath [eternal punishment], "For the *wages* of sin [the reward for sin] is **death** [eternal judgement], but the **gift** of God [salvation that comes by the atonement] is eternal life by JC [through his death on the Cross taking our punishment/judgement for sins]" (Rom. 6:23). I pray we do not take this for granted, nor disrespect the blood, and the Spirit of His Grace through a life and lifestyle of constant and continual SINNING!!!!! God, help us all not to choose a life of Sin, and sinning. God, does not truly really actually pardon sins; he pardons the sinner; and, he, God, did this only after the **sin price was paid** [paid in full] on the Cross; Therefore, God doesn't really actually forgive sins, he, God, really, actually, punishes sins [in Christ on the Cross], so, he can forgive the sinner [only after his sin debt is paid]. God, help!!! It is not unscriptural to say, God forgives sins; however, it is unscriptural to understand it incorrectly and apart from God's satisfaction of divine justice. God, help us to understand the difference between, God, forgiving our sins in an arbitrary way and, from God forgiving our sins through Christ's vicarious sacrifice and death [in order to satisfy God's righteous demands for justice in keeping with his Divine Eternal Law].

"Whom God hath set forth **to be a propitiation** through faith in his blood [through faith in the atonement or the payment made to forgive sins], to declare his righteousness for the remission [forgiveness] of sins..." (Rom. 3:25). The word propitiation *means* atoning victim, the **expiator**, the one *who appeases [satisfies] the wrath* of God against **sin** and the **sinner**. There is no remission or pardon for sins where there is no atonement, which *means* an atoning victim, someone who takes the place of another in the punishment of sins. The bible places the emphasis on the **payment [of the Cross]**: not on the pardon. As important as forgiveness is, it is impossible apart from the Cross. Christ is the atoning victim where God punished all sins in his body on the Cross appeasing and satisfying the wrath of God against sin and the sinner. We were **pardoned** by **his grace** and **mercy** when our sins were **punished** in Jesus Christ on the Cross. Paul said in Romans 8:3, "God sending his own Son in the likeness of sinful flesh, and **for sin, condemned** sin in the flesh." This speaks to the incarnation when God became a man, or, when the word was made flesh and dwelt among us. The *purpose* for the incarnation was **for sin** [and *means* he was made to be a sin-offering] that, Christ, might **condemn** sin in his own body on the Cross. He was born to die!! Christ came into the world to die for sinners [Mk. 10:45]. He came to take Sin upon himself and, **for Sin**, that he might *punish* that Sin on the Cross. The word condemned *means* in the GK to **damn** Sin, or, to **judge against** Sin; it comes from another GK word that *means* to **punish** sins. John 3:16, must be understood by Romans 8:3.

For God's love for the world is demonstrated in Jesus Christ being made Sin for us on the Cross, and, he, suffering the wrath of God against Sin and the sinner in his own body in divine punishment and eternal death [this spiritual death speaks to his humanity dying eternally]. He took our place in punishment [and he took our place in Divine Justice and divine judgement] that is why the atonement is both a **substitution** and a **satisfaction** [a payment]. The *sinless* Christ was made to be **sin for us** on the Cross in order to *satisfy* the demands for divine justice. **He took our place as a substitute that, he might judge all sin and the sinner in himself on the Cross, in order to satisfy divine justice and provide justification for sinful humanity.** For by <u>Grace</u> you and I are *saved* [for by His earned and deserved redemptive works on the Cross you and I are saved], through faith [through trusting in the atonement: the payment made for the forgiveness of sins]; and not of yourselves: it is the gift of God: not of works [man's own efforts to win approval and acceptance with God]..." (Eph. 2:8-9). Grace is unearned and undeserved toward you and me; but, for him, for Jesus Christ on the Cross, he, had to earn it [and, he had to deserve/win it]. Thank God for Jesus Christ our Lord!!

1 John 2:2 tells us, "And he is the **propitiation** for our sins: and not ours only, <u>but also for the sins of the whole world</u>." Christ is the atoning victim, and through his death on the Cross God punished all sins in him, turning away His wrath against all sinners [being appropriated by them through faith in his blood]. God has never once pardoned any sin in the sense of just overlooking or turning the other way [or turning a blind eye] [or, bypassing justice]. He has punished all sins in Christ on the Cross that he might forgive the sinner for all his/her many sins [transgressions]. There is no mercy and/or pardon [forgiveness] for sins **where there is not first divine justice** [punishment for sins]. This is why the Cross-is indispensable to Eternal Redemption [Eternal Reconciliation]. Knowing this we now understand that the true gospel, the preaching of the Cross must bring with it both a **fear** of God and **conviction** for sins [which leads to **hatred** for sin]. We have to understand the seriousness of sin [sins]

and our sinning. For most who claim the gospel for salvation, they have a very low view of **sin** and the **sinful** condition. Many see grace as God just doing nothing, and/or requiring nothing; **this is why grace is so cheap in the eyes of the ignorant** [those who are **uninformed about the true gospel**]. The reason why true and genuine biblical faith requires the absolute abandonment of oneself to Christ, through faith in his blood [through faith in the atonement] is, because, the **grace** of God is tied to the **Justice** of the **Cross**. Many people fail to see the grace of God toward the sinner, as that which required the death of His Son. God gave all in his Son: in his death on the Cross to purchase man's redemption, **and this redeeming work on the Cross is the payment made that secured not only our forgiveness but as well, purchased [bought] our very own life** [the total man: spirit, soul and body]. Generally speaking, the bible teaches, that, God on the Cross provided for mankind, the forgiveness [pardoning] of sins; however, technically speaking, He [God] did not really overlook sins [he did not just pardon sins outright]: He punished all those same sins in Christ on the Cross. This is the Pauline revelation, our sins were punished [judged] in Christ [and Christ was punished for ours sins]; we as sinners were planted in the likeness of his death, and there we died with Christ on His Cross. God judged the *sinner* in Jesus Christ on the Cross. The old sinner man now crucified with Christ and now dead and buried with him, and now [we are] raised to new life, having become a new man [a new creation in Christ Jesus]. **Did he really just pardon our sins??** Did he really just pardon the sinner??? From man's point of view, the bible presents it as such; but, when the Christian begins to grow in his/her sanctification they come to understand salvation from God's point of view, and **are now empowered to live the new life** by the revelation knowledge of JC [Christ and Him crucified]. This is why so many so-called Christians are still struggling with sins unnecessarily; they just do not know nor understand their full redemption [their full salvation] in and by Christ Jesus. I do not want to be misunderstood; **salvation for the babe in Christ is the "forgiveness" of sins**. However, when *the babe* becomes a man [mature] in the things of God [putting away childish things] he/she begins to understand; now, their faith in the gospel [the truth of the gospel] [the atonement] involves so much more than just **pardon** [the forgiveness of sins], "For I am not ashamed of the gospel of JC [the atonement; the payment that was made for my reconciliation] for it is the power [ability; and miracle] of God unto salvation [deliverance, healing, and wholeness] for all who **believe** [for all who *comprehend* and come to trust in (and rely upon) and apply its truths and come into its full spiritual **experience**]" (Rom. 1:16). God did not just, pardon sins, He judged it on the Cross!!!! Now, He can justify the *sinner* who is now planted into the *likeness* of His [Christ's] death, burial, and resurrection, and ascension [unto new life as, a new creation in Christ Jesus: being delivered from sinful Adam and, being set free from the presence and influence of a sinful fallen root-nature that, before conversion, was formerly identified with Adam's first transgression]. For the believer, the genuine Christian, sin is no longer a matter of one's root-nature; nevertheless, sin is still found operating in the carnal unredeemed human physical body [and, the unrenewed soul]. However, the gospel has made every provision for victory over this body of sin; which, Paul also called the body of this death [what death, the death or, fallen condition that belongs to the Old man, Adam, still resident in the human body]. This unredeemed condition is found in our members or, in the parts of our physical body and, as well, it can be found in those many parts of our unchanged unrenewed soulical anatomy [of the mind, the will, and the emotions]. God, help.

PART TWO

IMPUTATION
Imputation and Impartation of His Grace

*Your acceptance with God is not based on what you do, but on what He [God] has already done in Christ Jesus [on the Cross-in the Atonement].

*In Romans 5:10-11, we are <u>reconciled</u> by His death [changed, by Christ putting away the Old Man in our Baptism], much more, His Life now **saves** us [by ushering in that which is New] [through our spiritual regeneration].

***Life** here in the text is the GK word Zoe, and *means* the <u>spiritual life</u> [the God kind of life or the God quality of life].

*Here in the text, the first application speaks to the resurrection life, this life is the New Life *ushered* in by the resurrection of JC. This is what Paul called the New Creation [the treasure now within the earthen vessel].

*But there is another application here in the text: the **perfect obedient life** Christ lived while under the Law [of Moses] (as described throughout the *four* gospels) [the imputation of His righteousness to our spiritual account is based upon his perfect life of obedience under the law].

Life** here in the text has a double reference: it both speaks to the ***new birth or, the new life we have received through faith in JC, and, as well, it speaks to His sinless life [or, perfect life of obedient] by which **imputed** righteousness is made possible [is made *both* available and provisional].

*This imputed righteousness depends on His obedient life [to make it possible and available for exchange]; the Cross, and his/the Resurrection of JC was necessary to make this same righteousness transferable [and, is the means by which this righteousness of JC is transmitted]. This means, to, convey [to cause to pass] from one person to another; to give over [or rather, to share in] the legal possession of something.

*A True [real, tangible, touchable] righteousness [merits, obedience of another] imputed us!!!!!

*In His death in the Atonement He has declared us **innocent** [pardoned; acquitted] [this is where our disobedience and transgressions were imputed to him]; in His Resurrection he, Christ, has *imputed* his righteousness to us that, has made us Just [legally right standing before God; and it is because of and through his resurrection we have received the impartation of new life] [this is when we received his very own life] (Rom. 4:25).

*His *sinless* life under the Law; his *sin-bearing* death on the Cross and, His *resurrection* from the dead, has accomplished our justification [has *forgiven* our sins and has *imputed* his righteousness to us. In this thing, his redemptive works, he has declared our **innocence** and has made us **just**], **and has imparted new life** [to us]. Praise God!!!!!!

*Christ's work of *mediation* on the Cross is not just His death [not just anyone died for your sins]. A **just** man died for your sins. The Just had to die for the unjust. This *means* in order to **qualify** [to die as a substitute] He [Christ] had to *live* a **life** of perfect obedience under the Law. He [JC] had to *fulfil* the righteous demands of His divine eternal Law for perfect obedience, first, before he could *qualify* as our Redeemer [our expiator]. Where Adam **failed** [in his disobedience to God] [in the fall], He [Jesus Christ under the Law] would now have to succeed [he would now have to overcome where he, Adam, failed]. This is the contrast between Jesus Christ and fallen Adam as stated in Romans 5:12-21.

*Before Christ could *satisfy* the demand for Divine Justice on the Cross, making the Atonement legal [possible for redeeming men], He had to **qualify** [he had to be made eligible for the task]. This is why the perfect life of obedience under the law was necessary as a part of the redemption our justification. This is why Christ did not just come down out of heaven, and, just immediately go to the Cross.

Eligible** *means* to meet the requirements **[He had to legally qualify]**; by being tested and ***proven to be **fit** for office/service [He had to be found worthy before the Court (of heaven), before, he could be an atoning sacrifice] [he had to legally qualify to make atonement] (Heb. 5:5-10).

*On the Cross-we have a *double*-**imputation** [two-transactions taking place on the Cross].

***Imputation** *equals* [means] the Divine Exchange, which, in turn becomes our justification.

*How can an unjust person be justified, or, how can a sinner be forgiven and restored to divine favor?? "Abraham *believed* God and it was counted to him for his justification [righteousness]" (Rom. 4:3; James 2:23). This is you and I putting our faith in what He did for us on the Cross.

***Faith** in Christ, and him crucified is the *instrumental* cause for our justification [**faith** in the atonement is our acceptance with God that won His approval and, has accomplished our reconciliation].

No Cross, no pardon! Faith is a necessary requisite, indispensable, and essential for salvation. Faith serves as the crucial means, tool, or agency through which men are saved; however, notwithstanding, the legal ground for our justification is the Cross of JC [and, his subsequent resurrection]. Redemption/reconciliation is impossible without the Cross and, putting our faith in it.

*On what basis [on what ground] are we declared righteous?? It is on the **merits** of Jesus Christ both *before* and *after* the Cross [in both his sinless life and, in his sin-bearing death: and, through his resurrection]. It is based upon *both* His **obedient life**, and **his obedience in death**.

*This <u>justification</u> is a **real** [tangible, and touchable] righteousness [an earned, and merited obedience] [wrought by Christ under the Law] and imputed [and imparted] to us by the Cross and through resurrection. Through the Cross, our sins imputed to Christ; in his resurrection, now, his righteousness imputed to us [to our account on the legal ledger in heaven] [as well, now, imparted to us in new life, within, a spiritual rebirth].

*It is a **double-imputation**: the *first* transfer [transaction] takes away our **sins** [and puts our life of disobedience into Jesus Christ on the Cross] [He is the original sin-eater]; the *second* transfer [transaction] gives us his **righteousness** [His very own perfect obedient life]. Our sins *imputed* to Christ [and put into him on the Cross], and His righteousness *imputed* [and imparted] to us [through the resurrection].

*Our sins *imputed* to JC; His righteousness [and new life] *imputed* [and imparted] to us [the sinner] [now made righteous] [now called saints].

*This **righteousness** is you and I receiving His earned [merited] obedience under the Law. The New Life we have now received is His very own **righteousness** and perfect **obedient** Life under the

Law [this is the treasure in our earthen vessels]. This is not just his right standing [his personal bearing] before the Father, but as well, we have received His very own life of obedience imparted to us [in and through the resurrection].

*All of this is what is meant by being Under Grace!! We have received [not just the forgiveness of sins, but] the unearned, unmerited, and underserved *righteousness* [his very own perfect obedient life] through faith in the Atonement [this **double-imputation**] [this Divine Exchange] [this divine transfer] [through faith in the blood of His Cross: in his death, burial, and subsequent resurrection, and ascension].

***How shall we escape if we neglect such a great salvation** (Heb. 2:3): if we turn this great gospel of our salvation into a cheap grace [into easy believism]. Many have simply reduced the gospel [the grace of Christ] to just the forgiveness of sins. God, help us not to do this thing!!

*Remember, **Justice** is you and I getting what we deserve; **Mercy** is you and I not getting what we deserve; **Grace** is you and I getting what is underserved. **Justice**, is eternal judgement; **mercy**, is divine pardon; and **grace**, is spiritual empowerment [is you and me receiving **new life**].

*This is where Justification is tied into your Sanctification: Grace *extends* both mercy to pardon sins [justification], and as well *extends* power for holy living [power for sanctification and transformation]. *Grace is you and I getting [receiving] something from God that both **atones** for sin [sins] and *empowers* us for **sanctification**. Many confused these two, grace, and mercy. **Grace** extends mercy from the Cross-for our atonement justification, but then [Grace] through the **resurrection** [the **power** of His resurrection] we have been raised to New life (Rom. 6:4, 7:6). This power [and **grace**] is the God given *ability* to **duplicate** [to walk in] the life of JC by the faith of

JC. All of this is made possible as we *yield* to the **sanctifying** and perfecting work of the HS, who is the Spirit of Grace [Christ] at work within [from within us]. This is *both* **imputation** and **impartation**. Salvation has accomplished *both* imputation and impartation. *The sinful condition of man transferred to Christ [on the Cross]; God laid these things [our sins] on Jesus, and God poured out his wrath [judgement] on Christ as a substitutionary work. He was *made* to be sin for us: he took on the *likeness* of sinful flesh on that Cross, that through death, he might atone for sins, and reconciled men to God. Praise God!!

*On the Cross, Christ was JUST [righteous] in himself, and made to be **sinner** by imputation [he was made to be sin for us; this does not *mean* he became in and of himself, sin, or a sinner, but through his substitutionary work and the *imputation* of our sin, he, was counted among all sinners [transgressors]. Legally he took our place!! So that *both* in himself he still remained righteous [without personal sin] but, was through imputation numbered among the wicked [made a sinner]. This is exactly what we find on the **Day of Atonement**, both, **two goats,** one for the **Sin-offering**, and the other for the **Scapegoat**. Because, in Christ Jesus, in the gospel, through his redemptive works on the Cross, we find him *both* **righteous** and, **sinner!!** We find in him, both, righteousness and transgressions [this is where, in and of himself, he retains his our righteousness: he retains his own personal innocence under the law; notwithstanding, in the atonement, he was made to be sin for us through imputation, **by taking on our sinful state and our fallen Adamic condition**]. The Sin-offering is where the sinless spotless lamb was offered to God for atonement; the other goat, the Scapegoat, is where the sins of all the people were transferred, and then, the goat was sent away out of the camp, to never return. One is clearly positive and, the other negative. The Sin-offering represents his perfect sinless life being offered up for atonement: this represents his own personal righteousness under the law; however, it is in the other goat we find Christ being made sin for us when God laid on him the iniquity of us all. Christ, the righteous, took our place on the Cross, now made a sinner, in our stead, on our behalf, and died, and was judged to atone for sin.

*On the Cross [in the atonement] Christ paid the price for our sin [sins], this is both a work of expiation and propitiation. By **expiation** he took away our sins, and by **propitiation** he appeased the wrath of God against the sinner, thus, satisfying his righteous demand for divine justice [he took the **penalty** for our guilt and stain, and, he took the **punishment**/judgment due us because of our sins]. Thanks be to God for Jesus Christ.

*This justification has now imparted to us new life. This new life is his positive righteousness set to our account [his life of perfect obedience under the law imputed to us] [and now residing *within* as a treasure in the earthen vessel]. It is *in* and *through* this **new life** [which is his active righteousness *within* wrought *within* by his active grace] that makes sanctification possible. This is why our justification [being declared legally just] [and the impartation of new life] must never be divided from nor ever separated the one from the other [justification anticipates, demands, sanctification, and sanctification *both* proves and demonstrates our justification]. God, help us not to make this eternally fatal mistake!!!

*Just as the **Cross**-precedes the Resurrection, and just as His **Death** precedes our new life, so also **Justification** precedes [and comes before] Sanctification. In order for there to be **resurrection life**, there must first come **a death** [on the Cross]. Many have missed the point; **justification anticipates** [*demands* and commands] [automatically assumes] **sanctification**: as much as sanctification *proves* [and demonstrates] justification: these are not separated but joined together in the same one salvation process from start to finish [the *first* stage is, Justification; the *second* stage is, sanctification, and the *third* stage, glorification]. **Life is not separated**; and, life must not be separated; so, it is important we do not separate these two from one another, and must never be seen as such. **Justification** was never intended to be separated from our sanctification; while there is **a distinction**, there is no division nor separation. To separate justification from **sanctification**, will bring spiritual death. I understand how this sounds to those who believe in, once saved, always, saved; notwithstanding, to separate normal life, from its normal growth, will ultimately bring death [it will ultimately bring ruination to life]. It is important we do not look at the salvation process mechanically; but, **as something alive**, and **living!!** Justification has not only atoned for sins but, imparted new life; this new life is a living thing, not, some, mechanism or, mechanical thing that follows some precise pattern or, some logical step by step process. First justification, and then, sanctification, and then, glorification; **while this is true in principle**, it is not how these things work, **practically**, meaning, how these things are actually, **actively engaged**. Salvation is new life; life doesn't happen/operate **in predictable ways** or, *through* some **prescribed set of principles!!** This is why, to think you can be justified, today, and have and hold salvation, and then, to **suspend** your Christian life of obedience and growth, to some future time, even 20 years down the road, thinking, you can just pick it up at any time along the way, and it will still be there. These [persons] are those who John Calvin would say of, have never truly come to saving faith. To suspend something means, to, **put off to another time**: sometime in the future; it means, **to cause to stop temporarily**; it means, **to hold** in an undetermined and undecided state, awaiting **further decision**. In other words, I have accepted Jesus Christ as Savior, but not Lord; so, my sanctification awaits further decision. So, the new life within, **is halted**, and **stunted**, and now **awaits further commitment** to God. Christians really believe this, that, it is ok **to remain in this state of suspended** and **interrupted [postponed] life**. This is *both* biblically and logically, **absurd!!!** It is only when life grows, and continues to grow, **do we find life sustained!!!!!!** To think we can receive new life, and then, to put it on hold, for any real length of time, and then, to expect it to still be there, and thriving. NO!!! **It will die!!!!** I do not care what you call it: losing your salvation or, never really truly having saving faith to begin with. **Growth is a struggle for Life**; life will always struggle on its way **to new growth**. Without this struggle, life will die!!! Justification is not only the atonement for sins, it is also you and me receiving new life; which, it order to thrive and survive, it must be active, in faith and obedience to God, that growth will take place, and live. It is true; salvation can be understood by its simple biblical principles, with its corresponding precise and prescribed pattern for growth; however, it is a living thing, and at times, very unpredictable; notwithstanding, both biblically and logically, for this new life to survive and thrive, it must immediately be actively engaged in sanctification and transformation of the human soul, or else, this new life with its new growth, is threatened.

This <u>Salvation Process</u> is compared to the *growth* of an ordinary **plant**. <u>Justification</u> is like the planting of a **seed**. The <u>seed</u> *germinates*, sprouts, and springs forth as **new** life. The only *means* by which this new life can protect itself [defend itself] against the harmful elements is to grow!!!!!!! As a seed, the hard outer shell protects the [new] life content within. However, once the seed is broken [ruptured] now the [new] life within is exposed and vulnerable to the harsh conditions. Forcing itself to grow is the only way to ensure its own survival. Its new *growth* and coming **to harvest** will guarantee its future posterity [its perpetual and continued existence]. <u>Sanctification</u> is the **time** [space; growth] between ***germination*** and **harvest**. What sanctification is, is the ***new*** **life** received in justification growing and bearing its fruit!! There is no separation between justification and sanctification. **If the <u>plant</u> fails to *grow* it will die!!!!!** Paul said, **"For the invisible things of Him...are clearly seen, being understood by the things that are made..."** (Rom. 1:20). Some have tried to say, that, **Justification is a past event, alone,** and thus, we are [made] **secure** in this past event. No matter what happens to us here after we can never lose our <u>salvation</u> [this new life we have *first* received through justification]. This, is just, illogical *both* biblically and naturally. If [new] [real] growth *fails* to occur to help protect this vulnerable **new life** now exposed to the harsh and sinful elements [conditions] of a perverse sinful wicked world, it, will once again, **die** [it will be swallowed up and choked out of existence] [I do understand we are speculating about those things that are ultimately hidden from us: we cannot be entirely sure in how all these things work, but, that is the whole point. To make justification a past event, alone, now separated from sanctification, is a critical error. This is the lesson of the parable of the sower. The seed [or, the new life] falls on different types of soil [ground] that works to help or either to hinder the growth. Three out of the four different types of soil failed to harvest [failed to bear fruit]. Without a harvest [without fruit], **the plant would pass out of existence** [the plant would fail to survive]. **Its perpetuity is found in its harvesting of new seeds for planting!!!** It's [the seed's] [the new life's] continued existence depends on a successful harvest!!! Why do we think it is any different with a Christian who is born-again by the **seed** of the word of God (1 Pet. 1:23). If this **new life** in us *fails* to grow to harvest, it will be lost [2 Cor. 6:1]. This is exactly what the bible *means* by its counter argument to Eternal Security. Eternal Security is a true biblical doctrine; but, its [continued] security is found and guaranteed *in* and *through* its growth in Christ. IT IS IN HIM WE HAVE LIFE; he who has the Son hath the life. It is only as we continue in him do we continue in [eternal] life. To divorce justification from sanctification is like, you and me **divorcing our salvation from His life**. The doctrine of Eternal Security cannot and must never be divorced from the overall Salvation process. Our growth in Christ is what helps to protect the **seed** [the new life] from extermination. This is those invisible things being understood by the things that are made [understood by those things we can see and understand, naturally]. Why is this so hard to understand and believe, and why have we made salvation [justification] a past event [alone] [standing all by itself] that can never be altered or lost?? Justification is not a past event, alone, but a continuing event, that, started in the past but continues in the present through spiritual growth, **which the bible calls sanctification**. Justification, alone, is obtained through faith in Christ's redemptive work on the Cross, alone, but, it is **solidified** and made **real** [actual] to us by the new life received. This **new life** found in our initial justification is not separated into neatly confined spaces [boxes] for our private consumption. [New] life starts out [and begins] and, it will continue on uninterrupted **as one single solitary flowing stream of existence changing** and **expanding as it grows**. Salvation is a single solitary process flowing from **one stage** [from one manifestation] of life **to another**. These are joined together and cannot be separated; to do so, brings, **certain death!!!** This does not take away from the biblical fact, that, **justification [the new birth] has occurred the moment we believe the gospel**. But, this new life cannot **be stagnant**, nor isolated or, **it will die!!** If the new life [the new seedling] **fails to grow, it dies!!!!!** To claim a justification devoid of sanctification is a spiritual counterfeit [a false gospel]. The word **devoid** *means* being without a usual, typical, or expected attribute, or accompaniment. There is no doubt, that, sanctification is the usual, typical, and **expected accompaniment [and companion] to justification**. I am trying my best not to be misunderstood. Justification is a work [an act] of God in the life of those who believe the gospel. This happens the very moment we believe and put our trust in the atonement [the Cross]. However, notwithstanding, this salvation imparts new life. This new life is intimately tied and connected to our justification. To lay claim to the **judicial transaction/divine exchange** [the atonement] that pardons our sins **and brings us into right-standing with God**, only to reject, deny, neglect, and/or **even to treat with contempt the new life purchased for us** on the Cross, which includes His subsequent resurrection, is to trampled underfoot **the blood of the Covenant wherewith we are sanctified** (Heb. 10:29). Sanctification is really not something I do [works], but something that He does that grow within [me], and manifests its [new] life [force] present within [and is guaranteed to manifest its fruits/works of righteousness] (Gal. 2:20). I understand, that, the believer has a part in his/her own sanctification, however, **it is not the actual works of the believer that sanctifies**, but, the [new] **life** *within* **growing** being *stimulated* by those same works [and now producing works] (Gal. 2:20-21; Col. 1:29; Phil. 2:13). All that the *works* of the believer does, is to cooperate with the Work of the Spirit, within. I understand, that, those who are very familiar with the arguments on Justification between the Catholics, and the Protestants of the 16th Century, can see what I have just wrote here in this paragraph as addressing this controversy. The argument/controversy was focused upon the <u>infusion</u> of grace, and/or, the <u>imputation</u> of grace. I will say more on this later throughout these three series of books. For now I will say, this controversy [confusion] between these two different approaches to justification was quite heated, and was never truly entirely reconciled. I believe, the Protestant understanding of *imputation* is the correct understanding of justification, but, however, the problem comes in when we stop there. **True justification must be seen as both an <u>imputation</u> and <u>impartation</u>!!!** Both a judicial transaction [imputation], and as well an impartation of new life [which needs to be understood **as an infusion** of His grace]. **God, did it for us**; and, as well, God, **did it in us. Imputation** is God doing something for us; however, **infusion**, must be understood as something **invested within**. Infusion is God doing something in us!!! Imputation, is, **for us**; infusion, is, **in us**. Justification is *both*, imputation and, impartation. An **imputation** of his righteousness and, an **impartation** of his life [you and me receiving new life]. Again, to believe it is ok to remain in this **state of suspended and interrupted [postponed] life** is a travesty and, a spiritual counterfeit. This is *both* biblically and logically, absurd. It is only when life grows, and continues to grow, **do we find life sustained!!!!!!** To think we can receive new life, and then, to put it on hold, and then, to expect it to still be there, and thriving. NO!!! **It will die!!!! Growth is a struggle for Life**; life will always struggle on its way **to new growth**. Without this struggle, life will die!!! Justification, is not only the atonement: it is also you and me receiving new life; which, it order **to thrive** and **survive**, it must be active, and it [the new life] must remain active in faith and obedience to God, that growth will take place, and the <u>seed</u> [the new life], **live**. Our salvation [the new life] in Jesus Christ is a living thing, it is alive, and yet, at times, very unpredictable; nevertheless, both biblically and logically, for this **new life to survive** and **thrive**, it must immediately **be actively engaged in sanctification** and **transformation** or else, this new life with its new growth, within, **is threatened to pass out of existence**. God, help us all to understand the balance between our justification, which is the work of God in those who believe the gospel, with sanctification, a cooperative work of the believer in yielding to the work of the Spirit, within. To risk delay, or to neglect, or, even to reject this necessary immediate response in our Christian sanctification, can, and will, put the Christian at risk of the loss of [new] life. Again, for the Calvinist this would mean, this person who claimed the gospel had laid a false claim; nevertheless, for those who believe you can lose your salvation, this would mean just that, the **miscarriage** or the **abortion** of new life. God, help us all!!

In John 3 Jesus compared biblical salvation to the reproductive process that gives birth to new life. Justification [spiritual regeneration] is understood as an inward spiritual conception. This pregnancy must be guarded at all times and at any cost in order to ensure it will be brought to full term. This is the true biblical testimony [witness of the scriptures] and cost of true discipleship for all who have received this new life. Just as any pregnancy can be deliberately aborted, so also a Christian can deliberately choose to turn away from the faith [aborting the new life]. True, it may take quite a bit of doing but, not entirely impossible. This is the point!! To take on an attitude [to hold a mindset] that we can never lose what we have received under any circumstance no matter what is, just biblically and naturally illogical. Just as some have experienced a miscarriage, losing the pregnancy through neglect or some other physical or medical reason, so also a Christian who refusing to *yield* to the initial changes and **spiritual growth** taking place *within* that, **demands sanctification** [commands a harvest] we, could risk losing the pregnancy. For a believer who has received new life to continue to choose the life of the flesh and resisting Christ within could suffer a miscarriage. While this may take a lot of doing; it is not an absolute impossibility. For a Christian to backslide and to go back into the world, and to forsake the faith, and then, to persist in this rebellion could bring ONE to spiritual bankruptcy [this is repeatedly substantiated in the scriptures]. Notice that Paul said, "For Demas hath *forsaken* me, having loved **this present** [evil, sinful] world, **and is departed...**" (2 Tim. 4:10). The New Testament calls Demas a fellow-laborer of Paul, the Apostle (Col. 4:14; Philemon 1:24). The statement made by Paul, was, not that Demas just abandoned the ministry, but as well, he abandoned the faith!! Peter spoke of those who were leaders [teachers] but turned aside and returned to their former [sinful] state/life, "For if after they [you] have escaped the pollutions of the world through the [saving] knowledge of our Lord and Savior Jesus Christ, and, are *again* entangled therein [have gone back to your past, or have returned to the world], and overcome [and are once again overcome by your former sins and lusts], the latter end is worse with them [with you] than the beginning" (2 Pet. 2:20-22). Salvation is by grace through faith, alone, but, this new life is not stagnant, nor isolated. Justification [new life] anticipates and demands growth and change as a natural and spiritual part of its normal inherent innate nature [this is sanctification]. Sanctification is the proof of, and, the demonstration of our justification, "If a man say, I love God, and hates his brother, he is a liar: for he that loves not his brother **who he hath seen**, how can he love God **whom he hath not seen**" (1 Jn. 4:20)? We love to claim something we cannot see [nor prove], and yet the way we live our lives proves we have seen nothing!! Sanctification is simple and easy, if we understand it as nothing more than the [new] life received in justification growing and doing what comes natural to it [what is normal]. The **branch** cannot help but bear fruit because of the new life of the True Vine within [it]. We as branches are engrafted into the True Vine: this is our justification; we remaining and continuing, enduring in that same One True Vine is what the bible calls our spiritual [and practical] sanctification. We cannot and must never **separate the new life from its growth!!** I am trying my best to balance all these things that concerns our justification and our Christian sanctification (Jn. 15:1-16). It is not right nor biblical to put these things in neatly fixed and separate boxes, this is error!!

His *imputed* righteousness [that is, his imputed (transferred) life of obedience] credited to us [counted to us] through our <u>identification</u> [association, recognition of, and connection] with him. God has *exchanged* our sins [our life of disobedience] for his righteousness [his life of obedience]. Christ is our legal representative [both *in* and *through* his sinless life and sin-bearing death] and, we are in living union with him by the indwelling presence of the Holy Spirit [He is the True Vine: the life-giving sustenance; and, we are his many branches purposed for fruit bearing; and, the Holy Spirit is the *supply* [the life-giving force] of the Vine that makes fruit bearing possible, Jn. 15:1-16]. The phrase **"in him"** or "in Christ" is found over 130 times in Paul's writings. This term used by Paul to *identify* the believer [in union] with Christ is our **placement** [being placed] in him. In him [his death], our sins [our life of disobedience] *imputed* to Christ [on the Cross]; and, in him [in his resurrection] his righteousness [his life of perfect obedience] *imputed* to us. All that is ours [under the curse] in fallen Adam is *imputed* to Christ on that Cross-and all that belongs to Christ [in his perfect sinless life/righteousness (his right-standing before God) and all the **benefits** that go with a perfect life of obedience under the law now belong to me/us] through his sinless life and sin-bearing death [and subsequent resurrection] is now mine [in him]. This is the Great divine Exchange. It is you and me daily living in the *reality* of this divine Exchange that makes all the difference!! It is believing that in every instance where I have failed to obey, Christ has obeyed in my place. His death is my death!! His life is my life!! His righteousness is my righteousness!! His obedience is my obedience!! His favor is my favor!! It is our daily embracing of the Cross [the gospel of His Grace], and, **looking outside of ourselves to Christ's shed blood** and **righteousness that releases His power** and **divine ability within.** This is the double-imputation of the Cross!!! This is the Great Divine Exchange!!! He took it all away; and, has given me all of himself. Praised God!!

The Cross of JC is a Divine Exchange [a divine transaction] that *imputes* our sins to Christ and His righteousness to us. This is a

Divine <u>transfer</u> of our Old *life* in Adam to Christ on the Cross, and His resurrection **life** to us in the New Birth. This **new birth** is his very own sinless perfect life of obedience imparted to us in spiritual regeneration. Now, Roman 8:4 makes sense, "that the *righteousness of the law might be fulfilled in* us...who walk *after* the Spirit [who yield to and live in agreement with the new life]" (Gal. 2:20; Rom. 12:2). This Divine Exchange [transaction] is a double imputation: his **death** took away our sins and put them into Christ on the Cross-and cancelled sin [put an end to sin]; and his **resurrection** has given to us/me his righteousness and has imparted to us/me new life (Rom. 4:25). The word <u>transaction</u> *means* something transacted or exchanged; to <u>transfer</u> goods and services. The word **transfer** *means* to move to a different place; or, to move from one place to another. To REMOVE FROM and to MOVE TO another place!! To *transfer* is to cause one to pass from one place to a new and different place. It *means as well* to **transplant**: to *both* take you out of one thing and bring you into another thing, and as well, **to take out** of you one thing and **to put into** you a new thing. "Who hath delivered us from the powers of darkness, and hath <u>translated</u> us into the kingdom of his dear Son" (Col. 1:13). This is a change in location [relocated] in the spirit. This is not only a change [in location] in the spirit, but, also a change *inside* within the spirit of the man. "For he is not a Jew, which is one outwardly; neither is that <u>circumcision</u>, which is outward in the flesh: but he is a Jew, which is one **inwardly**; and the **circumcision** is that of the heart, in the spirit...not of men, but of God" (Rom. 2:28-29). In Romans 6 Paul said, we have been Crucified [dead; died] and *buried* with him, but in Colossians he said, we are **Circumcised** [cut out: removed] and buried with him (Col. 2:11). To **circumcise** in the GK *means* to cut around, to remove: even to cut away. Paul said in Romans 5:10, "We were **reconciled** to God [GK-changed] by the ***death*** of His Son [on the Cross]." What specific change took place at the Cross?? My Old [sinner] Man was *crucified* with Christ and [my *sinful* **spirit** as a partaker of Adam's fallen sinful human condition] **cut out** of me [the sin-nature], removed, and *placed* on the Cross-cancelled [neutralized]. In [at] the resurrection, **his resurrection life** *infused* into my human spirit has **regenerated** *within* new life that, is now made to be a partaker of his very own obedient life [His Divine nature] (2 Pet. 1:4). Jesus said, "I am the resurrection and the life..." (Jn. 11:25). He did not say, I am the life and the resurrection, but if he had said this, it would still be true. He is the life; and, has always been the source of all life, but here, he is referring to the *new life* that comes to us, and is born out of his resurrection. This new life is the new creation; and, he, **is the firstborn of every new creature** (Col. 1:14-15). The word <u>firstborn</u> in the GK *means* **first begotten** [from the dead]; and is a reference **to his resurrection life** (Heb. 1:5-8). We have been brought [put] into the kingdom of God, and the kingdom of God is now put into us/you (Jn. 3:3; Lk. 17:21: 2 Cor. 4:7, Col. 1:27). This double imputation [transaction] has affected *both* **my standing** before God [made righteous] and, in the spirit world [we went from the conquered to the victor], and as well, has affected me and changed me from *within* [we have received new life and have become a new creation]. Grace has **imparted** something new to me, something undeserved!! The word **exchange** *means*, to receive something in return for something given. **It is life for life!!** So many say, you can have Christ as Savior and still reject him as LORD; can you have Egypt and still have Canaan at the same time?? Impossible!!!!!!!!!!! Many want to claim salvation but remain in Egypt. This is *both* illogical and a biblical impossibility. "For whosoever will **save his life** shall **lose it**: and, whosoever will **lose his life <u>for my sake</u>** shall find it [shall obtain it]" (Matt. 16:25-26). Our salvation has to be understood by you and I [the branch] being *engrafted* into Christ [the True Vine]. To **engraft** *means* to become successfully incorporated into the host body; to implant; to firmly put into in a permanent way: **to graft** from one plant to another **and cause to grow together**. It is possible to attempt to join what they call *a cutting* from one plant, to another, and it fail to take!! "Every branch **in me that bears no fruit** he takes away: and every branch that bears fruit, he purges [he prunes] it, that it may bring forth more fruit" (Jn. 15:2). Here in the text, Jesus is speaking of those who claim Christ for salvation but it does not take, and, they *fail* to **grow** together with him. However, those who were [are] **successfully engrafted into Jesus Christ now grow** [and continue to grow] and [until they] *bear* the fruit of the True Vine. Help!!

This is found in our *union* with Christ, "I am the Vine, ye are the branches...**abide** in me" (Jn. 15:5). This **treasure** *within* the earthen vessel is understood by the parable of the Mustard Seed, "...when it is *sown* in the earth, **is less** than all the seeds that be in the earth: but when it is sown, it **grows up**, and **becomes** greater than all herbs..." (Mk. 4:30-32). The **new life** [in him] we have received is Christ's very own life; but it starts out as something very small [indistinct] and has less influence over our lives at spiritual conception in comparison to all the other desires of the flesh and the world. These competing *desires* pull on us and influence us to satisfy its immediate demands!!! However, when this new life begins to **grow** [in our sanctification] it begins to *transform* the believer until the **new life** *within* becomes the one ultimate driving force in his/her life. This **seed** [of new life] starts out as the smallest influence in one's life, but, will eventually become the greater force *within* that will dominate the man [the believer]. The growth of this new life and new *influence* within the believer is what **transforms** him. Notice, we **grow** and, we **become**. This is sanctification!!! All of this is brought forth from the divine deposit [treasure] [wealth] from within the earthen vessel. "Abraham *believed* God, and it was counted unto him for righteousness" (Rom. 4:3; James 2:23). Righteousness here is speaking of Christ's sinless perfection. His sinless perfect **life** of obedience under the law imputed to us [this life does not sin, or get sick; it commands demons and, commands the elements, and multiplies the fish and the loaves, and works miracles, and its *authority* is found in our union with Him]. This righteousness *imputed* to us is Christ's very own earned righteousness in obedience to the Law. There are three branches [divisions] of the Law: Moral, Civil, and Ceremonial. He *first* fulfilled the **first** and **second** *divisions* of the Mosaic Law in Loving God with all his heart, soul, mind, and strength; and *secondly* loving his neighbor as himself, [he perfectly kept every *jot* and *tittle* of the letter of the Mosaic code thus fulfilling it]. All that remained, now, was to *satisfy* the demand of the third branch of the Law. The Ceremonial Law [the third branch] demanded a death!! This death would satisfy the demands for divine justice [in the breaking of the first two branches (divisions) of the Law]. Christ became [and was proved to be] the perfect sinless Lamb for atonement through his perfect obedience and complete fulfillment of the first and second divisions of the Law. Once he paid the sin price on the Cross [thus, fulfilling the third branch of the law], the Law was now complete [finished; satisfied; fulfilled; perfected]. He, in his sinless perfect humanity [and through his perfect obedience under the law] he fulfilled and perfected the first two branches of the Mosaic Code; it is in his sin-bearing death, he perfectly and completed finished the third division of the law. The word <u>counted</u> in the GK *means* to reckon, or to impute, and is the same GK word used in James 2:23 and is translated as imputed. This GK word *logizomai* is an accounting term, and pictures an accountant's ledger. On the one side: you have **debts**, and on the other side: you have **profits**. Here, Paul is saying we are *transferred* and moved from the debt side of the ledger to the profit side [to the gain] [surplus] [the profit margin] of the ledger. No longer do we owe; we now, **own!!!** Imputation is a legal matter and transaction that moves us from *debt* to **solvent** [able to pay all legal debts]. We go from the Red to the Black in accounting terms. From debt [owing], to solvent [profit; gain; to ownership], "And if children, then heirs; heirs of God, and joint-heirs with Christ" (Rom. 8:17). This is a double imputation-In him [in his death] our **sins** [our life of disobedience] is *imputed* to Christ on the Cross; and in him [in his resurrection] his **righteousness** [his life of perfect obedience] is *imputed* to us [both positional and experiential]. All that is ours under the curse in fallen Adam is now *imputed* to Christ on the Cross; and all that belongs to him, in his sinless perfection [in his sinless humanity] [in his life of perfect obedience under the law] now *imputed* to us [now belongs to me]. This includes all the **benefits** that go with a ***life*** of perfect obedience under the law [all made possible by his **sinless life** (fulfilling the first *two* divisions of the Law), and **sin-**

bearing death (satisfying, finishing, and completing the *third* branch of the Law), and his subsequent resurrection]. This is the Great [Divine] exchange!! This is not only an **imputation** but as well is an **impartation**!!! Romans 5:10-11 says, "...we were *reconciled* to God by his death," which *means* we have been changed by his death on the Cross-the Atonement. Here, the word reconciled in the GK *means* both changed and made different [#2644-236 in Strong's]. "Much more [to an even greater degree] we **shall be** saved by his **life** [this speaks to not only our justification but as well to our sanctification]. Life here is the GK word ZOE and speaks to the God kind [quality] of life [this is spiritual/eternal life]. All of this is made possible by that Divine Exchange, "...by whom [Christ] we **have now** received the atonement [GK-reconciliation; **exchange**; restoration to divine favor]. The **Cross**-put an end to the Old and his **resurrection** life brought into the world the New. To **take out** [the old] and to **put in** this [new life] is the double imputation. Reconciled [changed] by what He **took out**, even more so by what He **put back in**!!! Salvation is not just about what he *took out* but even the more what *he imparted* to us by way of new life. Double imputation is what he *first* took out and then what he *replaced it* with [and put back into man]. This is the Old Testament story of the Exodus. He brought us out to bring us in!!! We are saved according to his **purpose** and grace. His purpose is what He wants the most: to put into us the new life, and to see it [the new life] **grows** and comes into **fullness** [wholeness], **maturation**. This is why he delivered us and brought us out [he removed, took out of us our sinful condition] that he might put into us new life. He *took out* of us **the old fallen sinful nature** that he might put into us a new nature that is now a partaker of his divine nature. Do you see where Paul said, "much more," God is placing an even greater emphasis on what he **put into us** than, what he took out [of us]. Sanctification is His end game!!!!!! To bring us into his fullness!! This sanctification *anticipates* glorification [the resurrection of the body]. Paul said, "**We were** *reconciled* [changed and brought into new life, and made different]," and "**We shall be** *saved* [delivered from the power of sin, and healed from all its negative effects, and brought into soundness:

fullness] [sanctification]," because, "**We have now** *received* the atonement [reconciliation: we have now received that divine exchange]. We **were** [past-has happened], we **shall be** [future-will happen: this is a process from start to finish], and, we **have now** [present-is happening]. The word now *means* at the present time. This *means* the atonement is not just some past event; but, it is as well an ever-present reality. The Atonement is not just one big divine transaction on the Cross, but, as well, it is a daily divine exchange of one's life, yielded, and turned over on a continual, consistent, and daily basis to Christ. "As you have received Christ Jesus the Lord [meaning, in the very same way you *first* received him], so walk ye in him [so, continue to follow after him, and continue to be occupied with him and by him]: rooted and built up in him, and established in the faith" (Col. 2:6-7). **This is that** *daily* **exchange in our daily sanctification.** Thank God!!! The atonement is not just a past event, seen and understood through Christ's historical death on the Cross; and, it is not only a future promise as seen and understood through and by his resurrection and, our promised resurrection: it is an ever present power and provision [and reality] found in **the power** of this **gospel** of JC: to save, rescue, deliver, heal, protect, preserve, and to make whole, and the like.

Salvation is a *process* that begins with **Justification**, then continues with **Sanctification**, and then finishes with **Glorification**. Justification is our spiritual *regeneration* and the New Birth; sanctification is *transformation*, and is where we **grow** in His grace *first* received in Justification (2 Pet. 3:18). Glorification is the *resurrection* of the body and the completion of the Redemptive Process. Paul said, "And the very **God** of peace **sanctify you** wholly (completely); and I pray God your whole spirit and soul and body (GK-complete in every part, i.e. perfectly sound in the entire person) be **preserved** blameless [unblamable; faultless] *unto* the coming of *our* **Lord** JC [who is Master, Owner, and Controller, having all authority over our lives]" (1 Thessalonians. 5:23). Notice that God is the **sanctifier**, "And...God...sanctify you," it is He who will *preserve* and **keep** you unto the end [GK-To keep, and to guard against loss: to watch by keeping the eye upon]. The promise here in the text is, that God [the HS] Himself will work *within* you **to will** and **to do** of his good pleasure <u>to present you faultless in his sight in His presence</u> at the end of time at the Bema Seat of Christ [Completed in our **spirit** [regeneration], **soul** [transformation], and **body** [glorification], a completed redemptive work]. Notice in the text again, the word <u>unto</u> and Paul connecting it to Christ's very *own* **Lordship** over the life of the believer. Many have divorced His Lordship from our Salvation. Peter said, "For if after they have escaped the pollutions of the world through the [saving] knowledge of the [our] **Lord** and **Savior** JC, [and] they are again entangled therein, and [are] overcome, the latter end is worse with them than the beginning" (2 Pet. 2:20). Notice in the text it says, "*...they are **again** entangled therein, and [are] **overcome**,*" here Paul is speaking of those who fell back into what they came out of to the losing of their soul. Notice, Peter ties our Salvation to His Lordship!! Paul said, "And that he died for all, that they which **live** [have new life] should not henceforth live unto themselves, but unto him which died for them, and rose again," "And ye are not your own. For ye are bought with a price: therefore glorify God in your **body**, and in your **spirit**, which are God's" (1 Cor. 6:19-20; 2 Cor. 5:15). We have been **redeemed** [purchased] by His precious blood and, **we no longer belong to ourselves** and, now, **have no right** to our lives any longer.

The Divine **Exchange** [the Atonement] is He giving up His life in order to purchase ours [yours]. In order for you and me to receive this so great a salvation, we must believe the gospel and willingly lay down our lives for His, that we might receive His very own life and share in His inheritance. Remember, this is a choice [a decision] we have to make: to surrender one's life for His life [JC]. This is the preaching of the Cross-that **divine exchange** without which <u>salvation</u> would be an absolute impossibility. It is not a *mental* agreement with the facts of the faith [where the life remains unchanged], but a *heart* change [a decision] and commitment [conversion] to live the New

Life that abandons the old one. You cannot remain in the Old life [the old land of Egypt] and receive at the same time the Promised Land and Eternal Life [salvation] in Christ Jesus (Rom. 6:23). **It just does not work this way; many are being deceived!!!!!!** Paul said, "With the mouth *confession* is made **unto** salvation," again, there it is that word unto, which *means* into salvation or to **enter into** salvation, where one must make a *profession* of faith. Paul further states, "That if thou shalt *confess* with thy mouth the **Lord** Jesus... thou shalt be saved." Here again Paul connects His **Lordship** to our salvation (Rom. 10:9-10). So many want to *separate* His Saviorship from His Lordship; Peter did not do this (2 Pet. 2:20). Here the GK word is **kurios** and *means* supreme in authority, Lord, master, and controller. In order to receive this so great a salvation we must **confess** and **bow** our knee [life] to His Lordship. We must confess JC as Savior and **Lord**, and acknowledge at every point His right to rule over all of our life: spirit, soul, and body. Without this true knowledge, understanding, and true commitment to the facts of the gospel one will not receive [mercy] grace for salvation. The *confession* of our mouth is our **power** of attorney and is our **address** [location] in the spirit world. The entire world of the spirit knows where you are and knows who you are by the confession of your very own mouth. This is why salvation requires it; and, this is why salvation is called the great Confession. This confession and profession of your faith *both* locates you and relocates you in the world of the spirit!! If your confession does not line you up with Him, and, puts you under the Lordship of JC, then, it will not locate you, relocate you, and **put you into salvation** [and put you into eternal life]. God, help us all to believe in the gospel of Jesus Christ, correctly, rightly, and bow our knee to it [bow our knee to him].

The instrumental cause for our justification is faith alone; this faith is not the grounds for our justification, but rather, the *means* by which justification is **obtained** [that through which we are linked to Christ and by which the objective benefits of his saving work (grace) is subjectively appropriated by the believer]. Faith is the *means* by which we receive our justification [this is an *imputed* righteousness by which we are saved; before, his righteousness is ever inherently present within us]. This is an **imputation** before **impartation**. Imputation is for our justification, and impartation is for our sanctification. The **legal ground** for our justification is found in the **Person** and **Work** of the Lord and Savior Jesus Christ on the Cross [in the/his atonement] [in his redemptive works] [and, in him and he crucified, alone]. We are **justified** by faith in Christ and, in him crucified, before, we are **sanctified** [by the inner workings of His grace] [by the Person and Work of the indwelling Holy Spirit]. We are all first considered [righteous] **justified** through faith in Christ's atoning work, *while* we were yet <u>sinners</u> [enemies of God] (Rom. 5:8-11). Sanctification does not *qualify* one for justification, it demonstrates it [it is the atonement/the Cross alone that qualifies one for true justification]. This does not *mean* a **justified person** is an unchanged person: a justified person is **spiritually regenerated** and has received new life [now, the new life *within* has to grow up (in him) to be enabled to **bear the fruits** we now call our Christian sanctification]. The believer is *first* [up front] made or declared **just** [innocent] [righteous] before this process of sanctification [ever] begins. It is very important to always keep in mind that though a *justified person* is a changed [new] person, those changes wrought in him by the grace of God are not the grounds for his justification, that ground remains exclusively the righteousness of Jesus Christ that is *imputed* to him through faith in the Cross-the atonement. We are made-declared **just** [made right with God] by virtue of the *imputation* of Christ's righteousness alone, while we were yet sinners. **Imputation** *refers* to that act by which God will count or reckon us **righteous** [just] by legally transferring the righteousness of Christ to our own personal account [this takes place in the Court of heaven], this involves the *transfer* of Christ's **merit** to us [his life of perfect obedience under the Law]. Just trying to keep it real. I apologize for the redundancy but this is the only way to ensure there is no confusion between justification and Christian sanctification. For you and I to claim a justification which comes by faith in Christ's redemptive works [alone] on the Cross, and then in turn [to turn around and] live a life in contradiction to this [our] profession of faith is biblically illogical and dishonest [a false gospel] [a false conversion]. The consequences of ideas, by R C Sproul, chapter 21, Audiobook 2010. God, help us all not to take this for granted!!! The gospel is justification, and sanctification!!

IMPUTED OR INFUSED?

Christian Theology over the last number of centuries has seen this concept of justifying grace, either ***imputed*** or ***infused*** as contradictory throughout its history. Does this have to be the case? There is no doubt, they both were applied as enemies [as opponents] operating on opposite sides of the fence. Is there a place for both ***imputed*** <u>grace</u> and ***infused*** <u>grace</u> to participate on the same team? Imputed *means* to freely give: to reckon, or to count one as righteous as a gift. It *means* to put to the account of someone, such as an accounting ledger. It is a *transfer* from the **debt** side of the ledger to the **profit** [surplus] side of the ledger. We have gone from owing **a debt** [from **sin**] to now having **that debt** [the **law**] satisfied, and now we are relocated to the profit margin. We longer owe, we now **own!!** Again, to **impute** *means* to put to the account of, while **infused** *means* <u>to put into</u> or to cause to be filled. The *former* is outside of the man and put to his account. This is a legal transaction, while, the *latter* [to be infused] *means* <u>to put into</u> [to put inside] the man, this becomes a living union with him. <u>Imputation</u> speaks to our justification, while, **impartation** [infused grace] applies to our sanctification. There is no doubt; the **merits** [righteousness, and obedience] of Jesus Christ is **imputed** [and reckoned] unto us, thus we are declared [counted] as just or righteous. This is a righteousness by which we are saved [alone]. It is **an alien** [outside] righteousness that belongs to **another** [imputed or counted to us] coming from elsewhere [or from another]. We are justified [saved] [clear of all guilt] by faith in his blood [by faith in his redemptive works]. This <u>reconciliation</u> is God restoring man [the believer] back into divine favor with Him. We are now **in right**

standing with Him through *faith* [through trusting] in the promises [the gospel of our salvation] [the Atonement-what He did for us on the Cross]. This **imputed** grace is an *imputed* righteousness for [our] justification. There is no doubt; when it comes to justification, it is always an imputed [free] grace!!! Now on the other hand, **infused** grace is equally valid as a *sanctifying* grace [not for justification]. This controversy [argument] [confusion] has persisted for the last 500 years between Catholics and Protestants over the Doctrine of Justification. There is a place for *both* principles [concepts] [truths] [doctrines] to coexist together on the same one gospel team. Thank God. Both believing Protestants and true believing Catholics can reconcile their differences in this way!!! It is both an *imputed* grace for justification, and an *infused* grace for our sanctification. Praise God. Justification is that which is applied from the outside; sanctification works within!!!

Now, after **imputing** [justifying] grace for salvation [which is a legal judicial acquittal], in addition to this, this same *imputed* grace is now **infused** for sanctification, which becomes His very own **obedient life** now within us [as a treasure within the earthen vessel]. It is clear; this **grace** of His very own life *within* is the sanctifying force [power] that now operators within (Phil. 2:13). This **infused grace** is his very own obedient life, that same life He lived out in perfect obedience to God under the Law. This **infused** grace [impartation] *within* becomes our new birth [and is a part of our spiritual regeneration] and becomes the *means* by which the believer [the saints] are sanctified [set apart]. Now, through this *sanctifying* work of the Spirit of Grace, working through *the means* of His grace **infused** *within* as his very own obedient life now at work [changing us from] within. Christ in us [His infused Grace] is **the True Vine** within [His very own obedient life within us], and the FATHER through the *sanctifying* and *perfecting* work of the Holy Spirit becomes the Vinedresser. The Spirit of Grace operating from *within* is the Holy Spirit himself; and the **infused grace** *engrafted* within is none other than Christ's very own life!! This is why Paul would say, "Christ **in me** the hope of glory" (Col. 1:27). This **infused** sanctifying grace becomes the life *transforming* grace within our born again spirit [within our spiritual regeneration], that will bear the fruits of the Spirit *in* and *through* [the transformation of] the human soul. This **infused grace is His very own merits, righteousness,** and obedient life imparted [given] to us, that [if yielded to] will bring forth **fruit** and *fulfill* the righteousness [the righteous standard] of the law (Rom. 8:4). Grace is **something received yet undeserved** [it is something we do not deserve or, could ever earn by our own merit]. Many look at Grace as simply a covering for sin, that, actually really does absolutely nothing about sin itself, and, the sinful life. Many look at Grace, simply as an exemption, simply something we do not have to do, and, something that simply overlooks sin and bypasses His divine justice. **Grace is a very, very powerful action that overturns a bad situation and now makes it [puts it] into a favorable condition.** It does not overlook nor ignore the sinful or, the sinful condition: it undo's it; and *transforms* the situation making reconciliation possible. When we say, we are made righteous in Christ, we are saying, we are in Right-Standing with Him [before God]. This is a legal or judicial standing *binding* in a Court of Law. The two terms **Justification** and **Righteousness** are interchangeable and inseparable and *mean* the same thing, and are applied in the same way in the Greek. We are now justified, and made righteous!! Grace will extend mercy to the sinner; while, at the same time, grace, is **looking to empower the new life of righteousness for holy living** [grace has purposed to bear the fruits of this newly regenerated life]. I do not want to be misunderstood!! Grace will extend mercy to sinner for the forgiveness of sins; notwithstanding, grace with then, **impart new life. It is here, within our sanctification,** grace will go to work **to empower transformation** and, **holy set apart living**. There is no room for carnality to go about and to continue in the old life. Grace is a divine ability and empowerment given [within] for change!! God, by his grace, will continue to extend his mercy to the sinner, or rather, to the backslidden carnal Christian; however, these who call themselves Christian and continue to live in sin, prove, they are not [living and operating] under his Grace. So many have defined, "under grace," as, under license to sin [or rather, no longer under any obligation to obey God]. Under Grace, means, **in Christ**: and, under his supernatural empowerment. This is why Paul said, "Sin shall no longer have dominion over you!! Why?? Because, we are now under his divine Grace!! To be under law is, to be under sin; to under grace is, to be in Christ. To be under law means, to still be in fallen Adam; notwithstanding, we are in Christ Jesus, thus, we are under his grace. Grace is not a license to sin; it is not a get out of jail free card; it is not an exemption, where, we are allowed to live in sin **with impunity** [which means, without punishment] (Rom. 6:14-15). This is further proved by God's response to the Apostle Paul's plea for deliverance and healing: My grace is sufficient for you (2 Cor. 12:1-10). You will notice in the text, that, what Paul called GRACE in verse nine, he turns around and calls that same grace, STRENGTH, "And he said unto me, My **grace** is sufficient for thee: for my **strength** is made perfect **in weakness**." Paul's weakness was his infirmity; however, God's strength, was/is **his grace!!** Grace is not a covering for sin; God, will extend his mercy to atone for our sins, which of course comes to us by the grace of God [which means, it comes to us by his undeserved favor]. However, notwithstanding, immediately, this same grace will go to work in our Christian sanctification to transform the human soul, thus, completely transforming **human behavior/works**. I do not what to be misunderstood; Peter speaks of the manifold grace of God (1 Peter 4:10). This word manifold should be understood as, grace, coming to us in manner different forms. This is understood as the **multiplied ways** in which grace can and will be applied to the Christian. But, it is very important we do not reduce grace to a simple covering for sin and, a permission to commit vice [as if grace is consenting to sin]. It is not my desire to box grace into this one specific definition; however, this definition for grace as an empowerment for living is rarely taught. Help!!

It is important we understand that this new life [in Christ] within us, which is Christ's very own life, cannot steal, will not commit adultery, cannot sin, fall ill, get sick, catch a disease, and will never die. This new life within is given authority over every manner of sickness and disease, will command demons, and will command the elements (1 Jn. 3:9; Rom. 8:9-13). This is his very own resurrection life living within us!!! The bible tell us, "In him was [is] the life... [and] he that hath the Son hath [the] life; and he that hath not the Son of God hath not [the] life...that you may know that you have eternal life...I have come that you might **have** [the] life, and that you might **have** it more abundantly" (Jn. 1:4; 10:10; 1 Jn. 5:12). In the GK **to have** *means* **to hold** this life *within* ourselves in Christ, to have this [new] life and **to hold** this [new] life in abundance. "And this is the record, that God hath given to us [eternal] life, and this [new] life [that will never end] is in his Son" (1 Jn. 5:11). This **new life** comes to us by His [the] **grace** of His Son, through faith in his death, burial, and resurrection. It is clear; **we have received an imputed [free] grace for righteousness unto justification [salvation]**; but we have also received an **infused** [imparted] grace [put into us] for [our] Christian sanctification that in all things in the life of the believer He [Christ], might have the **preeminence** [might be Lord over all: spirit, soul, and body] (Eph. 1:13-23; Col. 1:13-22; Rom. 8:15-39). Jesus said, **"...Make the tree good, and his fruit [will be] good"** (Matt. 12:33). Both the TREE and the FRUIT!! The **tree** [that is made good] is the *imputed* grace for justification, while, the **fruit** [which represents our outwardly changed lives] is the *infused* [imparted] grace for our Christian sanctification. We are *both* **brought into** His grace and **clothed by** His grace [imputation], and His grace [Christ] is as well *infused* and put into us [for our spiritual growth and transformation]. This is a real change that has happened *within* us the believer, where **imputation** now, as well, *corresponds* to our **impartation**, and where [grace for] justification now *anticipate* and demands [grace for our] sanctification. Salvation is *both* an ever present imputation [not just a past imputation] and, an ever present impartation, where the *former* is outside and **done for us**, and the *latter* is inside and done **to us** and **within us**. This is justification demanding a real change, and, sanctification responding to that demand. These are like two peas in a pod, and are inseparable and irreplaceable. To do otherwise, would made it a false gospel.

In Justification, union with Christ makes a real change in us. Justification makes a real change in us because it gives us Christ. Martin Luther said, "There are two kinds of righteousness: <u>Alien</u> Righteousness and <u>Proper</u> Righteousness. The *first* [the former] is God; the *second* [the latter] is us [man]. **It is through this Alien Righteousness I become a good tree**, and it is by the **Proper Righteousness** [which are good works that follow faith] that I bear **good fruit**. The real change in me is the change in me where I become a **good tree**!! A good tree now *capable* of doing ***good works*** or bearing **good fruit** [that which accompanies faith]. Therefore, the **inward-change** is precisely the change of an Alien [outside] Righteousness, this is Christ's very own righteous merit [obedience] earned under the Law, which is given to me as a <u>possession</u> [a free gift] now residing *within* **as an active infused Grace**, whereby I grow and bear fruit. These *fruits* are nothing more than the **corresponding actions** to true <u>faith</u> [faith **rooted** in the gift: the imputed grace]. The **imputed** Grace that *justifies* is the **Good Tree**; and then afterward it becomes an **infused** Grace, and a real <u>change</u> within me, that I now really <u>possess</u> in me that now <u>works</u> *within* in order to bring forth **good fruit** [true sanctification]. **Imputed** Grace for <u>justification</u>, and an **infused** Grace for <u>sanctification</u>. The real righteousness, the *inward* change, is not my righteousness nor my good works, but an Alien righteousness and an **imputed** grace, which is Christ's very own righteous merits/works, and obedience under the Law **imputed** to me and *counted* as mine through faith in Him and His Cross [the **Atonement**], and is now *imparted* to me as an **infused** grace. It is quite clear; this Alien Righteousness has become that deep inner-change that has taken place within each born-again believer!! This **infused grace** [impartation of Christ's very own life] is Christ's very own perfect obedient life now imparted to me, as a gift, a promise, a provision made possible for me **in my union with him**. May God Be Praised!!! [History of Christian Theology by Phillip Cary, "Catholic Theologies of Grace," and "Protestant disagreements," and the Teaching Series by R C Sproul, the Cross of Christ, lessons 2-4]. God, please help us to understand and comprehend **your fullness!!!** Praise God, and our Lord Jesus Christ for **mercy** and **grace**, in **our justification** and Christian **sanctification**.

PART THREE

Knowing, Reckon, and Yield

We will not be able to *believe* to receive if we do not first have a proper knowledge of the thing we believe. We must first properly comprehend the thing we believe [in the spirit] before we can properly apprehend that same thing [in this world]. What does communication mean? It is the *transmission* of ideas; the process by which information is *exchanged* between individuals. What are the keys to communication?? If it is an exchange of ideas and the transmission of information, what then would be necessary for successful communication? The *need* to properly explain one's position and the *need* for the other party to properly understand said position. For communication to be successful there is both the need to rightly explain the proper meaning of things, and then for the other party to properly understand, otherwise, an appropriate response to those things believed for would become impossible. The **word** of God properly taught will ***ground*** the people of God in the truth that will help them to properly believe and receive from the promises of God. We have to come into the **knowledge** of the truth to be free (Jn. 8:30-32). This is why bible doctrine is so important. Not just the right understanding but as well using the proper terms. Those who promote [and push a] false doctrine [those who promote false teaching] will often attempt to do one or the other, if not try to change both the **terms** and there **meanings**. It is important to use the right biblical **term**, and then **explain** [break down and make clear] the right [proper] biblical **meaning** of the term. This is why we find over the 2000 years of Church history the fight for [the fight to retain] biblical inerrancy. Not, just, that it is the Word [and words] of God, but as well, we must maintain its proper **terms** [the right verbiage; or the use of the right words] and there proper **meanings**. Biblical **inerrancy** is the belief that the Bible is without error or fault in all of its teachings. In other words, the Scriptures are **infallible**, which means, totally and completely trustworthy as a guide to true biblical [Christian] salvation. The Bible is the only true guide in the life of true faith. The bible is true concerning what true biblical faith and Christian practice truly and really is. The right use of its **terms** and their proper meanings are paramount to true biblical faith and Christian practice. Inerrancy means, **without error**; however, it is possible to **incorrectly interpret** and **misapply** the scriptures!! It is always important to keep in mind: all scriptures are interpreted by all the other scriptures. The bible warns us not to give to any scripture a private [or separate] interpretation, which means, to interpret a text in an **isolated** manner: to interpret [or, to give meaning to a text] apart from [or separated from] *both* its context, and, the overall meaning and purpose for the bible itself. The bible teaches that we are to search the scriptures, and, to compare spiritual things, with other spiritual things, within the context of the scriptures. This is the only way we can rightly divide the word [or message of] the truth contained within any given text (2 Pet. 1:20; 1 Cor. 2:13; 2 Tim. 2:15). Peter, warning those who attempted to interpret the bible but did so in error, "Which they that are unlearned [either not taught or, incorrectly taught] and unstable **wrest**, as they do also the other scriptures, unto their own destruction [ruination and the loss of eternal life]. **Wrest**, here, in the text, means, **to pervert** the scriptures, as if to twist out its proper shape into something unintended and incorrect [to contort into a new and improper form]. To contort means to twist into a new and different shape. In other words, **to contort the gospel**, means, to twist it into a different and incorrect [false] gospel (Gal. 1:6-9). Here, it refers to these [people] **as unstable**, which gives us the word picture of one **vacillating** [or, halting] between two places/positions. This speaks to immorality: vacillating between a life of **virtue** and a life of **vice**. This was the exact **mindset** of many of the Greeks and Romans in Peter's day that were in the **pursuit of virtue**, only to succumb **to vice** (2 Pet. 3:16). Peter said, "those that **were clean** [are those who] escaped from them [from those persons] who lived **in error** [both doctrinally and morally] (2 Pet. 2:18). It is no different today, many Christians vacillate between biblical morality and the human value systems of this world [walking somewhere between the flesh and the Spirit] (Ps. 1:1-6). A **term** is a **biblical word** or expression that has a **precise meaning**; so, when we say it is important to use correct biblical terms and their proper meanings, we are speaking specifically about the Bible's true intention, prescribed purpose, and applied meaning of any given text. All of these things must be understood and applied in their proper biblical context. The proper meaning of a text, is, the thing intended [the thing it purports]. To take any word or text [of scripture] out of its proper context is guaranteed to contort and pervert the intended meaning in the text [of scripture]. Help!!!

THE RESURRECTION

In the resurrection, Christ was <u>vindicated</u>, [in and of himself] he was sinless, and death had no direct claim upon Him [he was exonerated: he was found to be just and innocent, and proved to be holy]. Death is God's punishment for sin!! For Christ to remain in the grave [because he was utterly without sin], would have been unjust of God to leave him in the grave [to punish him forever for sins]. Now, Christ willingly took upon himself the imputation of our sins and, the suffering he endured on the Cross was not for his guilt and sin, but, God declared him to be righteous [innocent of all guilt and sin] by acquittal in terms of his own personal resurrection. The Bible teaches, it was impossible for death to hold him!! Romans 4:25 tells us, "[He] who was delivered up for our <u>offenses</u> [trespasses and sins], [was also] raised for our justification." For Christ to die and, to fail to be raised from the dead, the bible teaches, we would all, still, be yet in our sins, and our faith in God would be yet in vain (1 Cor. 15:12-17). His resurrection was not only his own personal acquittal and vindication [that proved he was innocent and righteous] (Acts 17:31); but as well proof that God accepted his sacrifice for sin to make atonement [for us] [in appeasing the wrath of God against sin and the sinner]. This is why Paul said, that, faith in the ***gospel*** requires one to believe on the **resurrection** of Jesus Christ from the dead in order to be saved (Rom. 10:9). God, in the resurrection, bore witness to His own satisfaction [approval for all] of the redemptive works of Christ on the Cross [his Son] to make atonement [for mankind] [by raising him from the dead]. It is through faith in the **gospel** [both his death and resurrection] that we have received the divine assurance of our own personal future resurrection and promised eternal life [the forgiveness of sins]. Not only the power of **sin** *broken* in the atonement [on the Cross], but as well the power [and force] of the **grave** *neutralized* and set aside, which is evidenced by and through His [Christ's] resurrection. Not only is new life given and, eternal life promised, but as well, a new body is guaranteed on the last day at the return of JC, which is the first resurrection [the resurrection of the just] [The teaching series by R C Sproul, Understanding the Gospel, Resurrection and Justification Part 6]. It is important that we not only *identify* with his **death**, but as well with his **resurrection** [life]. To *identify* with his death is to *identify* with the death and burial [removal] of the Old; and to *identify* with his resurrection is to *associate* oneself with His [new] life [which puts us into Christ] [This is the true Vine, and his many branches]. This is what the *writer* of Hebrews calls, **"so great a salvation"** (Heb. 2:1-4). "Therefore <u>we</u> ought to give the more earnest heed *to the things* which <u>we</u> have heard, lest at any time <u>we</u> should let them slip...how shall <u>we</u> escape, if <u>we</u> neglect so great [a] salvation..." (Heb. 2:1, 3). The word **neglect** here *means* to make light of; to be careless toward: to hold with little regard, and to show [very] little interest in. <u>Neglect</u> in the Old English [OE] *means* to pay little attention to, or to show little respect for, to fail to give the proper time to: to bypass; disregard; forget; ignore; and overlook. This is the great falling away of the Church!! The **neglect** of the gospel [and the scriptures] have caused many **to drift away** from the faith. Notice how the word **neglect** is tied to those things that are *slipping* away. **Five times** in the *text*, in verses 1 and 3 the word **"we"** is found. Notice, Paul is addressing <u>believers</u>, "...we ought to give the more earnest heed to these things **we** have heard, lest **we** should let them slip. No doubt, the writer of this epistle [Paul] was including himself in the warning. Is Paul saying, **we** [the believer] could slip away [drift away] from the faith? Is Paul saying, how shall the believer **escape** the judgment of God if they **neglect** the [great] salvation [they have received] and, drift away from the faith? Again, this is somewhat controversial. This is used as a counter-argument to the doctrine of Eternal Security that helps us to balance its understanding and application to the faith. The things we have heard according to the text is referring to the gospel of our salvation. Paul here is making it clear, the need <u>to contend for</u> the faith (I Tim. 6:12; Phil. 3: 10-15; Jude 3; Jn. 10:10). Here, Paul is not pointing [referring] to <u>justification</u>, but to our <u>sanctification</u>!! **What does it mean to slip away?** The word in the GK *means* to flow by [as running water], or, to carelessly pass [time] and to miss or to let slip. How many Christians *waste* their time with temporal things, and *waste* most of their lives on things that have little to no eternal value. The word picture here could be applied to a boat or ship at sea aimlessly **drifting** without direction or navigation. Paul is saying, we must pay the more careful attention to *these things* [truths] we have received in our knowledge of this gospel lest **we let them slip** and we *drift* away from the faith [the gospel of His grace], **the truth** about the gospel. The reason why many drift away from the faith is that they are no longer [or not at all] **tethered** [anchored] to the truth [of the gospel]. To **tether** *means* a line to which someone or something is attached [to fasten or to restrain by or, as if by a tether, rope, or chain]. **Like a boat on shore tied to the dock.** The reason why many Christians are *drifting* away from the faith and from biblical morality is, that, they are no longer **anchored** [tethered] to the truth of the Scriptures [the gospel]. This is like a boat on shore [or, near to shore], but those in the boat have failed to let the anchor down, and they just allow the boat to move with the current, and they just *drift* away from the shore and are lost at sea. Those who fail to keep their **anchor** in the water [who fail to keep their lives in the word of God everyday of their life] are drifting away. Paul said, we are to be "**rooted** [grounded in the truth] and **built up** in him [transformed in **our union** with him], and **established** in the <u>faith</u> [having a deep and accurate and abiding knowledge and devotion to the gospel], as ye have **been taught** [the scriptures], **abounding** therein [being a doer of the word, not just a hearer only] with **thanksgiving** [maintaining a grateful heart at all times]" (Col. 2:7; Phil. 4:4-9). Paul was applying **these truths** to all believers [and warning them] to pay careful attention to all of these things. The immediate context found in the book of Hebrews is Paul attempting *to warn* the Christian Jews not to **drift away** from the Christian faith [the meaning of the gospel] and returning to Judaism. Today, we find so many believing Gentiles **drifting** away from the true gospel to a spiritual counterfeit. Many are now returning to vain philosophies of men, and false ideologies [based on the rudiments of the world] and not on Christ and him crucified [new creation realities]. These are those who labor for [seek after] **the meat** [food] that **spoils!** These are just as the great multitude who sought him to make him their king because they did eat and were filled [these have turned the faith of our fathers into a material gospel]. (John 6:1-27; Matt. 6:19-34; 1 Tim. 6:3-12). So many have placed so little value on the **new life** [treasure] they have received in their spiritual regeneration, having forsaken it [and now neglect it] for the life in their body [For Demas hath forsaken me, having loved this present world (2 Tim. 4:10)]. When Paul spoke of this great salvation, he was picturing in his mind's eye the great Exodus in Egypt. If those who **rejected** [were indifferent to] the first great salvation in the OT were subject to loss and judgement, how much more **we** who neglect this so great a salvation [in Christ] will not escape the coming wrath (Heb. 10:26-31; 2 Pet. 2:1-[20-22]). Just as so many in the time of the first great Exodus out of Egypt looked back, today, many are entangled once again [with their old sins, and old lifestyle], and **are overcome** [find themselves in bondage once again to those same things Christ had once set them free]. Many [people] who were delivered out of Egypt [both Israelites and the mixed multitude] began to **backslide** the very moment they left Egypt. How many of those who claim the gospel for the forgiveness of sins are no different?? They lay claim to the gospel for salvation, only then [and for some immediately] go back to the sin [and a sinful lifestyle]. God, help us to see there is no recourse to return to those former things!! God, help us to make a true and genuine commit to the gospel through a true and pure devotion to Christ, and he crucified.

"...And therefore it was **imputed** to him for righteousness. Now it was not written for his sake alone, that it was *imputed* to him; but for us also, to whom it shall be **imputed**, <u>if we *believe* on him</u>

that raised up Jesus our Lord from the dead; who was delivered for our **offenses** [on the Cross] [our willful transgressions; our sins, trespasses, error; from another GK word that *means* apostasy or falling away; our slipping, sliding, and side-stepping], and **was raised again** for our justification [acquittal; to pardon for sins, to declare innocent or just]" (Rom. 4:22-25). Notice how his *imputed* **righteousness** was/ is received by the person who believes on him in His resurrection (Rom. 10:8-10) [this **righteousness** we have received in him, through faith in him, will *increase* and *expand* through the **knowledge** of him] (2 Pet. 1:1-4). Here, this **righteousness** must *mean* more than just a judicial pardon, but as well, speaks to the **new life** that was received in the **new birth**. This **new birth is our spiritual regeneration** [unto and into new life]. The righteousness we have received which is tied to the Cross is a **judicial** righteousness that has provided the forgiveness of sins [and has declared us just or innocent in a Court of Law]. This is the *imputed* righteousness of Jesus Christ; however, this same righteousness that is now tied to the resurrection is an **active** righteousness that has *imparted* new life. "For with the heart men *believe* unto righteousness...and shalt *believe* in thine heart that God hath raised him from the dead, thou shalt be saved" (Rom. 10:9-10). This one act of making us righteous in the atonement is a single solitary action [righteousness]. I do not *mean* to divide righteousness; however, for the sole purpose of explaining some of its intricate workings I have divided it at this time. This righteousness is **imputed** and **imparted** to us through faith in his death, burial, and resurrection. This is why Paul spoke of *being made righteous*, and as well exhorting the saints to *bring forth the fruits* of righteousness (2 Cor. 5:21; Rom. 5:16-17). "And this I pray, that your love may abound yet more and more **in knowledge**...that ye may approve things that are excellent... **being filled with the fruits** of righteousness which are [imputed and imparted and *brought forth*] by Jesus Christ (Phil. 1:9-11). [Not just a Judicial righteousness (pardon), but as well **new life** (an *active* righteousness that is His [Christ's] very own **obedient life** under the law). This is both an **imputed** and **imparted grace** [a righteousness for salvation: Justification, Sanctification, and Glorification]. Not just what **He did for us** [imputation] [on the Cross-in our justification], but as well what He **has given to us** by way of **impartation** [for our sanctification and glorification]. **Imputation** has taken place at/on the *Cross*; **impartation** has taken place [and is made possible] because of the *resurrection*. You will notice in Romans 10:9-10, that Paul says, we believe *unto* [or into, or to enter into] **righteousness** with the heart [or through *faith* and believing from the heart]. However, he tied this *faith* that **brought righteousness** to those who believed: **to faith in [believing on] the resurrection**. Why did he not mention the Cross?? I believe, here, in the text, the Cross can be *implied* [here, the full atonement can be implied]. So, why did Paul draw his attention to this specific part of the atonement [the resurrection]? Here in the text, I believe Paul is speaking of more than just our justification. Here, Paul is speaking of our **full** and *complete salvation* from start to finish. This is as well *confirmed* [supported] in Paul's previous statement in Romans 1:16, "For I am not ashamed of the **gospel** of Jesus Christ for it is the **power** [and ability] of God *unto*/into [or to enter into] **salvation** for all who believe." The word *salvation* here in the GK *means* to **deliver**, and **to heal**, and to bring into **wholeness** [soundness, completeness, or fullness]. Our **deliverance** out of sin and the Old life is our justification; **healing** [from the effects of sin] and coming into **fullness** is both our sanctification [the transforming of the human soul], and our glorification, which completes the redemptive process that is our *bodily* resurrection. He [Paul] first said [in verse 9], "and shall believe in thine heart that God hath **raised him** [up] from the **dead** [the resurrection]," and then he proceeded to say in the following verse [10], "For with the *heart* [faith] men believe *unto*/into righteousness." I believe Paul here is placing an emphasis not only on the **imputed** righteousness [for our personal justification] but on the **active righteousness**, that *brings* one into healing and wholeness [fullness] [where justification is just a part of the whole]. It is important to note that the *meaning* and application for biblical resurrection is more than just **some promised future event**. The word [to rise] **resurrection** is just as much **a principle** [a concept] as it is a future promise. *It is not only a future promise but as well a present* *reality*. **What is resurrection as a future promise: but the body glorified or raised from the dead into something brand new.** So, what does the bible teach the resurrection is as a principle?? The word principle *means* a rule, what is *the rule* or principle [law] [ground] of the resurrection?? It is LIFE!! Jesus said, "I am the *resurrection* and the **life**" (Jn. 11:25). The word **concept** *means* to be organized around **a main idea** or some main **thought**. The *theme*, or main idea [or, the rule or principle, ground] of the **resurrection** revolves around [His] LIFE [the new birth] [the new life] [eternal life] [and **the power** inherent within this <u>new</u> life to bring forth the fruits of a changed life]. God, help us to understand this **present active principle** for life!!

*The Cross-precedes the Resurrection, as Death precedes [new] Life. Pardon, then new life!!!

***2 Corinthians 5:17-behold [look and see] [the new creation] [that] all things are NEW!!!**

Resurrection *means* to make alive again [to make the body alive again]. To *rouse* from death; to *rouse* from disease; **moral recovery**: to *excite* to "new" thought and "new" action [from <u>inactivity</u>: from dead works/dead religion]; it gives to us the *idea* of collecting one's <u>faculties</u>: (WD any of the powers of the mind, such as the will, reason, or instinct. Inherent capabilities, power, or function). Here in the GK, this word <u>resurrection</u> not only applies to an end time event, on the last day the bodily resurrection of all believers, but to so much more!! Resurrection *means* to **rouse**, which *means* to **excite** or **stimulate** to action. Notice its direct word meaning is to *rouse* from disease, to *rouse* [or to excite] moral recovery [to stimulate the right and proper action]: to excite or stimulate to action a new and right way of thinking, to excite or stimulate to a new and right course of action. This is not just a promised provision for/in our salvation for future inheritance, which is a part of our **hope** of eternal life, but as well a **present provision** [a present power and ability] and inheritance accessible now [Heb. 6:1-5 "...tasted the good word of

God, and the <u>powers</u> (dunamis: abilities) of the world to come"] (Col. 1:12). It is clear; this **new life** we have received from God as **a treasure** in our earthen vessel is a resurrection *life* and *power* able <u>to rouse</u> [excite] and stimulate to action every principle fulfilled and provision promised in Christ Jesus. This is why Paul said, not just **"dead to sin,"** but as well **"alive to God."** This is why Paul *addressed* the believer's need to **<u>awaken</u>** from sleep, and **<u>rise</u>** from the dead (Rom. 8:4). It is the resurrection that must be understood as both a *future event* [future promise], and as well a **present** *active* **principle** [concept; thought; reality; provision]. **Alive** to God [the resurrection], and *indeed* **dead** to sin [dead to sins and the sinful lifestyle] [through the Cross]. Again, when Hebrews 6:5 speaks of the powers [or the dunamis] of the world to come, it is speaking of the **abilities** and **abundance** of the future world to come **enjoyed now**, in this **present time**, in this present dispensation of the gospel of his grace [the church age between Christ's first and second advents]. God, help us to understand the resurrection in all three prophetic time zones of **past, present,** and **future.** The resurrection is *both* a past event and future promise; notwithstanding, the resurrection, today, is a present active principle for power!!

"Wherefore he saith, **Awake** thou that sleep, and **arise** from the dead, and Christ shall give **thee light**" (Eph. 5:14). The words *"awake,"* and *"arise,"* are translated elsewhere in the scriptures as *arise, raise up,* to *raise,* to *rise,* and *risen*. These are all terms used to speak of the resurrection and is a part of the GK word cluster applied to the Resurrection. In the context of this chapter Paul is speaking to born again believers who need to be *awakened* [aroused from their sleep and spiritual slumber]. This is to be understood in the context of resurrection [the new life], not to be confused with the last day event called the resurrection. <u>Light</u> here in the text is not speaking of salvation itself but rather, our **understanding** of this salvation [here, Paul is not referring to Christ giving us salvation but to Christ giving us *understanding* of our salvation], *"That the God of our Lord Jesus Christ…may give unto you the spirit of wisdom and revelation in the* *knowledge of him:* ***the eyes of your understanding*** *being* **enlightened**; *that ye* **may know** (have the knowledge) (Eph. 1:17-18). Here, in the text, the word <u>enlightened</u> *means* to illuminate, **to give light** or, to make to see. Notice Paul said, they were sleeping!! What is Paul trying to get at in the text? Romans 13:11-12, and 14, will give us even greater insight into Paul's mind and meaning. "And that, **knowing the time**, that now it is high time to **awake** out of sleep: for now is our salvation nearer than when we *first* believed. The night is far spent, the day is at hand: *let us therefore cast off the works of darkness*, and let us put on the armor of light...**put ye on the Lord Jesus Christ**, and make no provision [avenue] [opportunity] for the flesh to fulfil the lusts thereof." While, it is clear, Paul is drawing special attention to the end of the Age, and, our salvation drawing nearer [closer] to us, which clearly speaks to the resurrection of the Just and the redemption of the body. However, **Awake** out of your **sleep**, and **put on** the Lord Jesus Christ, for the time is short? The word *awake* here is the same GK word in Ephesians 5:14, and implies resurrection, and means to *arise, raise up,* to *raise,* to *rise,* and *risen.* Here when Paul says, *"Put ye on the Lord Jesus Christ, and make no provision for the flesh to fulfil its lusts,"* he is saying, **"put ye on,"** and <u>reckon</u> yourselves **"alive to God,"** and **"put off,"** <u>reckon</u> ye yourselves indeed **"dead to sin,"** and make no provision for the flesh!! When the **new life** *within* becomes *active* [aroused] [excited] [stimulated] [operational] by the [power of the] Holy Spirit it will begin to *rouse* to new thought, and *excite* to moral recovery; and, as well stimulate to a new course of action [obedience to God]. "**Awake** to <u>righteousness</u>, and sin not [and **sin no more**]; for some have not the <u>knowledge</u> of God: I speak this to your shame" (1 Cor. 15:34). Here, the word **"awake,"** is a different GK word from Ephesians 5:14, and Romans 13:11, and *means* to **rouse** [oneself] out of a **stupor** [it means out of a <u>lethargy</u>: it means out of drowsiness; laziness; dullness, and indifference]. What does Paul mean by Righteousness?? What about the Knowledge of God?? Here, *righteousness* must be understood as a **present active principle**: the **new resurrected life** *imparted* within. Paul here is directly connecting [and uniting] the **power** and **ability** to operate in this righteousness [new life] to their own personal knowledge of this righteousness. **"Awake to righteousness**...for some have not the **knowledge** of God." To **sin no more**, and to come into that **promised experience** of Christ's death, and **to awaken** to *righteousness*, or to experience being **"alive to God,"** [His power] is contingent upon [and depends on] our **knowledge** [and understanding] of this death, burial, and his resurrection [and all that it means and has provided for us as believers]. Paul is exhorting the believers to *awaken* to something [to His righteousness] because Paul taught them the *knowledge* of that righteousness [he is exhorting them to come into an understanding of the truth of His righteousness]. The **new life** *within* us all is His **active righteousness** that will bear fruit [that will harvest] if aroused [excited], and stimulated to action through the **knowledge** of Him, and He crucified: **an understanding of the gospel of His grace** [the/his Cross: his death, burial, and resurrection]. Our justification or acquittal [our right-standing with God] is a judicial righteousness. However, this acquittal and judicial standing before God has **imparted to us new life** [an **active righteousness** at work *within us*]. The one issue or problem, today, in the Church of JC, that has ushered in the great apostasy of those who claim the gospel is found in their failure to *awaken* to righteousness. **Biblical morality** is at an all-time low!!!!!! Why?? The reason why many are not **experiencing** this promised **"death to sins,"** is that many are not currently **experiencing** being **"alive to God."** Remember this new life is a resurrection life, and it must and will arouse, excite, and *stimulate* to action **moral recovery** [obedience to God]. This **new life** *within* us is His **active** righteousness that will bear His fruit [that will harvest] if and when it is *aroused* [excited], and **stimulated** to action!! It is through the various **tools** given to us to help us grow in the faith that will work to excite to action out of its dormancy [sleep; slumber, and **hibernation**]. These **tools** are the spiritual disciplines of **prayer**, the **word**, and **fasting**, and the *like* will all **stimulate growth** [Paul said, **giving of our substance** will *increase* the fruits of our righteousness; **fellowship** is another very powerful tool that will provoke **to love** and **good works**]. Obedience to the Word itself will stimulate growth!!! **Forgiveness** is very important [necessary] to keep from blocking or hindering the growth of this new life within. We must take the **right action** [apply these tools] in order to *arouse, excite,* and *stimulate* the new life within. Dormancy *means* suspension of activity [sleeping, slumbering, resting, and/or drowsy, etc.]. Hibernation *means* to be inactive or to be in a dormant state. The bible calls the **believer** and the **new life** *within* [which is His, Christ very own life], the True Vine and His many branches. The [Zoe] **life** [force] and **supply** [of His Spirit] found in the **branch** comes from the true **Vine**, "Except it [the branch] *abide* in the Vine [it cannot bear fruit]; no more can you, except ye *abide* in me [for without me you can do nothing]" (Jn. 15:1-5). It is clear, that, **our relationship to this life** [to the new life] that we have received from God that is found in Him [in Christ] should be understood in *terms* of **living** and **growing things.** In the winter season: most plant life [vegetation] will **hibernate** or **go into stasis** [the slowing or stopping of normal functions]. Most plant life will draw [pull in] all of its normal functions/resources close to itself [and sleep]. During those months, some of its outward life and living will die [dead limbs and other debris]. This is why the bible speaks of God **pruning** and **purging** the believer of dead works!! It is during the early spring when the **sunshine** is plentiful and, there is an **increase of rain** [moisture], and the *suppling* of other **nutrients** in the soil that, help **to excite to action, life**. The change in the season and the *supply* of these external stimuli help to rouse to action the [new] life content within. This *new stimulation* will produce the **new growth** *within* and *without* that will go with the new season. This is sanctification [the believer's own personal experience with spiritual transformation]. Our sanctification should be understood in *terms* of **living** and **growing things!!!** This is why, **to separate,** our **justification** from spiritual growth **and change** [our sanctification] must be understood as a counterfeit [false] gospel. Salvation is distinctly **justification,** and then it continues to *bear its fruit* through **sanctification.** To turn away from [and to neglect] this so great a salvation, which if *supported* and *promoted* will **bear its fruit**, is to fall away from the faith altogether [apostasy] (2 Thess. 2:1-17; 2 Tim. 3:1-17).

The word <u>**substitution**</u> in the OE means *to take the place of another*. This word means to *replace* or a replacement: to put something or someone in the place of another. Christ's death on the Cross is a **substitutionary** work. Christ died for me!! Moreover, since Christ died for me, thus his death now becomes my death. Because he died, I died, and because he rose from the dead, ***with him*** I also have been raised to new life. I have become a new man [a new creation] in Christ Jesus, through *faith* and by **identification** with his death, burial, and resurrection. This is where it all begins!!!!! It begins with his **substitutionary** work, and our **identification** with that work. Without identification with Christ in his substitutionary work on the Cross: in his death, burial, and resurrection *salvation* [and sanctification] would not be possible. I must **identify** with him [and believe on him in] his ***death***, and [His] <u>resurrection</u> as my own death and resurrection [as my own personal redemption]: or salvation, [deliverance and healing] on an individual basis would not be possible [this applies to every other promise of God contained in the scriptures]. His ***substitutionary*** work must come *first, second,* then our ***identification*** with that work must follow, **or nothing moves** and/or **nothing changes** for man. The <u>first</u> action is His work; the <u>second</u> action is our response to it. To <u>identify</u> means to join to, and to associate with, and to share in, **to treat as the same**. We identify with Jesus Christ as one who is joined to the heir and, is now a part of the heir in all of his fullness. Praised God!!

The word <u>identification</u> means taking on [and receiving] what belongs to another; the act of <u>ascribing to oneself</u> the qualities and characteristics of another person [<u>that which belongs to another</u>]. This *means* to be the same as, or, to come into the same [as that person]. "He that *believe* on me [looks to me] the works I do he shall do also" (Jn. 14:12). This is identification. They are his works and his works alone, but we can participate in [become a part of] all these things [works; blessings] when we look to him [and identify with Him and simply come into the same]. This is identification, "Because [just] as he [JC] is, so [also] are we in this world" (1 Jn. 4: 17). **Identification** is to believe on Christ and become one with Christ in that same place. "He [God] spared not his own Son, but *delivered him up for us all* [substitution] how he [God] **with him** shall also freely give us all things [identification] (Rom. 8:32). To identify **with him** [Christ] in everything will enabled [open the door for] the believer to access the provision [the spiritual blessings] made possible by the Cross [which are held in Christ Jesus]. To *identify* with him [to believe on him] in his death, burial, and his resurrection **means to become one with him in that death** and resurrection, "Likewise **reckon** ye also yourselves to be dead indeed to sin, but alive unto God through Jesus Christ our Lord" (Rom. 6:11). To **reckon** means to *think* it to be so or to *conclude* it as such. To **count** it to be so *means* we must *consider* it done [finished]. We **identify** with Christ in his death and resurrection as our own, and then we consider it done. To **reckon** [to count it as so] *means* to consider it [presently] a forgone conclusion. To *reckon* yourselves dead to sin and alive to God *means* to take these things as an absolute fact [and a present reality]. Until the believer [Christian] takes his **stand** on the **word of God** [His promises] and fights the good fight of faith, he/she **will never** *endure* **the battle** involved in laying hold onto life [and to have and hold that life in abundance]. **Faith must labor, and war!!!** That labor is the battle or struggle for faith!!! This faith comes by hearing, and hearing, and hearing by the word of His Grace [the Covenant]. We **comprehend** the life we [the believer] have *received* that we might **apprehend** the *life* promised!!! The word *fight* in the GK means **a** struggle or it means **to** struggle. We are fighting a spiritual enemy that does not fight fair or open to view. We need to know our *rights* and our redemptive *benefits* [privileges] in Christ Jesus. Our battle must always be based upon our Spiritual Covenant, the gospel of His Grace. All of this is contingent upon our [**reckoning**] laying **hold on** [eternal] *life* [Zoe] in Christ Jesus. This means to *seize* or to take possession of life; to apprehend that for which we are also apprehended of Christ Jesus (Phil. 3:12). Life has taken hold of us [in the new birth]; now we must take hold of [possess] that life!!! Again, we **comprehend** [reason] the [new] life [the Zoe life] we have *received* that we might **apprehend** [take possession of] the [Zoe] *life* promised!!!!!!!! All these things *promised* [in the word] are spiritually discerned. This *means* these things must be comprehended [understood] first. [Zoe] means spiritual life, the God quality/kind of life received as a **treasure** [wealth], [as a divine deposit], [benefits], [blessings], in Christ Jesus: in us (Jn. 10:10; 1 Tim. 6:12; Jude 1:3). We are taking hold of all that, which first took hold of us. Paul, after 30 plus years of going after [and serving] God, he, was still, near the end of his life and ministry, attempting to take hold of that which first took hold of him 30 plus years earlier on the road to Damascus. This is a spiritual **work** and as well a spiritual **warfare**. "Let us **labor** therefore to *enter* into that rest [into His provision], lest any man fall [short of it] after the same example of unbelief" (Heb. 4:11). This is a *labor* of faith [knowing, reckoning, and yielding] (Rom. 6:3, 6, 11, and 13). The word rest here in the text within the context of the chapter is referring to the Promised Land [the land flowing with milk and honey]. This is the place that God made ready and provided for the people to meet their every need. This speaks to the believer's place of provision in Christ Jesus that has already met our every need (Eph. 1:3; Rom. 5:2; 8:32; 1 Cor. 2:12). In the OT, we find that this place of provision, the Promised Land, was not only a **labor** [in traveling to get there] [from Egypt to Canaan] but also a **warfare** once they arrived at their destination (Num. 13-14; Heb. 3-4). The bible says there were giants in the land [many enemies that had to be put down (deposed) (removed) and dispossessed (striped) who were standing in the way of their inheritance]. This is why, Paul, called the *gospel* of our salvation a fight or, **a contest of faith**. We fight the good fight of faith!! This faith is a fight [a contest] or, **a warfare**. We fight this warfare in the arena [in the battle ground field] of faith!! According to Romans 6:1-23, the application [and the stand] of our faith is in **knowing** the *promises* of God, then, to **reckon** it true, and finally to abandon oneself [to **yield**] over to these promises, our thoughts, speech [words], and action [deeds], which James called our faith **made**

perfect or complete by its corresponding action. There are five major operating principles to faith: *hearing, confessing, believing, doing*, and *enduring* (Rom. 10:8-10, 17; James 2:14-26; Heb. 10:32-39). The last principle [enduring] is simply you and I continuing to do what he said, promised [its corresponding action], while under tremendous pressure. The word labor in Hebrews 4:11 *means* to make an effort or to endeavor, which *means* to make every effort [it also means to study]. There is no doubt; this labor of faith is first in *knowing* [the truth], second, to *reckon* [count] it to be so [true], and third, to *yield* oneself [your life] over to its practice (John 8:30-32; Rom. 3:3-4; James 1:21-25): to abandon yourself over to the **new life** and all that is provided for in Christ Jesus by consistently applying your thoughts, words, and actions, to the promises of God, by faith [and obedience to God].God, help!!!

Converting our position, i.e., what we are, in God's sight, into possession, i.e., into what we enjoy **in our experience** is on a twofold basis: we must **know** what we are and what **we have** in our [legal] position in Christ Jesus; and we must **act in faith** on what we know to be true *according* to the Holy Scriptures [and, in agreement with what God has purchased for us by way of the Cross and, his subsequent resurrection]. We are to ***constantly*** count as true [in the present tense] the word of promise as a present statement of fact [that, the promises of God and, the provision God has made available to us through the gospel, is, the absolute truth]. We become so **in our experience** [as the word of God promised] only after *we count* upon our position in Christ Jesus, by faith. This requires *yielding* to [and coming into agreement with] the word of promise. Our victory is in our **knowing** and **acting on** our position of grace in Christ Jesus, and thus **experiencing** it's [his] power and provision [of this gospel] to meet every need [The New Unger's Bible Handbook by Moody Press, Page 480]. God, help us to believe, and act, and take our stand!!!!!!

The problem is we often judge our situation by our own personal experience, and then, discount the word of God as untrue or, not for today, rather than *counting* our experience as the liar and, his word, true. This is why we cannot believe for what we do not first have knowledge of. Again, we comprehend in the spirit, and then, and only then, are we able to apprehend in this world. In Romans 6:6, 11, and 13, reveal the key approach [steps] to Christian Sanctification [victory]. The secret to a holy and sanctified life!! A life characterized by you and I being "dead to sin," and "alive to God." The secret is found in **three** words in Romans 6, to KNOW, and then to RECKON, and lastly to YEILD. We must be continually aware of these words as we seek to understand and receive His sanctifying grace. [King James Bible Commentary, Thomas Nelson Publishers, Page 1417]. To know in the GK *means* to perceive or to understand. We then take this ***knowledge*** of the truth and we put it into our everyday **conversation** and **action**, "But what saith it? The word in nigh/near thee, even **in thy mouth**, and in thy heart: that is, the word of faith, which we preach [which we speak]" (Rom. 10:8; James 2:22, "...and **by works** [a corresponding action] was [is] faith made perfect [complete, having accomplished its task]). To **reckon** something to be so *means **to count*** it **as done** [as an accomplished fact]. This will as well involve the ***renewing*** of the mind. The mind is now **convinced** of its truth and reality and is now **converted** over to it; this is what it *means* by one who comprehends in the spirit. Finally yet importantly, we are then to yield over ourselves, to this new reality, and now, our every thoughts, words [speech], and actions are now in line with the word of promise. This is what Paul *means* by, "Abraham **believed** God and it was *counted* to him [it was imputed] to him for righteousness" (Rom. 4:3). This is what Paul *means* when writing in Galatians 3:2, "This only would I learn of you, Received ye the Spirit [and He working miracles among you, vs. 5] by the works of the Law, or [was it] by the ***hearing*** of faith? The hearing of faith *means* the thing heard, and *means* **hearing** the word of promise, and this must as well include **knowing** the word of promise, then **counting** it to be true [to reckon it to be so], and lastly, we must **yield** to it and to come into **agreement** with it where all of your ***thoughts***, and ***speech***, and ***deeds*** [actions] conform to what is promised. What man *thinks* in his heart [both, its knowledge and corresponding action], so is the man!!!

Hence, we *enter into* His **life** and become a partaker of Him, and all that is His, spiritually, and eternally, and now *yielding* to him our every need, and desires, and ourselves. This is not a matter of striving to be holy, but *knowing* that he is our holiness and we are now a partaker of his holiness through faith in the **gospel** [his redemptive works: his death, burial, and resurrection]. Sanctification is all about you and I *knowing* what Christ has already done [accomplished] on our behalf through his death and resurrection: and then, **to *reckon*** these things to be so!!!!! To **reckon** *means* we **know** something to be true, and then, moment by moment, day by day, we count it as true, and there, we take our stand. Not only do we **know** what he accomplished for us in our justification: we count ourselves indeed, **as dead to sin** [this is past], and now living daily in the *reality* of this/his resurrection life [we live as though we have already attained and have entered into his fullness]. This is a real and ever-present reality that can be **experienced** by the believer through the sanctifying and perfecting work of the Holy Spirit *from* within. The HS has come to make these things [that the gospel has already accomplished for us in Christ, and him crucified] effective in us [producing a decided, decisive, and desired effect] and to make what Christ has done for us, real, tangible, and touchable, enabling us to become in our daily experience, what we already are **"in Christ Jesus,"** and, what we will fully be, in the resurrection. Our Sanctification is in *knowing* our justification [and all that this entails], and then, ***to reckon*** ourselves **dead to sin** and **its power** [dead to the Old life]; and then, we *yield* our lives [abandon ourselves] over to him, and, all that we have [by way of all that we possess] is now given over to him: the one who has spiritually raised us up from the dead [and has now given us **new life**]. Paul's concept of the maturing of sons [sanctification] (Eph. 4:13-15), is, when we **rest** in his finished work on the Cross, *knowing*, we have been **reconciled**, there [changed; made different, there] and, daily *reckoning* that work to be finished, and constantly [daily]

yielding ourselves over to the **new life** resident and growing within [King James Bible Commentary, Thomas Nelson Publishers, Page 1418]. God be praised!!! **Sanctification, is, a cooperative effort that takes place between the Holy Spirit's work, and, our response to it. Justification** is, his Cross; **sanctification** is, my Cross!! Without the help of the Holy Spirit, and my **Cross**, my/our **sanctification**, would not be possible. Sanctification requires both, the Cross, and the sanctifying and perfecting work of the Holy Spirit, from within. The next book in the series, will, address our Christian sanctification, in light of the new creation realities. Sanctification is, not only what the Holy Spirit is doing, but, it must be understood, that, what he, the Holy Spirit is doing, is, the gospel, the Cross, the resurrection, and all that Christ has already accomplished for us in this new life and new creation. The Holy Spirit will take that which belongs to Jesus Christ, in all that he has accomplished on the Cross, for us, in and with and through his redemptive works, and show it unto you [and go to work: to work it into you]. The gospel that brings salvation, begins, with our justification; however, it must by necessity as well continue its work of redemption [its work of bringing us in his fullness, the abundant life] through our Christian sanctification. God, help. The spiritual fruit that comes about through our Christian sanctification is designed to manifest and demonstrate **the power** and **victory** of the Cross [in his death, burial, and resurrection, and ascension: this is the gospel of Jesus Christ]. My prayer, is, that God will greatly bless you in the reading of this book, on the gospel of his grace, and, that, all that God has promised us by way of this gospel, will be yours!! GOD SPEED.

FINAL THOUGHTS

My hope is that this book is enriching and fulfilling in its attempt to satisfy the hunger of the soul, for God. I'm not a professional writer but, I am a professional teacher. So, I understand that the writing style of these series of books may be a bit tedious!! I set out from the beginning to make available to the body of Christ study notes [bible study material] that would help to equip the saints for the work of the ministry [Eph. 4:11-16]. Being repetitious was by design. I am very much aware of the fact that these books are not an easy read [it is not a Sunday stroll in the park]. It will take a lot of **effort**, **time**, and a real **commitment** to the material to draw out its truths and make them stick [in your consciousness]. Meditation and prayer over these things will be of the utmost importance. Remember, this is not just something we are striving to learn [study], but it is as well a spiritual transformation. I guarantee, these three books will absolutely change your life.

It is not my desire to be controversial; however, for some this material contained in all three volumes maybe troublesome. For the last 500 years the church as a whole has failed to take the things of the Cross any further than the forgiveness of sins. Many in the church today, and over the last 500 years have even rejected the biblical testimony of divine healing. For some reason we are skeptical of all things supernatural!!! While it is true, there is a spiritual counterfeit; however, in order to have a counterfeit there must as well be the genuine article. In these series of books, I am attempting to address the truth about all these things that concern the supernatural. **Without the supernatural we would have no gospel!!!** The supernatural element is prevalent throughout the scriptures: to deny, or to even reject the supernatural is to reject the scriptures themselves. It is in the scriptures where Paul said, "I am not ashamed of the gospel of Jesus Christ, for it is the **power** of God unto salvation" (Rom. 1:16). This power is the GK word *dunamis* and it means miraculous power [the supernatural]. This references a divine intervention where it concerns the gospel of JC. Without the operation of the supernatural power of the Holy Spirit no one would be saved, delivered, healed, protected, preserved, etc., without this divine intervention. Man will not and cannot save himself; without the divine supernatural intervention of the Spirit in the lives of those in need, salvation would not and could not take place. Because the church has failed to draw from this source [the supernatural God] and, preach a supernatural gospel of power to the world, we find today a weak, compromised, and apostate church. To even confess Jesus Christ as Lord with **power** and **signs following** it must be by the Holy Spirit. God help us to be open and willing to receive these things written herein, and to take seriously all these things written in all three books that concern the gospel of our Lord Jesus Christ. God, help us to see that the GOSPEL of JC is the supernatural power [the divine intervention] promised us throughout the OT Writ. Where all the LAW and PROPHETS point!! We no longer need the law of God to intervene, direct, instruct, and to hold accountable; notwithstanding, this is the work of the Holy Spirit of God *within* all those who are regenerated and transformed through the power and authority of this gospel. The law is still useful as God's divine standard for biblical morality; again, notwithstanding, the gospel of JC is now the new divine biblical standard for moral living in keeping with the sanctifying [and perfecting] work of the HS. The HS will write these things contained in the Law of God upon the hearts of men!!! This *means* Christian growth and changed will occur/come by the HS [putting the law/word of God into the heart and minds of those who believe the gospel (Heb. 10:16)]: not by keeping the law. The gospel is the power of God!!!!

With all this in mind; we the Church cannot and must not deny our past, nor our historical and **theological underpinnings**. In Matthew 13:52 we find, "Then said he unto them, therefore every **Scribe** [writer/teacher] which is **instructed** [a disciple] unto the kingdom of heaven is like unto a man/a person that is a **householder**, which brings forth **out of his treasure** *things* **new** and **old**." The word householder in the GK, means, the **head** of the family or, the one responsible to teach Doctrine. Out of his treasure in the GK, means, wealth, deposit; in other words, out of this man's accumulated wealth of **knowledge** and **learning** of the word of God he will bring forth **doctrine**. Both GK meanings for *old* and *new* must be understood with respect to age. New, will speak of *freshness* [which *means* recent or current revelation]. Old, means, not recent or, antiquated. It is very clear; the bible speaks of drawing from *both* the **past** and the **present**. From this text, it is quite clear; we are not to reject the knowledge and experiences of the past, and, at the same time, **we are not to get stuck in the past**. We must operate today **in ministry** and **in doctrine** having this perfect balance *between* what God said and did in the past, with what God is currently saying and doing, today. God, help us, where it concerns our understanding and practice of this gospel of Jesus Christ, **never to ever forget**: to bring forth **out of our treasure** [chest of learning] [out of our Christian knowledge and experience] things, **new** and **old**. I pray that, as we go forth in this **world of sin** and **death**, we will do so graciously and, in the simple truth of the gospel alone, as the power of God to enter into this full and complete salvation, through faith in our one and only crucified Lord and Savior Jesus Christ. Help!! Thanks be to God for Jesus Christ!!! When Jesus speaks of the Scribe in Matthew 13:52, he, is speaking of the Old Testament teacher of the Law of God. So, this would easily refer to *both* the Old and New Testament writings when he speaks of *both* the **new**, and the **old**; however, notwithstanding, we must also, today, being 1900 years removed from that first century church, as well, apply **this/the new** to what God is saying and doing in today's church, and, to what he has already said and done [the **old**] over the last 2000 years of church history. This is why, in these series of books

I wrote on the EVANGEL [on the Gospel], I thought it necessity, at times, to also include **the old** [as *both* aspects of the Old Testament writings that reinforces the New Testament gospel, as well, to draw from those things written throughout church history that pertains to a right understanding of the gospel of JC]. My hope is that this book and, the other two books in this series on EVANGEL, the Gospel, will be a blessing to all those who read [it], and take heed to those things written therein. GODSPEED!!

ADDITIONAL MATERIALS

The Passion Translation of the New Testament 2018 Book
The Expositor's New Testament by Jimmy Swaggart 2003 Book
The Amplified New Testament 1987 by Zondervan Corporation.

The New Testament, an expanded translation by Kenneth S. Wuest
The ESV Study Bible 2008, Crossway Publishing ministry of Good New Publishers.
The New Unger's Bible Handbook by Merrill Unger, Moody Press Chicago
King James Bible Commentary 1999, Thomas Nelson Publishers, Inc.
The Reformation Study Bible, R C Sproul, Reformation Trust

The Gospel According to Jesus by John MacArthur 2009 Audiobook
The Gospel According to Paul by John MacArthur 2017 Audiobook
The Discipline of Grace by Jerry Bridges 2010 Audiobook

The Transforming Power of the Gospel by Jerry Bridges 2012 Audiobook
Foundations Of The Christian Faith by James Montgomery Boice 2017 Audiobook
Foundations An Overview of Systematic Theology by R C Sproul 2013 Audiobook
Everyone's A Theologian An Introduction to Systematic Theology R C Sproul 2014 Audiobook
All Essential Truths of the Christian Faith by R C Sproul 2017 Audiobook

ABOUT THE AUTHOR

Pastor's Curtis and Lynne Schulze has spent thousands of hours over the last forty years studying and researching genuine biblical spirituality. In today's world, there are countless avenues and many different streams of thought where it concerns true spirituality. There is a lot of confusion in the minds of many people concerning those things that relate to sacred matters. Many extra biblical schools of thought dominate the landscape worldwide: from eastern philosophies to western traditions, there are countless instructions given and practices performed on how to be one with the divine (or, on how to experience the true God). However, many fail to connect with the true source. God help us all to find the true God!!!

The church has failed to respond to this influx of extra biblical ideas and, mystical systems now flooding the western world. Because of this, a void or vacuum has formed in today's world that has opened up the door for private interpretation. The world is transforming before our very own eyes!!! Man is plunging into a spirituality like never before; a mystical approach devoid of true biblical interpretation and application. These books are designed to answer the longings of many to understand our relationship with the living God from a strictly biblical worldview, what the Bible calls the deep things of God and, in agreement with the true gospel (1 Cor. 2:10).

For Christ Ministries is a church of Spirit-filled believers acknowledging God as Father; Jesus Christ as Lord, Savior, Redeemer, and Healer; and the Holy Spirit as Teacher and representative of God's power on earth. Love is our foundation [God's weapon of choice] to heal the broken hearted and to set the captives free!!!!!!!!!!! We believe as the body of Christ: we are Christ's ambassadors rooted in sound doctrine and, equipped as a house of warriors. We are an apostolic work, and representatives of the Kingdom of God: equipping, training, perfecting, and raising up the Lord's people to stand in these last and evil days. God is empowering His people!!!

Contact Information
Curtis L. Schulze
PO Box 3352, Stafford VA, 22555
info@pathfinderfellowship.org

www.ingramcontent.com/pod-product-compliance
Lightning Source LLC
LaVergne TN
LVHW021233080526
838199LV00088B/4335